Practical
Evaluation
Techniques for
Librarians

D1604718

Practical Evaluation Techniques for Librarians

Rachel Applegate

LIBRARIES UNLIMITED

AN IMPRINT OF ABC-CLIO, LLC
Santa Barbara, California • Denver, Colorado • Oxford, England

Copyright 2013 by Rachel Applegate

Library of Congress Cataloging-in-Publication Data

Applegate, Rachel.
  Practical evaluation techniques for librarians / Rachel Applegate.
    pages cm
  Includes bibliographical references and index.
  ISBN 978–1–61069–159–8 (pbk.) — ISBN 978–1–61069–160–4 (ebook)
  1. Libraries—Evaluation. 2. Public services (Libraries)—Evaluation. I. Title.
Z678.85.A67 2013
027.0029—dc23   2013012273

ISBN: 978–1–61069–159–8
EISBN: 978–1–61069–160–4

17 16 15 14 13   1 2 3 4 5

This book is also available on the World Wide Web as an eBook.
Visit www.abc-clio.com for details.

Libraries Unlimited
An Imprint of ABC-CLIO, LLC

ABC-CLIO, LLC
130 Cremona Drive, P.O. Box 1911
Santa Barbara, California 93116-1911

This book is printed on acid-free paper ∞

Manufactured in the United States of America

Contents

Introduction vii

Chapter 1: Personal Techniques 1
  Surveys. 1
  Interviews 23
  Focus Groups 32
  Usability. 37
  Instructional Evaluation 46
  Observation: Tallies 58
  Unobtrusive Observation: Reference Testing. 68
  Mystery Shopping 73

Chapter 2: Impersonal Techniques 79
  List-Checking 79
  Citation Analysis. 87
  Collection Mapping 94
  Use Analysis. 102
  Availability 111
  Process Evaluation. 117
  Transaction Log Analysis 125

Chapter 3: Technique Selection and Sampling 131
  Decision Factors. 132
  Summarizing and Analyzing Data 143
  Using Technology 155
  Using Consultants 159

Chapter 4: Planning for Evaluation. 163
  Library Operations Evaluation Plans (LOEPs). 164

Chapter 5: Reporting about Evaluation 181
  Targeted Evaluation Reports 182
  Periodic Organizational Reports. 185
  Reporting and Organizational Communication 187

Afterword: How to Handle Numbers 188

Appendix A: Study Questions Answer Key 193
Appendix B: Formatting Data 213
Index 229

Introduction

Practical Evaluation Techniques for Librarians is a *vade mecum*—a take-with you one-volume guide and tutor for the most useful techniques that you can use to evaluate your library, information center, or other organization: facilities, resources, services, everything.

Evaluation is the gathering of data for managerial decision making. This is different from research. The goal of research is to detect and describe generalizable ideas and relationships. For example, can online tutorials be as effective as in-person information literacy presentations? What is the information-seeking behavior of the new generation of college students? What kinds of books attract reluctant readers?

Evaluation is intensely local and specific. Here, you are examining your own resources and services. Your information literacy tools—are they effective? Your own students—how do they use the library? Your own collection of chapter books—are they used?

The two goals of evaluation are *proving* and *improving*. Many educational, nonprofit, and government organizations face intense pressure to demonstrate their value or the impact they have. In this way evaluation can provide evidence to prove the contribution of your library to a university's researchers, a school's students, or a community's residents. Evaluation also takes critical, constructive aim at your own services and resources. How strong you are? Where are your weaknesses? What can be improved? If you try this, has it really improved things?

You can find many books and articles about evaluation, assessment, and outcomes measurement in general. This includes manuals for specific techniques like surveys and focus groups. This book does not replace those resources. They provide important background and examples for the theories and philosophy of evaluation, and in-depth instruction and research on the methodologies.

What this book does is put in one place, in your hands, an intensely practical evaluator's kit with tools and plans. With this book you and your colleagues can examine individual projects and ongoing services. You can construct effective plans for keeping tabs on how your library is doing. With this book and a general-purpose suite of office software, you can gather, analyze, and report your own evaluation data. You will know what tools are best for what data, and requiring what staff time and effort. You will be able to knowledgeably solicit assistance and employ consultants, advanced training, or more powerful software.

Who are you? The descriptions and examples are designed for someone who has a bachelors' level of education, some library work experience, and some facility using spreadsheet and word-processing programs. The book does not require any previous knowledge of statistics. With an instructor's assistance, students in an MLS program without much work experience can use this. Library workers who are in managerial positions, especially with budget and reporting responsibilities, also will have sufficient background to succeed.

This book consists of five chapters after the introduction: two chapters on methods, one chapter on general concepts for all methods, one chapter on how to plan for evaluation, and a final chapter on reporting.

The first two chapters contain descriptions of particular evaluation methods. Chapter 1 covers "personal" methods, those in which the evaluator interacts with people. This includes surveys, interviews, focus groups, usability, instructional evaluation, observation by tallies, reference testing, and mystery shopping. Chapter 2 covers "impersonal" methods: list-checking, citation analysis, collection mapping, use analysis, availabililty, and process evaluation. These unobtrusive techniques mostly do not involve interaction with, or need cooperation from, human beings. Most of these methods are used to evaluate a library's resources, virtual or physical. In each of these methods chapters, for each method section (e.g., "Usability"), there is an *introduction* that describes strengths and weaknesses of that method as a guide to understanding when to choose it: the quality of data it yields as well as its feasibility. A *procedures* section describes how to carry out the method. Finally, *study questions* prompt readers to explore two existing studies as examples; answers are in Appendix A. In Appendix B are examples of how the data for each method is structured in a spreadsheet.

The general concepts in Chapter 3 are sampling, summarizing, using technology, and using consultants (experts). Sampling is the process of selecting items to be included in an evaluation study. It includes scientific random sampling and other types of sampling as well. The summarizing section goes over concepts and methods of summarizing qualitative data (text, into themes) and quantitative data (numbers, into percentages and averages), as well as statistical testing. A brief section reviews how technology can make the process better. In general, using more complex technology involves an initial investment in time (learning curve) or money (advanced software) to benefit from more speed and flexibility. A final section discusses what consultants can do for an evaluation plan or project.

Chapter 4, Planning for Evaluation, puts it all together. It is the equivalent to learning how to sketch a blueprint for a house after you know about framing, plumbing, and electrical systems. This chapter describes how to organize the best methods for your own particular situation and needs. Evaluation *methods* give you information on how your library is doing. For your own library (goals, staffing, and setting) an evaluation *plan* is that set of methods, and timing that gives you the important information you need to manage it on a daily, yearly, and strategic basis with the least effort.

The final chapter, "Reporting about Evaluation," reviews practical steps for creating evaluation reports. It describes different types of reports and the role of the audience. It gives tips on communicating results in terms of text, tables, graphs, and anecdotes. It is worth thinking through your planned evaluation all the way from the initial question to the imagined report: "Our library is proud to say that our X is doing Y." Discover at the beginning how to set up ways to gather the data that you need, not the night you are writing the report.

Chapter 1

Personal Techniques

Surveys

Introduction

Surveys are one of the most ubiquitous forms of measurement that we encounter in our daily lives. With every purchase we seem to be asked to fill out a survey; in close elections we get calls to answer polls; at conferences we turn in evaluation forms.

Here, the word *survey* is used to mean a set of questions, most of which have fixed answer sets, asked of one individual. This is sometimes called a *questionnaire*, but *survey* is the more frequent term in American society and in research. Most of the time, especially for evaluation, the people answering the survey are called the *respondents*, and they answer the questions either about a specific incident, episode, or transaction or generally. Think about the difference between "how was this afternoon's speaker?" and "how often do you visit your library?" or "please rate our children's collection."

Sometimes, a set of questions relates to an organization or an institution, and someone who knows the right answers is then called an *informant*. For example, "does your library offer homework help?" There is only one answer per library. This section will focus on surveys for the person-respondent type of survey because it is much more common in library evaluation.

Sometimes, a set of questions is meant to measure a phenomenon. A "depression inventory" is a set of questions that allow a psychologist to determine something about a person's mental and emotional status. These sets of questions are called *instruments* and are very technical endeavors for psychologists, sociologists, and other scientists. The LibQUAL+ library satisfaction survey is an instrument of this type, but that is quite rare in librarianship.

Some sets of questions are tests, meant to measure knowledge or skills. The "Instructional Evaluation" section covers this. A question like "Was this session interesting?" is an evaluative survey question; a question like, "Name two citation styles" is a test question; a question like "How confident are you in finding information after this session?" is something of a combination of survey and test.

Finally, a survey is not just a written paper or screen set of questions and answers. A survey can be delivered orally, as polls, or specialized surveys for elections, are: "Who would you vote for today?" As long as respondents select from a limited set of allowable answers, it is a survey, not an interview, even if it is oral. An interview allows people to use their own words and to interact with the interviewer.

The procedures section shows you the essential steps in designing simple surveys for both general and specific situations. Chapter 3 on sampling covers how to select and solicit respondents for your survey.

A survey means thinking inside the box. It presumes that you know the outlines and most of the inside of the box. You create questions with boxes for answers, and you can do so because you can anticipate somewhere between 75% and 90% of the possible answers to the questions. This means you know the "what." Survey data gives you the "how much" and "with what" answers.

Consider public library patrons. Some of the things that we know about them are that they have ages, genders, places of residence, work statuses, and numbers of children. We know some of their possible behaviors, like going to the library, shopping, or caring for children. We know the types of things that they can do at the library, such as check out books, look at magazines, ask questions, or attend programs.

Most survey questions are designed to get descriptive information about respondents. The summary of answers to descriptive questions tells you "how many." How many people visit the library more than once a month compared to those who visit less than once a month? How often does "get homework help" come up as a reason to visit the library?

Is this information available elsewhere? A library usually keeps tallies of people attending programs. This observational tally is undoubtedly a much better record of program attendance. However, other questions cannot be answered through observation. One can tally people at a program, but that tally has no information about people who do not attend. A general survey could show that people think programs are scheduled at inconvenient times or are not on interesting topics.

Even when information exists elsewhere, when you use a survey it is possible to combine information in ways that are usually not possible otherwise. An anonymous survey combines two library needs: the value we place on privacy for our patrons and survey respondents and the usefulness of seeing connections between different uses and users. For example, answers to a survey question on age can be connected to a question about desirable program times to see how to fit the needs of different groups. Answers to a question on where people live can be combined with number of visits per month to see if there are outreach needs. A particular collection or service can be very highly rated by one group and low-rated by another. Any two questions on any survey can be combined to see if there is some relationship or difference.

A survey is self-reported. How accurate or honest is that? We do not track patrons; we ask how often they visit. Because of this, some evaluators consider only traces of behavior to be "true" measures rather than the answers someone wants you to hear. Even so, there are some questions that only an individual can answer. Rating a collection, a program, or a service is the only way to see how real people perceive it. It is important to have questions worded so as to encourage honest and candid responses: not, for example, "Do you read to your child?" but "please check how often you do these activities with your child"—the more concrete the better, with wording and spacing that implies "never" or "seldom" are okay answers.

Interviews and focus groups are ways to gather unstructured, un-predefined information. In interviews you can probe for the "why" behind the "what" and for more details behind the "what": I visit the library only once a month because once a month I visit my mother. I visit the library almost every day because I'm in college and I can study while my children use the children's area. Until an interview study was done of students in public libraries, librarians often assumed college students were there because of their collections, or hours, or closeness, when "children" turned out to be a major factor.[1]

Few surveys get high response rates; 30% is generally good for surveys sent individually to people. Patron compliance is not a problem for observation or usage data or citation analysis. Behavioral tallies can be more accurate than self-reported data. Interviews are an opportunity to gather rich, contextual, unanticipated detail but can only include very few people.

Surveys are a quick, relatively easy happy medium between the opaque tallies of observation (what with no why, no human perspective) and the richness of interviews: much high-quality data for relatively little effort.

Procedure

Conducting a survey consists of three steps:

1. Designing the survey:
   - Content
   - Individual question design
   - Overall questionnaire design

2. Administering the survey: selecting, sending, receiving

3. Analyzing results

Designing the Survey—Content

The first step in designing a particular survey is deciding *what* you want to know and *who* knows it. For any given topic, some person whom you can reach with a survey has to be able and willing to answer questions relatively honestly.

Consider the question, "why do people visit the library?" You can think of this as, "of the people who visit the library, what are their reasons?" In this situation, your *who* is library visitors. If you conceive of the idea as, "what reasons are there for people to visit *or not visit* the library," then the *who* is both library visitors and nonvisitors. People have to be able to answer; few library visitors could be very precise in telling you exactly how many visits they have made over the last year and whether that number is different from the previous year. People have to be willing to answer. People reached through general mailings while trying to contact nonvisitors might not want to admit they do not visit the library.

Think about the perspective and knowledge of the respondent. Be as concrete as possible in wording questions. Pretest the survey questions with people as similar to the target respondents as possible.

Another content issue is *how much*: how long should the survey be? It takes a certain amount of effort to capture someone's attention enough to answer any survey at all. Once you have their attention, you need to strike a balance between taking advantage of this opportunity to ask many questions and having so many that people will not complete the survey.

Consider a standard end-of-session evaluation form at a professional conference or after a library event. Have the event presenter explicitly designate some of the event time for the evaluation form ("We'll stop now so that you have time to fill out the form before the next session/before leaving. It only takes a couple of minutes.") Next, ask questions about the program itself. Finally, add a few more questions that are relevant to the session attendees. These people are already available and willing to participate. This could be related topics like, "How likely are you to attend X program in the future?" or "What sorts of programs do you prefer?" or more general such as "To help us understand our users, please indicate your work status: full time, part time, other, retired" or "What is your favorite type of reading material?" Keep the additional questions fewer than the direct session questions, and keep the whole of it to not more than 5% of the entire session time.

Roughly, two pages or sheets or 10 minutes is about all that most people will want to volunteer for a general-purpose survey. For a transaction or incident survey, keep the time involved for the survey to less than half of the time for the incident. Within that length, keep all questions relevant to those particular respondents.

Similar to the "how long, how many" issue are "how else?" and "how often?" Any single survey does not exist in a vacuum. Every instance of asking someone their opinion takes place in a whole ecology of surveys. Survey burnout is a serious issue in many situations, particularly schools and colleges. It is so convenient to target students or teachers that they get targeted too often. Library survey designers should ask: Can the information be gotten any other way? Is there some existing survey that could include a few library questions? And how will a separate library survey fit within other surveys that the respondents are experiencing? This survey landscape is not always a negative. In some organizations a culture of evaluation takes root in which people expect to fill out forms after any type of program.

Lay out the general topic areas that you are interested in, with some indication of who will be targeted and how. Then ask peers to review it. This will show if you are missing some items ("why not ask about the interlibrary loan process?"), or if other data exists ("but we find out about that from professors"), or if an existing survey overlaps ("we asked about that just a month ago when the instruction department surveyed . . . ").

Designing the Survey—Individual Questions

The next step is turning content areas into concrete questions. Some considerations apply to all types of questions (see Table 1.1).

Tips for All Questions

Appropriate reading level
No jargon
Concrete
Complete sentences
Comparable
Single topic

Table 1.1 Tips for Survey Questions.

Consider the appropriate reading level for the target population. Surveys for fourth graders will be different from those for high school seniors. Avoid library jargon. If you think of it as "Access Services" but your signage says "Circulation," then patrons will think of it as "circulation" or "getting books." When you ask about frequency, be concrete: not "regularly" or "often" but "at least once a week" or "at least three times in the last six months." This includes specifying a time period: not "Have you used our website?" (ever?) but "Have you used our website in the last week?" Use consistent grammar and complete sentences. Complete sentences are easier for readers to interpret; too often, in sentence fragments, what the question writer is thinking about is not obvious to the respondent: "Visiting when" (visiting what?). Check to see if a previous survey covered some or all of the same topic. Unless previous questions were really poor or are now obsolete, use the same wording so that you can compare the results. Finally, make sure each question is about one, and only one, topic. More than one causes the double-barrel error discussed below.

Here are the six basic types of questions. Each creates a separate kind of data for analysis, so it is important to consider not only what you ask but also what the resulting summary should look like.

1. *Dichotomous* questions have only two answers. Sometimes these are two named alternatives, such as "male/female," "student/teacher," "less than/more than three years' experience." It also includes "check/not check": "Do you use these items: books, CDs, DVDs. . . ."

   If a question has "other" in addition, it is *not* a dichotomous question: "Married/Single/Other," "Student/Faculty/Other": these have three, not two, answers.

   Data: 1 and 0: 1 for option A, 0 for option B

   Summary: number and percent of those who selected A or B

2. *Multiple-choice choose any* questions are actually a series of dichotomous questions. "How did you hear about this program? Check all that apply." In effect, you are asking a series of questions: Did you hear about it through the newspaper, yes or no? Did you hear about it through flyers, yes or no?

   It is very easy to write a survey that has many questions: ask people if they know, use, or think "very important" for each of a list of 10 services or items, and you suddenly have asked 30 yes-or-no questions.

   Each of the options should be distinct and the same size. For example, "the economy" and "gas prices" overlap a lot and are not the same conceptual size. However, precision is not as important as with the *only one* type of question (next).

   Data: 1 and 0 for each option asked about: they select it, or they do not. Skipping it is the same as not selecting it.

   Summary: number and percent of total respondents choosing A, B, . . . or Z.

3. *Multiple-choice choose only one* questions are based on categories, or groups for respondents. Some people check "working full-time," others "working part-time," others "retired," and others "other." These are conceptual categories and cannot be converted into numbers: if "full time" is 1 and "part time" is 2, you cannot say that the "average" is something like 1.5.

   The set of question choices must be mutually exclusive and exhaustive. *Mutually exclusive* means there is no overlap. If you ask about age ranges, you do not say "10–20" and "20–30." If someone might fall into more than one category, either change the question to "choose any" or use wording that directs them to choose one: "Choose the occupation that *best* fits what you do *most* of the time." *Exhaustive* means all possibilities must be included. If your age ranges only go up to 65, you have left out 66+ year olds. An easy way to ensure coverage is to add an "other" category: "Married, Single never married, Single divorced, Widowed, Other." You know you have created good categories when few people choose "Other."

Data: one arbitrary code for each group

Summary: number and percent of those answering that question who select each option.

4. *Rating or Likert-type scales* have the very familiar wording, "On a scale of 1 to 5, where 1 is worst and 5 is best, how would you rate…" Good Likert-type scales have equal negative and positive points, with roughly the same distance between points conceptually, and the "best," "good," or " desirable" option presented on the right. This is consistent with the English language where we go from left to right and reach a climax at the end. It is also much easier to report results when a larger number (5) means *better* than a smaller number (4). Although you may see scales where 1 is best or the best result is on the left, there is no compelling reason to do that, and it is better for your survey and for surveys in general to be consistent.

It is not necessary to provide adjectives for each of the points along the scale. However, be sure not to include "does not apply" within the same scale. "N/A" or "does not apply" or "do not know" are not the same as a neutral feeling. Table 1.2 gives some examples of adjectives that can fit statements asking about opinions and behaviors.

Strongly Disagree	Disagree	Neither Disagree nor Agree	Agree	Strongly Agree
Very unlikely	Not likely	Neither likely nor unlikely	Likely	Very likely
Very poor	Poor	Neutral	Good	Very good
Needs improvement	May need improvement	Good but could use improvement	Meets expectations	Exceeds expectations
Disagree strongly	Disagree	Kinda-sorta *Cartalk.com*	Agree	Agree strongly
Never	Rarely	Sometimes	Often	Always
Very seldom		Sometimes		Very often
Not at all				Completely
Not important		Important		Very important
Not at all helpful		Helpful		Very helpful

Table 1.2 Likert-Type Scale Adjectives.

How many points should be on the scale? The more points you include the more distinctions you can make but the more difficulty people will have in deciding. Five is a familiar size and a good choice for most circumstances. Three can be useful for brief surveys. A 10-point scale is sometimes seen. If there is an even number such as 4, there is no middle point, and it is a *forced-choice* scale. While this may be useful in situations where you want to force a choice, such as a political poll, it is seldom useful in library surveys and tends to annoy some respondents.

Data: a number from 1 to the maximum. "N/A" or "not applicable" should be *ignored*, not recorded as 0.

Summary: an average of the scores and standard deviation for the "spread."

5. *Ask-exact* questions ask for a very brief answer to be written in. These could be verbal ("What kinds of books do you like?") or numeric ("How many children did you bring to story hour?"). Verbal questions give you the chance to see what words your respondents use about your library, services, and collections. Numeric questions give you more detail than providing categories (asking "Age: 10–19" does not let you know if they are 12 or 18). However, people find it more difficult to answer exactly, and sometimes they do not want to, particularly with income and also with age. Ask-exact questions can be used but should be limited to 20% or fewer of the questions.

   Data: textual or qualitative

   Summary: the numbers of respondents using particular terms or answers

6. *Open-ended questions.* Surveys do not just have closed-ended questions. Whenever a multiple-choice choose-any question includes "other," you should also include "please specify" so you have some idea about what categories you missed. You can also include truly open-ended questions: broadly worded with space for people to write a sentence or more. Most respondents find open-ended questions more difficult to answer, as they require cognitively coming up with an answer and practically writing or typing it, so you should not make an open-ended question mandatory. Narrative questions tend to favor more educated and more verbal respondents. On the other hand, there are respondents who feel confined by closed-ended categories and who need an opportunity to use their own words and provide their own input. Most surveys should have at least one open opportunity for people to provide comments.

   Data: textual or qualitative

   Summary: thematic (See the end of the Interviews section.)

A seventh type of question should be avoided, no matter how tempting: the *ranking* question. The ranking question asks respondents to place items in a rank order. It is a blatant forced choice and has several problems. First, when there are several items to be ranked, most people have difficulty making distinctions. Second, people generally resent being forced to make choices as in an even-numbered Likert-type scale. Third, the results are very hard to summarize and to convey accurately. The final reason is the most serious. Ranking loses valuable information. If I have to rank chocolate, vanilla, and strawberry, I would rank them 1, 2, and 3, and nobody would know that I really hate strawberry and would *rate* it 1 on a scale of 1 to 5, with vanilla a 4 and chocolate a 5. Rating them 1, 2, 3 erases that specific, individual valuation. Ranking is completely unnecessary. Ask people to rate items, then list them in order based on average ratings. Those averages will reveal where items are very close to, or very far from, each other (see Table 1.3).

Based on this data, we know to avoid fruit-flavored yogurt. It would be misleading to draw a line between ranked items if we will keep the top two flavors without knowing their ratings, because numbers 1, 2, and 3 might be very close to each other while there is a big gap between numbers 1–3 and numbers 4–5.

A big problem that can show up with any type of question is the double-barreled question. A double-barreled question includes more than one topic in the same question. It is

Ranking *Based on rating*	Yogurt Flavors	Ratings
1	Chocolate–Vanilla Swirl	4.8
2	Chocolate	4.7
3	Vanilla	4.0
4	Strawberry	1.2
5	Banana	1.1

Table 1.3 Ranking versus Rating.

true that a question can usefully employ two words—synonyms—to describe the same thing: "health and wellness," "library skills and information literacy," or "access services and circulation." Avoid using one question to ask about two distinctly different things: "How would you rate our library's collections and services?"

Unless you are consciously trying to get a global assessment of your entire operation, it is much more important to be specific and concrete. This requires careful proofreading and pretesting because double-barreled questions are a surprisingly easy mistake to make. Like ungrammatical apostrophe's (yes, that's an error), they pop up like weeds.

Designing the Survey: Putting It All Together

The overall presentation of the survey includes the introduction and conclusion, the question sequence by topic, and the screen or page formatting. Done well, all of these help respondents understand the survey better, enjoy the experience more, and learn more about your library. Every survey is in fact a marketing tool: it describes what you do and do not offer, what you care about and what you have omitted. It markets, so it should market well.

The introduction to a survey should create a social bond. *Social* means appreciating that it is a human being taking the survey. Normal interpersonal rules apply such as using *please, thank you,* and *here's why.* The survey introduction should thank people for responding and give some indication of why the survey is being done:

- "Thank you for taking the time to complete our survey."

- "We use this information to make changes in our programs and think of new things to offer."

- "The last survey showed that you wanted . . ."

If a survey is more than one screen or page and also if it is a global, not transaction-based, survey that covers several topics, include a brief indication of the topics that will follow:

- "We will ask you first about the programs for children, then about those for teens, and then adults. We have a separate section about our books and DVDs."

- "This survey covers what your liaison, your department's specially assigned librarian, can do for you in these areas: instruction for your students, special research help for faculty, and building our collections, digital and physical: books, journals, and other resources for your area."

This serves three purposes. First, it gets people thinking about the topics, a form of cognitive priming. Second, it assures people that certain topics *will* be covered. When respondents have particular concerns, they will try to shove those concerns into the first available space or question unless they know that they will be asked about them later. Finally, the list emphasizes what you think is important—what you are marketing.

Conclude a survey with two or three items. First, ask a global "do you have any other comments or feedback" question. Even if few people use it, it signals that you are interested in them "outside the box" of the preset questions in the rest of the survey. If you anticipate specific complaints, include a section where you tell them whom they should contact for personal feedback and that this particular survey is anonymous. End with a thank you. In short: "Any questions or comments? Contact us. THANK YOU."

Sequence the questions in the body of the survey in a relatively coherent fashion. It is certainly true in a scientific sense that the order in which you ask questions and the wording used do affect how people answer. However, an evaluation survey is usually not trying for instrumental precision. Instead, it aims to be user friendly and to get a reasonable reflection of the real world.

- Begin with some simple demographic questions, but do not make them required.

- Put the most common, most well-known, or simplest topics first. For a more complex topic, either place it after a related simpler topic, for instance, checking a book out, then asking for a hold, then asking for interlibrary loan; or if there is no other related topic, place it towards the end of the survey.

- Keep the format within each topic area roughly consistent from topic to topic. For example, begin with an overall question, "What is your rating of our X programs?" followed by more specific ones, "What affects your decision to attend programs? Check all that apply." End with an open-ended question, "Do you have suggestions for programs?" Where possible, repeat this rhythm in different sections. If different topic areas need different types of questions, try to make it obvious that there has been a change. Avoid making questions or question layouts *slightly* different. They should be the same or *obviously* different.

- All rating scales should be the same size, 3 or 5 or 10, and the same direction, best or most favorable to the right. Use the same anchor adjectives for similar questions.

In each question and consistently throughout, use special fonts to draw the reader's attention to the key points. Use them to indicate "choose any" or "choose all" and the main points of the question, especially those that make that question different from another question. Here are examples:

- Now, please choose the reasons why you visited the library *today*, choose **all** that apply.

- During your *last* visit to the library, what was the **most important** reason you visited?

To design a web- or screen-based survey,

- Pay attention to screen or page breaks. Ensure there is little or no scrolling. Signal when a new topic starts rather than another page on the same topic.

- Be judicious with requiring answers. Even if you are very interested in a topic, avoid requiring an answer unless it is needed for skip logic. Friendly respondents will answer anyway, and unfriendly respondents tend to resent the requirement and may abandon the survey entirely.

- Skip logic allows you to shorten the survey for each respondent. Skip logic is when an answer sends the respondent to different questions. That may be a very good thing, but remember that it will not shorten the data that is downloaded for analysis.

For a paper-based survey,

- Pay attention to layout and flow, including a reasonable page break.

- For each question with multiple responses such as either "choose only one" or "choose any," the set of responses should *only* be in one line horizontally or vertically; respondents have difficulty reading items in a word-wrapped list. This is a list where one or more words are on another line.

  NO:
  Your location: ____Within the city ___North, suburbs____South, suburbs ____Other

  YES:
  Your location: ____Within the city___North, suburbs____South, suburbs ____Other

  OR: Your location:____Within the city
  ____North, suburbs
  ____South, suburbs
  ____Other (please specify: _____)

- An exception can be made, with two columns, for lists where the categories are very familiar to the respondents and the grouping is tight;
  Your status: ____Undergraduate   _____Graduate Student
  ____Faculty   _____Staff
  ____Other: please specify: _____

- Place check boxes or lines, when possible, to the *left* of the items. This avoids the problems of varying word and sentence lengths:

  Select your favorite genre:
  NO:
  Romance   ____
  Suspense   ____

> Mystery   _____
> Science fiction and fantasy   _____
>
> YES:
>
>   _____Romance
>   _____Suspense
>   _____Mystery
>   _____Science fiction and fantasy

- For scales, always have the scale on one line, and use headers even if the question defines the score points:

For each genre, please rate how much you read books in this area, where 1 is not at all and 5 is all the books you read are from this genre:

	Not at all		Sometimes		All/Exclusively
Romance	1	2	3	4	5
Suspense	1	2	3	4	5

- When you use skip logic, make it very clear where someone should go next; use over-large fonts and directional arrows. Consider having the two options next to each other in columns. In this way, those who have skipped one question have the opportunity to see what they are missing, which is additional marketing (see Table 1.4).

During the last month, did you visit the library?	
YES	**NO**
If so, please check all of the reasons:	_If not, please check all of the reasons:_
Check out books	Have no library card
Check out videos	Out of town
Consult a librarian	Too busy
Attend programming	Inconvenient hours
Visit with children (programming)	Unaware of programming
Visit with children (books, materials)	Visited previous month

Table 1.4   Survey Design: Parallel Presentation.

Then, edit the complete draft with three sets of fresh eyes.

First, have a professional colleague who knows what you intend review it to see that everything is included and that the responses are detailed enough to give useful data. For every question, think, "how many people will answer it in various ways?" If you or your colleague can easily imagine most people choosing just one option, then it is time to reword the question or remove it. Too-broad questions are especially prone to this. If you ask if someone has used X item or service, have you narrowed down the time frame? "Have you used an e-book?" What kind? From what library? When—ever in my life? If I just clicked on one once, does that count?" Make each question more concrete. Make all responses reasonable, rational choices, not, "I read to my children . . . _never._"

Next, recruit two or three people who are like the people who will take the survey. These can be friends, as long as they are not experts. Have them talk their way through the survey. "Okay, when you ask about electronic services I think about putting a hold on through the website, which I think is hard to do. Oh, you meant databases? What's a database? Is that the catalog?" This is the way you see how people interpret questions. Do the different testers interpret questions in the same way? If not, try again and use synonyms, be more concrete, and ask for help.

Finally, a careful person who has had nothing to do with the survey needs to proofread it for grammar, spelling, and visual presentation errors. Nobody who has written or edited the survey up to this point can really catch problems at this stage: it needs fresh eyes. The survey should provide a smooth, readable appearance with no mistakes. Embed your library's logo in appropriate places. Now it is a marketing brochure.

Administering the Survey: Selecting, Sending, Receiving

Now that the survey exists, it needs to be sent, received, and returned. All of this will depend on your target population: its size, their addresses, and their capabilities. As far as size goes, sometimes you want to reach all of your population. This is common in school and academic library settings when you need to reach all teachers or faculty or all biology majors. In a public library setting, be sure about the distinction between all attendees at an event and a broader "all," all your patrons who might have attended. You can hand out surveys at all programming events. Those are "all," when the population is program attendees, and will be useful in rating the quality of the programs. They are not "all" of the population of potential attendees.

If the target population is smaller than 20 people, consider doing individual interviews on the topics of your survey. It is generally worth the extra time because it yields richer data and also builds connections between you and your users. If the target population is between 20 and 150 individuals, you will probably send surveys to all of them. For populations over 300, consider randomly sampling a number between 100 and 300 and placing extra effort into follow-ups to get responses from just those. These size numbers overlap because other considerations such as the availability of addresses come into the decision (see Table 1.5).

Target Population	Interview	Survey All	Survey Sample
5-20	X		
15–150		X	
100–500		X	X
1,000+			X

Table 1.5 Participant Numbers, Surveys versus Interviews.

You will need an address in order to reach each target. Note that just placing a link on your webpage is not a real survey. Nor, really, is putting a note on circulation slips. That is more like having a suggestion box available. Real surveys involve actively reaching out to people. These are the most common varieties of addressing prospective respondents:

- *Captive audience.* This is very effective. In this scenario, people are gathered for some other reason, and you take some of their time and ask them to answer a survey. Even though filling out the survey is voluntary, people generally comply. The in-person captive audience is one clear reason to keep producing paper surveys because this is by far the best method for getting a high number of responses.

  This method is very common in schools and universities. Either a required process such as orientation or a large-enrollment course is targeted in order to reach "all" students. Using the homeroom works in schools. Specific gateway courses reach students in a particular discipline. Parents waiting for children to finish programs are also a captive audience. The main drawback, a growing problem, is that it is so effective that too many people want to use it, and so those processes and classes get over-surveyed and burnt out.

  On the other hand, think about some unused captives. This could be asking a Chamber of Commerce meeting to include a brief library survey or asking a social service agency to make the surveys available for their clients.

- *Transactional audience.* In this situation, people are engaged in just the type of activity you are curious about, and you approach them as they are engaged. This includes attendees at the end of a program session, people picking up books on hold, or people having questions answered at the information desk. In each case, the main trick is to make the survey so quick and important that they do not mind a slight delay.

  A transactional audience is important when you only want people who have had certain experiences. Broadly surveying college students about interlibrary loan will bore many and reach few who are interested or qualified to talk about it.

- *Registrations.* This is available for most libraries. Generally, the best choice is to take a random sample of members from the registration lists and reach out to those particular people with an individual request for a response, either with a paper survey or response envelope and a survey link, or with an email and survey link. Make it appear individual, not like a mass email blast. If you envision doing several surveys with members of the same list, avoid oversurveying individuals by choosing, the first time, every 10th person starting at 1, then the next time every 10th starting at 2, and so forth.

- *Walk-bys.* In this situation, place survey distributors where they can personally ask people to fill out surveys. This is relatively feasible for public libraries, where volunteers can staff entrances during a survey week. It also covers situations in special libraries where you can give a survey to everyone who visits virtually or in person. One public library did a walk-by at a Wal-Mart to reach non–library users.

- *Random dialing.* Large national surveys such as those for political polls and for organizations like the Pew Center employ random-digit dialing. This is *sequential random sampling.* In this method, they use the next randomly generated number, over and over, until after dead ends and no-answers and refusals the desired number of actual respondents is reached. This can be very discouraging when you have 20 or more unanswered numbers attempted for every completed respondent. This is the most scientific method and the only one that will actually represent most of the potential members of a broad target audience, but it is not very feasible. Professional surveying organizations have the technology to conduct this type of study as efficiently as possible.

Listserv distribution is often used in research. People interested in a topic such as qualifications of catalogers identify listservs that are likely to have people who are able to answer the questions. In the case of catalogers, one of their lists is located and the survey is posted to it. This is more like a passive "check our webpage link" than an active survey and is not usually relevant for library evaluation projects. First of all, neither researchers nor evaluators really know who belongs to and pays attention to the listserv and how they are or are not like others who would be relevant but simply do not subscribe to that list. Second, responses are often very few. Finally, evaluators are usually targeting a well-defined user population, not everybody and anybody. Topical listservs usually do not map closely to that population.

Capability means how the target population is comfortable with communicating: paper or online, and if online, by what method. If paper or online, what reading level or background knowledge is needed? The main point is to realize that the method of surveying has a large effect on *who* answers and a small effect on *how*. On the one hand, people who would not have patience for a paper survey are often willing to do an online survey. It is very inexpensive to reach people via email. Surveys are in effect shorter, both because of the ease of presentation and because skip logic can present just the relevant sections. People can type longer comments than they might have the space or time to do longhand.

On the other hand, some people are not technologically adept. Librarians spend their lives with technology, but many of their patrons do not. If you use a technology that people find intimidating, it is the equivalent of using a screen of "are you comfortable with this? If yes, you can proceed." The same goes for reading level and sheer quantity of reading. Some people are less verbally fluent than others; a large quantity of questions that ask for comments and reflections will seem imposing to them, not open and inviting.

Librarians need to be thoughtful about orienting the survey format to what their respondents consider normal in their daily lives. Oral surveys have an important place in reaching people who are not text oriented.

Analyzing Results

Survey data summarization comes in four rough groups: percentages or frequencies from category data, numbers or averages from numeric-rating data, simple cross-tabulations, and statistical testing. Web-based survey hosts provide category and numeric summaries automatically; some cross-tabs may be available, possibly at a premium price level. Paper survey data needs to be entered into a spreadsheet. Often it is efficient for someone to enter these by using a web survey form, which funnels the data into the spreadsheet. Spreadsheet or statistical-package-formatted downloads are provided at various price points by web hosts. All survey data for analysis must eventually be structured within a spreadsheet.

The different types of questions listed in Table 1.6 result in different types of data and data analysis. *Frequencies* means the numbers of respondents choosing each option. For example, if 120 people respond and 14 choose "retired," then the frequency of "retired" is 14 and the percentage (of the total) is 12% (see Table 1.6).

Types of Questions	Types of Data
Dichotomous (two choices)	0, 1 = frequencies or percentages
Multiple choice, choose any	0, 1 for each
Multiple choice, choose one	A, B, . . . Z: frequencies and percentages for each
Rating (Likert-type)	1-max on scale; averages
Ask-exact (short)	A, B, . . . Z: frequencies and percentages for each
Open-ended	Text coding: see "Interviews" section
Not: ranking	*Create from ratings*

Table 1.6   Types of Questions and Types of Data.

For each dichotomous question the answer is either 0 for the first option, for instance "female," or 1 for the second option:

Where do you live?   ____In the city limits   ____Elsewhere
                                              1   0

For dichotomous questions *only*, if the person *skips* the question, leave the data space blank.

For multiple choice choose-any questions, if the choice is chosen, the answer is 1; if it is skipped, enter 0. Here, do not leave anything blank because if someone does not choose something, that itself is data.

What types of materials do you borrow?

1   __x__Fiction (general)

0   _____Westerns

1   __x__Graphic novels

1   __x__Science fiction or fantasy

In a spreadsheet, each *completed survey is a row*, and each *question or option is a column*. The way this works with dichotomous and choose-any questions looks like this (see Table 1.7).

Survey Number	Live Where	Fiction	Westerns	Graphic	Sci-Fi
1	1	1	0	1	1
2	1	1	0	0	0
3		1	1	0	0
4	0	1	0	0	0
Summary	67% *In the city limits*	100% *Chose fiction*	25% *Chose westerns*	25% *Chose graphic novels*	25% *Chose Science fiction*

Table 1.7 Report Example: Frequencies of Respondents in Categories.

In the spreadsheet, *averaging* the columns of 1s and 0s gives the percentages of respondents who have selected that particular option. See the last row in the table above. In this case, we see that fiction is very well used, but the other options have limited fan bases. For the "live where" column, if someone, such as person 3, has left it blank, the spreadsheet calculates as if this question does not exist. That is, if the response is "1 = within the city," then the result will be 67% of those who answered live within the city.

Multiple-choice choose-one questions are the most complex to analyze. This is because each answer is a mutually exclusive category. Take, for example, work status: "full time," "part time," "retired," or "other." You cannot average these all together, to say that the "average" patron is somewhere between full time and retired because 60 people said "full time," 45 said "retired," and only 20 said "part time" and 4 said "other." How these are handled in a spreadsheet or data program depends on which you use. If you use SPSS, SAS, or other statistical processing software, then each category is assigned an arbitrary number:

1 = full time

2 = part time

3 = retired

4 = other

These numbers cannot be averaged. Instead, they are used within the programs to sort the responses so that frequencies and percentages can be reported:

		Frequencies	Percentages
1	Full time	60 responses	46.5%
2	Part time	45 responses	34.9%

3	Retired	20 responses	15.5%
4	Other	4 responses	3.1%

If you are only using a plain spreadsheet program such as Excel, then it is best to treat these the way you treated choose-any questions, with each response in a separate column. The one selected will have a "1" and the ones not selected will have a "0," and percentages can be calculated just as above (see Table 1.8).

Survey Number	Work—Full Time	Work—Part Time	Work—Retired	Work—Other
1	1	0	0	0
2	1	0	0	0
3	0	1	0	0
4	0	0	1	0
Frequency	2	1	1	0
Percent	50%	25%	25%	0%

Table 1.8   Data Example: Survey Rows for Respondents.

You can also use Excel *pivot tables* to sort and summarize the data. In that case, the *name* of the choice should be used because pivot tables use the contents of the cell and not the column headers to label their results. You want it to use "part time," not "2" (see Table 1.9).

Survey Number	Work Status
1	Full time
2	Full time
3	Part time
4	Retired

Table 1.9   Data Example: Labels for Categories.

Therefore, the technique you use will depend on the software you use to analyze the data. This is also reflected in download options from web survey hosts (see Table 1.10).

Multiple-Choice Choose One	Paper into Spreadsheet	Download from Web Host
Plain Excel	1 or 0 in columns for each choice	Numeric
Excel pivot table	Names, one column	Actual text, condensed
SPSS or SAS	Numbers, one column	Numeric, condensed

Table 1.10   Multiple Choice, Choose-Only-One Data Choices.

For rating questions, such as Likert-type scales, the answers are very simple and just represent the numbers on the scale. Each question is one column. This provides a lot of data for little effort and allows interesting comparisons (see Table 1.11).

Survey Number	Quality of Service	Quality of Collection	Convenience of Hours
1	5	3	3
2	5	4	3
3	4	3	4
4	5	2	3
Average	4.75	3.00	3.25

Table 1.11   Data Example: Rating Scale Responses.

In this example, people appreciate the service more than the collection or the hours.

Ask-exact question analysis depends on the nature of the responses. Usually, someone has to review the answers to see what kinds of consistencies they show. They may already be very consistent. You could ask what someone's major is rather than listing all the possibilities to be checked, and you would find consistency (see Table 1.12).

What Is Your Major?	What Is Your Major (use the class code)?
Biology	BIO
English	ENG
Criminal Justice	CRJ
English	ENG

Table 1.12   Data Example: Coding Open-Ended Responses (College).

You might not find consistency in surveys that ask people their professions. If they are consistent, then they are treated like multiple-choice choose-one categories. If they are not, then someone needs to create that consistency by adding a column wherein each answer is given a consistent label or code (see Table 1.13).

Original	Codified
Teacher	Education
Teacher's aide	Education
Hospital social worker	Health
Business	Business
My own company	Business
Lawn care	Business
Law office	Professional
Store	Business
Nurse	Health
Grocery store	Business

Table 1.13   Data Example: Coding Open-Ended Responses (Public).

This process is very similar to cataloging from a relatively short list of controlled vocabulary. The goal is to use enough categories so that dissimilar originals are not put in the same group; for instance, are "nurse" and "police officer" to go into the "professional" category? Yet you do not want so many that there are one- or two-people groups, such as, "nurse," "hospital nurse," "home health nurse," and "medical technician."

Finally, when answers are lengthy enough, they become what is known as qualitative data and need a different type of analysis that is primarily not numeric. An explanation of this type of analysis is in the "Interviews" section.

Cross-tabs refers to creating subgroups out of the data and comparing their results. For example, consider a survey that has questions on both work status and the convenience of hours. With all respondents in the survey, the rating of convenience of hours may average 4.10. However, if you break it down, perhaps the hours were really rated highly only by retired persons—and there were a large number of retired people responding to the survey (see Table 1.14).

Work Status	Convenience of Hours
Full time	3.13
Part time	3.60
Retired	4.75
Other	4.23

Table 1.14   Report Example: Cross-tab Ratings.

With category questions, cross-tabbing can tell you who groups themselves on two different questions. Consider usage of electronic devices: do you own a smartphone, tablet, or laptop—yes or no? (See Table 1.15.)

Percent Checking They Use	Undergraduate	Graduate	Faculty	Staff/Other
Laptop	95%	98%	67%	65%
Tablet	21%	25%	52%	42%
Smartphone	34%	38%	55%	34%
The overall percent depends on the number in each category.				

Table 1.15   Report Example: Percentages by Groups.

Web-based survey software can provide cross-tabbed results. Statistical software is even more flexible and powerful. Within Excel, a pivot table is the most efficient method to produce these summaries. If plain Excel is used, the summaries can be done by careful sorting of answers.

Statistical testing is valuable even with limited evaluation results and even if you do not intend to transform your results into published research. The main purpose of statistical testing in evaluation is when you see that two things differ: to distinguish between a difference that appears because of sampling, natural variation, or inexact measurements and a difference that reflects actual, serious, important differences.

Here are some situations where things might differ.

- The convenience of hours score for retired people is 4.4, for part-time workers is 4.5, and for full-time workers is 3.3. The difference between retired and part-time is 0.1 and between retired and full-time is 1.1.

- 45% of faculty members have tablets; 33% of students have tablets.

- You survey all of your students, who are about 65% female and 35% male. The respondents to your survey turn out to be 50% female and 50% male. Are the respondents unrepresentative?

Here are some reasons why things might vary on their own rather than as a result of the two situations. That is, faculty members do not really own tablets more than students, retired people are not happier with library hours than full-time workers, and men were not reached more effectively with the survey.

- *Sampling.* If you select or invite only a random sample of a large population, then just by chance you may select people who feel one way or another in ways that differ from the whole population. This is what is known as the margin of error and is commonly reported in national polls. When conducting a random survey, a very rough guide is that for a sample of 400, results are within +3% to −3% of what they would be if you got everyone to answer, and to reduce that to 2% you need to survey 1,000 people, which is why a sample of 400 is so frequent in news stories.

- *Chance* also affects nonrandom samples. If you flip a coin 10 times, it is somewhat unlikely that it will land exactly 5 heads and 5 tails. Three heads and 7 tails does not necessarily mean there is something wrong with the coin.

- *Natural variation.* If something has a lot of variation on its own, then variation between two groups is not so distinctive. Think of this as consistency. The more consistent each group is on its own, the more real are the differences between them. The less consistent each group is, the more an apparent variation may just be chance. If every time you go to an ice cream stand your "single-dip" cone is a very different size, then when you get a smaller one, you know it is part of the natural and undesirable variation. If a single scoop has always been a certain size and then seems to be consistently smaller, the more you suspect that something has changed in the business's policy.

In Excel or in statistical software, the command "standard deviation" will tell you how varied or inconsistent the underlying data is.

- *Inexact measurements.* It is unrealistic to assume that people can make very fine distinctions in their answers. The more fuzzy the question and the more fuzzy the concept, the more likely it is that differences reflect people's reactions to the question and their ability to answer. This may mean they simply cannot make these fine distinctions rather their having more serious differences in judgments.

In statistics, a "t-test" measures whether two scores such as averages differ by groups. A chi^2 or "kai-square" analysis tests whether categories differ from each other and by how much. If 26% of faculty (18 of 68) in a survey have a smartphone and 32% of undergraduates (167 out of 522) do, is that difference real or just what might normally be seen, given that coins do not land head–tails–head–tails exactly and consistently? *Chapter 3 and Appendix B show how to set up these tests; only Excel is needed, though statistical software is more flexible and accurate.*

The main point of statistical testing is important to keep in mind even if you do not use it. Some variation is normal. Differences between groups may not signal anything really different but just this normal variation. The more respondents you have, the larger the differences between groups and the more consistent each group is within itself: each one of these factors increases your confidence that a difference you can see mathematically such as 4.5 versus 4.6 or 4.9 does reflect a real difference. This group really is more satisfied than the other group.

A simple plan for analyzing a survey as a whole goes like this:

- The survey itself should proceed from topic to topic. Provide basic summaries such as numbers, percentages, and averages for each question, grouped by topic.

- Consider if people can be divided into demographic groups and see if it makes sense to report their group averages or percentages in comparisons.

- Think about whether you think one item on a survey affects another. Are smartphone users more likely to say they "like" your Facebook page? Use cross-tabs for these.

- Read through all of the results and pull out the three or four most important or striking results. Arrange them in order of importance, not the order in which they appeared on the survey. Give the results three ways:
  o Bullet point sentences—a verbal description
  o Numbers, including the number of respondents (N)
  o Graphs such as bar, pie, or line charts. Make sure that all charts about similar items such as using the same five-point Likert-type scale are of the same physical size and use the same scale, or length of the X and Y axes.

General information on this is found in the Summarizing and Analyzing Data section of Chapter 3.

Study Questions/Examples

These two articles give the full text of the surveys as well as how they reached their audiences and the results. Each was conducted at a single site, although the authors of the first article attempt to draw generalized conclusions, which equals research, while the second intentionally focuses on a specific service or evaluation.

Bridges, Laurie M., and Tiah Edmundson-Morton. "Image-Seeking Preferences among Undergraduate Novice Researchers." *Evidence Based Library and Information Practice* 6.1 (2011): 24–40.

Bancroft, Donna, and Susan Lowe. "Helping Users Help Themselves: Evaluating the Off-Campus Library Services Web Site." *Journal of Library Administration* 45.1/2 (2006): 17–35.

- Who are the target (desired) audience?
- Who responded?
- Give an example of a(n):
  - Open-ended question.
  - Category question.
  - Rating question.
  - Numerical but not rating question.
- Do the authors report cross-tab results (table or graph)?

Interviews

Introduction

Interviews are another way to find out more about what people think about your library, systems, resources, and services. Their greatest strength is providing the information on *why* to complement information on *what*. Interviews are

- Time-consuming.

- Potentially inconsistent.

- Rich.

- Interactive.

They result in open-ended, textual data, either by taking notes or recording and producing verbatim transcripts. That makes it a qualitative method; *qualitative*, roughly speaking, means text-based rather than category- or number-based. The question is "What do you think about your study load?" rather than, "How many classes are you taking?" This introduction covers what makes an interview an interview and the pros and cons of interviewing as compared to other methods.

The key defining features of interviewing as an evaluation technique are that it is open-ended and interactive. That is, it allows respondents to say things in their own words, outside of predetermined categories, and the interviewer has the chance to follow up and to ask people to explain and expand on their answers. It is about listening and not presuming. This makes it especially valuable when you do not know enough about an issue to be able to create a really solid, unambiguous survey question. Here is a clue: if you have a survey question with category answers and "other," and more than a third of your respondents select "other," then your categories are not sufficient and you need to consider interviewing.

An evaluation or research interview is distinctly different from other library interview situations. A reference interview also involves listening, but often it includes "leading" questions, when the librarian is more familiar with the topic or the context than the patron is: "What class is this for?" or "what part of the job search are you interested in—writing a resume?" Most reference interviews also involve teaching: "Let me show you. . . ."

Those are not part of an evaluation interview. Interviewers should not hint at or lead into particular answers, nor should they help the patron. The interviewer must listen to a patron's frustrations, complaints, or compliments and concentrate on learning more, not on fixing the situation described.

When librarians do the interviewing, another challenge is to encourage the respondent to be candid about library problems. Patrons are reluctant to confess difficulties. Part of that is natural politeness, but it also happens because they do not want to admit they do not how to use a library. Just as in usability studies, patrons in interviews need reassurance that problems they report are chances for the library to improve, not confessions of the patrons' inadequacy. Asking respondents for ideas for the library to improve is often a good way to elicit criticisms where a more direct question might not.

An interview is a less efficient and a more time-consuming method than surveys, focus groups, or observation. Generally, you can involve far fewer people than you can reach with a survey or observe unobtrusively. Interviews can be a little more feasible than focus groups because of greater scheduling flexibility. They can also be biased and inconsistent if the interviewers do not keep to the same topics and allow everyone the opportunity to comment on the same issues while following up on individual comments—a difficult balance.

The solidity of the information gained in interviews depends on three things: the quality of the interview itself, the analysis done of the results, and the selection of those to be interviewed. Because there are so few people involved, their selection has a huge impact on the results. A survey can target a really wide audience, even though not everybody responds. Interviewees are selected and then solicited, and they are very few in number. It is important not to take their information as being generally true of all patrons. The section in Chapter 3 on sampling for qualitative information covers how to enhance the validity of this selection procedure, which is so important to the credibility of the results.

Why do interviews? Above all, interviews are valuable when you want to know *why*. Surveys and observations are excellent for "what," but not good for "why." Second, interviews are valuable when the "what" itself is not very easy to observe or is not distinct enough to precategorize in survey questions. What a child does at home because of a summer reading program would be very difficult to tap through observation, surveys, or focus groups.

A well-done interview is a real treasure of unanticipated information. It is one of the few ways to find out what we really do not know and our unknown unknowns.

Procedure

Interviewing for evaluation consists of four steps:

1. Recruiting interviewees

2. Preparing questions and formats

3. Conducting the interviews

4. Analyzing the results

Recruiting Interviewees

In Chapter 3 there is a section on sampling. This will help you understand the main points to keep in mind as you try to attract interviewees. These are considerations such as the variety of experiences you want to capture, whether people are experts or novices in a particular topic, and the range of user or patron types or categories you want to include. In real life, sometimes you simply will advertise as much as possible and take the participants that you can get. When that happens, keep in mind how the method you used to select interviewees forms part of the background of your results: that is, *whom* you have interviewed affects *what* information you gather.

For existing users, use your normal methods for communicating with them. This can be flyers within your facility, tear-off numbers or Quick Response (QR) codes provided, emails, and also personal invitations to in-person visitors. Not all interviews are lengthy affairs. Sometimes you can catch someone for a few minutes while they are waiting for something else such as a computer to boot up or a room to become available. Avoid trying to stop someone on their way out; catch them on the way in. Interviews also can be conducted by phone, email, or chat for those who are comfortable with those methods. Remember that each method will attract those people who are most comfortable with it. In-person interviews at midday will attract only those whose schedules and lives place them in your library at that time: residential students, children's caregivers, the retired. Chat interviews will reach a different, but still restricted, set of users.

Nonusers are the most difficult people to involve because by definition they have no established contact point with your organization. The added effort is worth it because these interviews will tell you things you will never find out from those with whom you are already succeeding; people interviewed at a program will not tell you that your programs are all uninteresting. The way to contact people who are not users is to find out what they are users of—to use their other connections to get in touch with them, including the local YMCA, Kiwanis, church, employment agency, workplace, and so forth. Because you are asking more of them to help this strange organization they do not use already, it is appropriate to offer them something in return for their time and input.

Two practical answers are given for the questions "how many interviews?" and "when do you stop interviewing?" You can confidently stop when you reach two goals at the same time: representativeness and saturation. First, ensure that the interviewees are representative of the groups that you are intending to question. Just because teenagers come up with nothing new does not mean that a senior citizen would not have a different perspective to add. Second, in your interviews you reach a saturation point: you hear the same things, and new interviewees do not add any additional perspective. Most evaluation interview projects involve between 10 and 20 individuals. More details are in the section in Chapter 3 about sampling.

Preparing Questions and Formats

Interviews are interactive, but they also need to be reasonably consistent. If you talk to 10 people primarily about adult programming, and then the eighth person mentions something about simultaneous children's activities, do you ask the ninth and tenth person about that? It is not accurate to report that "only" one or two or three people, out of 10, mentioned that, when persons one through seven might have if given the opportunity.

This seems contradictory to the overall idea that interviews will tell you things that you do not already know. This is a tension. The goal is to prepare in advance but still be open. One way to do this is to have one or two trial interviews so that you can test out just how you will ask the questions, getting any nervousness out of the way and learning a little about what might come up. These preinterviewees do not need to be selected as carefully as the real ones and can be family, coworkers, or friends.

Different interviewers have different styles. Some may be more comfortable writing out the main questions word for word, others with just having a topic noted and then speaking extemporaneously. If more than one interviewer is involved, write out the main questions entirely so that each interview starts out with a consistent framework.

The interview format has a range of formality and data-recording options:

- *Drive-by*. In this format, you have asked someone for a few minutes of their time as they are doing something else. In this situation, the most important thing is to ask simple, direct questions as quickly as possible while making limited notes at the time and taking some time after the interview to write down additional details. A clipboard and pencil are the essential tools. For each interviewee, have a sheet of paper on which the main questions are laid out, easily readable for you with space for notes.

Despite the brevity, do not forget to ask follow-up questions to make it a true interactive interview.

- *Scheduled.* Arrange with the interviewee a time of mutual convenience for 30 to 60 minutes. Some interviews will take as little as 15 minutes, but a 30-minute slot is the minimum.

  These interviews can be done in person or by phone. If done in person, be sure to arrange a place that is relatively private, neutral, and nonthreatening. The glass-boxed study rooms in many public libraries are ideal for this.

- *Email.* Interviews can be conducted entirely by email, or email can be offered as an option. In that situation, the interviewer sends emails to persons introducing the questions that the interviewer is interested in and asks the persons to either write his or her responses or suggest a time to meet or talk by phone.

  It is important to allow enough time for multiple email exchanges and for multiple interviewees. Only a few people out of those contacted in this way will be really prompt and responsive, but this technique does allow you to reach different people than those who can visit in person or who want to take the time for a phone interview.

Conducting the Interviews

An evaluation or research interview has the following overall structure:

1. Introduction

2. Main questions

3. Wrap-up

For the introduction, interviewers introduce themselves in relation to their organization, mention the purpose of the interview, and express appreciation. "As you know [from the arrangements for meeting], I am Madison Smith and I've been asked by MyTown Public Library to ask people about their experiences with and desires for the library. We really do appreciate this opportunity to listen, and it is great that you can give us this time."

The introduction also includes a few quantitative, survey-type questions provided orally. This would be things like age group, work status, frequency of visits, and other things that are mentioned in the section above on survey construction. This part has several purposes. It gives you context for the answers, such as "two people who are retired mentioned. . . ." It adds a little bit of personalization, which can be a good thing. People are alerted that they are representatives of a group, perhaps "working mothers," and their opinions will not be taken as individual comments or personal criticisms. Finally, it warms up both interviewer and interviewee, getting them into a rhythm of question and answer, and priming them in terms of memory. A question about how often you visit the library starts the interviewees thinking about library visits.

In the introduction, name the areas that will be discussed. This gets the interviewee thinking and also heads off a common problem of people hijacking the first question because they really want to talk about X. If they know that X is on the schedule, they can relax about questions A, B, and C.

The main questions have to do with the purposes of the interview. Scheduled interviews should not only be about small, simple items such as "How do you like our parking?" Think about all the topics that your interviewee can reasonably talk about, and fill a half an hour. Parking is one thing, but also ask where the library visits fall within weekly activities; ask about programs but also collections; and ask for overall impressions and any details.

Some interviewees talk a lot; many provide only limited answers. Here are some techniques for the latter:

- *Tour*. Ask them to describe the areas of the library that they are familiar with; probe with "what did you like or dislike about that?"

- *Incident or process*. Ask the interviewees to recount the last time that they did X. A key probe for this is to ask in as neutral and open a tone as possible, "Why?" "Can you tell me what you were thinking when . . . ?"

- *Critical incident*. Ask the interviewee for the best experience with X and for the worst, or ask for the most memorable. In your analysis, be sure to note that this question was leading and these are not representative incidents. Instead, this technique is used because people find it easier to talk about memorable events.

- *Secondhand*. Ask them what they say about X to others or what they have heard others say.

It is very important to use wording and vocal tones that are *open* and *neutral*. Even a question phrased as, "How satisfied were you with X?" presupposes that the respondents were satisfied or that satisfaction is the issue. "How was X" is more neutral in tone. You can guess that "Why didn't you do X?" is a very judgmental question; it implies that the interviewee is ignorant and wrong. However, as far as tone goes, it is also very hard to say, "Why did you do that?" in a nonparental tone: "*Why* did you do *that*?" Either practice the tones so that it comes out truly neutral or rephrase the question, "Can you tell me a little about why you chose to do that? What was going through your mind?"

Avoid dead-end questions. If a question can be politely answered with "yes" or "no" or one word, that question belongs on a survey. If you use it in an interview, it should only be an introduction followed by a probe. "Do you like our video selection?" Do not stop with "yes" or "no" but follow up with, "What do you like or not like?" When you are preparing, write out all of your questions. If you find that more than half of the questions are closed-ended, you probably are really thinking of a survey. Switch to a survey or collaborate with a colleague to rewrite the questions in a more open way.

After interviewees respond, it is appropriate to rephrase the person's statements, and this step also helps gather more information. It shows the person you are really listening and are interested in further details. "You said that you don't use the e-books. Can you tell me more about that?"

Finally, *do not help*. At that moment, in the interview, do not offer advice or assistance. If someone says they have difficulty with X, the right response in an evaluation interview is, "Can you tell me some more details? We'd like to get things fixed," not, "Oh, you need to click on. . . . Let me show you." Complete the interview; then, if appropriate, offer some assistance. Not only does offering help immediately cut short what the person is telling you, you are subtly indicating that they are wrong or ignorant and need instruction.

During the wrap-up, broadly restate a few themes that the interviewee has mentioned. Check your notes and make sure you have covered the important areas. At this point, asking for suggestions can also be a way of uncovering additional problem areas: "Well, you could try some online RSS" is another way for the interviewee to tell you that you are not communicating well enough.

Express thanks and appreciation again, and mention the way in which your interviews will be used, such as "The board will be hearing about what our patrons think," or "We will use these suggestions for next fall's orientation."

Analyzing the Results

When there are just a few interviews, it is fairly easy to review your notes or transcripts as a whole, note down major themes, and identify any areas for follow-up. From a small number of interviews, it is not possible to state that something is definitely an issue, but it is possible to counter the negative. If you believe that your staff members are *always* friendly, then even one incident of unfriendliness disproves it, and when several people mention it independently, that is a cause for concern.

Be sure to report the quantitative information and to place comments and summaries, which are the *what* that was said, within the context of *who* said it.

Analyzing more material such as lengthy interviews with more than five or so interviewees can be done through word processing or through specialized qualitative software such as N*Vivo. In the past, this was done by literally cutting parts of transcripts into bits, pasting them onto index cards, and then sorting the results into thematic piles. The following is a low-tech, pragmatic approach that is suitable for the amounts of information that most librarians can collect on their own without consultants.

Using Word or another such program, copy the transcript and then break the transcript or notes down into separate comments. For each comment, add a small source code that indicates the source or the interviewee. It can be useful for this to have some content as well, such as F1 for the first female interviewee, or FR1 for "female, residential student, number 1."

Read through the comments. Think about broad themes and individual items. Researchers generally take two different approaches, called "grounded theory" or "thematic coding." Essentially, these are ground-up or top-down approaches. In ground-up approaches, you read through the comments with an open mind and allow the comments themselves to suggest themes. In this light, a word cloud or other text-analysis program can tell you what individual words are used most frequently. In a top-down approach, from your experience, discussion with colleagues, or reading of the literature, you have some idea about the topics or types of comments people will make, and coding the actual comments is somewhat like cataloging them from an existing controlled vocabulary list. In practice, you will probably go into the coding with some preconceived ideas and make modifications as you encounter the actual interviews.

Mark individual comments with codes representing themes, for example "negative" or "positive," while "building" can be used for comments about lighting, air conditioning, or bathrooms or "technology" for computers and wireless.

Sort through and group the coded comments into sections. Looking at these groups, check for consistent themes, comments that offset each other such as "You open too early" or "You don't open early enough," or a section that is just too big. This might be one where there are so many comments about the physical building that you can zero in on different areas.

Within each group or theme, sort comments by the source codes. These can indicate if there are demographic differences. Is it the male residential students who kept mentioning all-night hours? Among audiovisual (AV) materials, are men more interested in DVDs and women in audiobooks? For particularly vivid or problematic comments, you can use the source codes to return to the full transcripts to see the context of the comments and the quantitative information about the person who made them: is this person like your typical user?

All of this will give you a sense of the combined perspective of the interviewees. The end result, or findings, will be sentences that summarize and faithfully represent the bulk of the comments. But then, how is the comment summary "Interviewees said they like our library" different from the day-to-day sharing of anecdotes and personal impressions among librarians about what they think patrons have said? People should have confidence in the results for two reasons: the process and the analysis. First, the process is not anecdotal because it is, instead, systematic. You have recruited and selected interviewees intentionally to seek out information; you are not relying on comments people feel motivated to volunteer. Second, in the analysis, the results are reliable when they can be replicated, just as in any other form of evaluation or research.

You can demonstrate the replicability of your findings in two easy ways: inter-rater and split-half. In an inter-rater approach, have two or three people independently code or organize the comments. If different people are seeing the same thing, it means it is probable that most people will see those things and that your findings are reliable.

The second technique is to set aside a portion of the comments, about a quarter to a third of them. This set-aside part should be similar to the rest of the comments, that is, not just those from particularly unusual interviewees. Then analyze the remaining part. Take the thematic results from the larger section and see if they match what is in the set-aside part. For example, you might find that a difficult-to-use website was mentioned by more than half of respondents. Note these down and then look at the one-quarter of comments that were set aside. Are the themes reasonably present in those? If they are, that is good. If they are not, consider if there is some reason that that group was different from the others or if the entire group of interviewees was just too varied to generalize at all. If too much remains individualistic and too difficult to summarize, consider the whole exercise just the first step in working your way towards understanding. Consider another round of interviews or a survey.

More information on interviewee sampling and on analysis of quantitative information is in Chapter 3, "Technique Selection and Sampling".

Study Questions/Examples

These two articles give the results of studies using interviews and are unusually clear about the methodology. Both of these articles are research, not evaluation, although note that the first study gathered its participants from only one site, so it could be characterized as being about that library, not libraries in general. The second study, by Dulock, included a fairly large number of quantitative or survey-type questions.

Adkins, Denice, and Lisa Hussey. "The Library in the Lives of Latino College Students." *Library Quarterly* 76.4 (2006): 456–80.
Dulock, Michael. "New Cataloger Preparedness: Interviews with New Professionals in Academic Libraries." *Cataloging and Classification Quarterly* 49.2 (2011): 65–96.

- What is the general group about which the authors wanted to find something out? What was their main question?
- Who exactly participated as an interviewee?
- What was one question used?
- Give two findings, each in one specific sentence.

Focus Groups

Introduction

Focus groups may be a bigger pop culture phenomenon than even the interview, from which they came. "We'll focus group that" or "That movie's ending came from focus groups" are heard in general news and conversation. From these examples we can see a primary area for focus groups: marketing and products. This leads to some of the most important features of focus groups for library evaluation. This introduction defines the characteristics of a focus group, with its strengths and weaknesses, and gives tips about when to do a focus group. The procedure section will describe the process. Refer to the end of the "Interviews" section and the section in Chapter 3 about summarizing to handle the transcripts of focus group sessions.

A focus group is a group of people who spend an hour or so discussing a topic or set of topics with a moderator and usually an assistant. Like an interview, the discussion is free-flowing and is not confined to the preset responses of a survey's quantitative questions. This makes it a qualitative method resulting in text. Unlike an interview, a participant's responses can be sparked or suppressed by the other people involved in the group, not just by an interviewer or moderator.

Focus groups are interviews that are more social and more efficient. They are more efficient in that you can receive input from up to 10 people in the space of one hour. Because only one moderator is needed per group, it can be more feasible to hire moderators than to hire interviewers. This is a key reason why focus groups were and are so well developed for marketing and product companies; they are less expensive than some other methods while they give detailed feedback and ideas very useful for the formative stages of product development.

Focus groups are also intensely social experiences. Generally, participants in each particular focus group are homogeneous, meaning persons in the group are like each other. For example, if you have senior citizens, teens, and parents all available for focus groups, they will be more comfortable in three separate groups. More comfortable generally means more forthcoming. The importance of the "interviewer," now the moderator, is diminished; the participants outnumber this person. This reduces people's reluctance to speak up against an authority figure. People who hear others mention a topic that concerns them and who agree with the points raised feel freer to add their own experiences because they have the comfort of a group. They do not feel alone or personally inadequate with their frustrations and can discuss them in more detail.

Socially as well, focus groups can involve suppression of opinions in two ways. First, people who are slower to speak can become shy when there are more vocal participants, although a skillful moderator, using deliberate pauses, can counter this somewhat. Second, if a participant has an opinion or an experience that seems counter to those of the group, it is very unlikely that he or she will discuss them. Silence, in other words, does not necessarily mean agreement with what others are saying. A possible counter to this is to offer participants a way to send their opinions separately and anonymously after the session.

These cautions are not as important to marketers as they are to librarians. Marketers are almost always interested in targeting specific, segmented audiences, where most libraries have a wider mandate. Products often are very social experiences, while many library services and materials, by library ethics, emphasize individual freedom and choice.

Because of the power of the social setting, it is usually best not to consider that a focus group of 10 participants has 10 opinions. You can report 10 interviews by counting: "Six people mentioned X and four people mentioned Y." Instead, report that comments made at one focus group included X and those in another focus group included Y. This makes it very important, whenever possible, to have multiple focus groups. Issues that emerge in more than one independent focus group are far more persuasive than those that happen to occur in just one.

Like interviews, a focus group is excellent at providing a window into users' perspectives, a way of seeing the library from their point of view. For the participants, talking about what they like is far easier and smoother than being asked to write a lengthy explanation of their opinions and experiences. Unlike quantitative survey questions, focus groups can tell you things you would not think to ask about. A librarian who runs evaluation only on surveys will miss exactly what he or she does not know enough about to ask about.

Both interviews and focus groups are useful in getting at this unknown, open-ended information. Each is more or less suited to particular patrons and particular types of libraries. Many teens, for example, generally have time, are talkative, and are appreciative of the chance to give their opinion and also of the food that is a requirement of a good focus group session. Busy adult college students would be far less likely to participate but could be reached individually for interviews. As with interviews, it is important not to generalize the results from those who happened to be able to attend focus groups to represent larger populations.

One of the most feasible and unbiased forms of focus groups is the preexisting, friendly groups such as Kiwanis, Toastmasters, or AV Club. If they can give you a portion of their existing meeting time, you have a chance to reach that rarest of evaluation participants, the people who are not already in your library.

The following section provides the steps in conducting a focus group. Note that if you are in a university setting, a focus group needs some extra attention for research approval because it cannot be as anonymous as an interview or questionnaire. Chapter 3 includes general advice on selecting participants for qualitative methods such as focus groups and analysis of the transcripts that result, with the special issues that the social aspect of focus groups involve.

Consult the "Interviews" section for the basics of question types and analysis.

Procedure

Using focus groups for evaluation consists of four steps:

1. Recruiting participants

2. Preparing questions

3. Conducting the sessions and recording the comments

4. Analyzing the results

Recruiting Participants

In Chapter 3 there is a section on sampling. This describes the main points to keep in mind. Focus groups involve a relatively small number of people so it is important to be very mindful of how the time, place, and conditions of your particular focus group meetings affect who is able and willing to participate.

As noted in the section on interviewing, when you involve your usual patrons, use your usual methods, including things like flyers, email contacts, newsletters, and organizational listservs. You will need a group of people to be together at one time, and those groups should be relatively homogeneous—people similar to each other. Think about the characteristics that make your users like or unlike each other: the harried parents, the teens after school, the residential or commuter students. When you make contact with potential participants, you will need to maneuver people into not just any group but the right group. Usually, this will mean setting up times and then recruiting people into those specific times.

Mealtimes and break times, occasions on which it is normal to offer food or refreshments, are especially useful. Offering food or cookies is a way of entering into an exchange with the participants: your time, our food. It creates a bond. Also, food and drink create a more social atmosphere among participants, diminishing the authority-figure barrier that a moderator might represent.

An especially useful method is to contact a leader for an existing group and ask to become part of their usual meeting. The wonderful thing about this method is that it can reach out to people who would not normally consider you and therefore not consider helping you with your evaluation. Availability bias, or getting easy answers from easily contacted people, is a hazard to all qualitative or low-numbers evaluation. The main drawback is that the leader or leaders of the group will present their own sense of authority, and they may overinfluence the input from the group.

For all of these drawbacks, and in spite of the overall difficulty in getting people to come to focus groups, the main weapon in the fight for validity, or results that are a reasonable reflection of reality, is to have multiple focus groups. What is said in one group may simply be a quirk of that group, that time, and that social dynamic. What is said in two or three groups, especially two or three quite different groups, is much stronger and more valuable in terms of telling you about people's real experiences.

Practicalities count. Ensure that all participants know where to meet, can park, and have someone to contact for questions and assistance.

Preparing Questions

For focus groups, one needs to be both more prepared and more flexible than with individual interviews. Lay out a set of questions or specified topic areas ahead of time. This is vital for consistency between groups, so that each group has the chance to provide input on all areas. *Pretesting* the questions is difficult but very valuable. That is, if possible, take one group and have a skillful moderator go down a list of questions or topics. He or she can see how much discussion each area seems to generate, and with that information, the people conducting the evaluation can adjust their questions for the next groups.

Conducting the Sessions

A focus group session has the following overall structure:

1. Brief introduction
2. Main questions and member participation
3. Wrap-up

The introduction to the focus group generally should be included in emails or phone calls ahead of time. When confirming the session day and time, the evaluator should briefly state the general purpose of the session. As participants arrive, have them fill out cards with relevant demographic or status-type questions, such as age group, frequency of use, work status, and so forth. People should be able to fill out the cards anonymously. You will not use this information for individual-comment analysis but to describe the group as a whole, for instance, "A group consisting of six freshmen and two sophomores."

The moderator starts with thanks, then briefly mentions the overall purpose, the general topics to be covered, and how long the session will last. Mention of time softens the impact of the moderator later having to cut a conversation short in order to keep within the time frame.

With an interviewer, most of the advice has to do with what not to do. Do not use closed-ended questions, do not presume knowledge, do not display an attitude of having the "right" answer, and do not help. With sufficient care, almost anybody can be a good interviewer. For a focus group moderator, the task is more difficult and is more along the lines of what should be done, not what should not be done. Good moderators have open, engaging, interested body language. They know when to pause to encourage people to gather their thoughts. They can use gestures and questions to involve more than just the most vocal participants. The good moderator keeps an eye on both the dynamics of the interaction and the question list to be gone through. Participants need to be brought back from diversions, but if there is intense relevant detail emerging, the schedule needs to bend to allow for it.

Questions for focus groups follow many of the same techniques as for interviewing. Begin with broad questions. More specific prompts such as "describe a visit" may not be needed because comments from all participants tend to draw people out. If broad questions get only general responses, make the questions more concrete, such as "Can you describe the last time when. . . ." Generally, the more specific or concrete the question, the easier it is for people to talk about.

An assistant is very valuable, especially with logistics and gathering the quantitative survey-card information. It is also valuable for the assistant to take notes on body language. Even when a recording is being made, there will be times when the moderator asks people to nod or otherwise agree or disagree; this will not be audible.

Wrap-up questions, at the end of topics or segments and again at the very end, are essential in a focus group. A wrap-up question is one where the moderator asks if X is what he or she has heard the participants saying and adds, "anything else?" Repeating their themes reinforces to participants that they are being listened to, and it gives them an opportunity to correct or to add or remove emphasis: "Yes, but Y is more important."

It is neither feasible nor appropriate for the moderator to do individual follow-up with participants. You do not say, "You mentioned wanting Y—let me tell you we already have it." However, there should be brochures or other contact information ready to hand out.

Analyzing the Results

Focus groups take a lot of effort to arrange. It is a particular waste of that effort to treat their data casually. For some focus groups, especially when you take advantage of existing groups, it may be appropriate simply to take notes, as one would take minutes of a meeting. If you have gone to the trouble of inviting, scheduling, hosting, and conducting formal focus groups, the additional expense of recording the audio and having someone create a transcript is best. Then you can make the most of the effort.

Once a transcript exists, then the steps of content or text analysis take place. A description of the basics of this is found in the "Interviews" section. This simplified Word-based method of analysis is sufficient for three, four, or five focus groups of an hour or so each. If there are more groups, consider engaging a consultant who has expertise in qualitative data analysis. See the sections in Chapter 3 about technology and about consultants.

To get a brief read of the data, there is a simpler route. Have three or four people independently read through the transcripts and note what they consider to be the most common or important thoughts, then compare. If different readers notice the same things, then those are literally the notable findings of the focus group process.

Study Questions/Examples

The academic library study took place at one site, but it is research rather than evaluation because the topics were about mobile use in general, not the mobile services at that particular library. The public library study used focus groups to complement a larger-scale quantitative survey.

Howard, Vivian. "What Do Young Teens Think about the Library?" *Library Quarterly* 81.3 (2011): 321–44.
Seeholzer, Jamie, and Joseph A. Salem Jr. "Library on the Go: A Focus Group Study of the Mobile Web and the Academic Library." *College & Research Libraries* 72.1 (2011): 9–20.

- What is the general group about which the authors wanted to find something? What was their main question?
- How many groups were there? Who participated?
- What was a question used?
- Give two findings, each in one specific sentence.

Usability

Introduction

A usability study is simple, powerful, tricky to arrange, and worth the effort. In a usability study, typical users perform key tasks while being observed and interviewed. It includes both quantitative behavioral observations such as "how much?" or "how long?" and qualitative interviewing, "why?" A formal usability study is a way to get past two problems: inconsistent information from random anecdotes, and people simply not using something for reasons they will not tell you.

Some of the most classic usability studies in library science happened during the development of automated library systems, particularly in the generation that switched from command-line to graphical user interfaces (GUI). Usability studies need not be confined to computer applications, however. A usability study can be conducted whenever there is any system that a person needs to use. This includes how signage and layout hinder or help people trying to find books on the shelves or find the bathrooms. This can be the workflow or task sequence in book or materials processing or even how to use a photocopier. In each instance, the particular goal of usability studies is not to learn how to teach the users to be better users or to change the users, but to learn how to change the system to fit normal, ordinary users. Mistakes by users are not errors that need to be eliminated. They are normal actions that designers must allow for.

The "Procedures" section describes the steps in conducting a usability study. While specialized equipment can track keystrokes, cursor movements, and even gaze, careful observation with just a pencil, paper, and timer can record useful information. Usability testing pulls together several methods so the some of the steps are similar to those in the interview, observation, and transaction log analysis sections.

One key element is recruitment of participants. Like other qualitative, in-depth methods such as interviews and focus groups, usability studies involve a relatively small number of participants. This means selection is very important and affects the validity of the results, or how closely they reflect real life.

Usability testing has one great strength and one small weakness. The great strength is that it is a thorough, multifaceted look at our systems, services, or procedures from the point of view of the user, not the library or the librarian. It combines the concrete actuality of observing the "what"—behavior such as clicking on a choice or not clicking, paths followed or not—with a window into the "why," the users' comments on their thought processes. "I always read the whole screen," one may say, but he or she does not click on the button labeled "next." "I ignore the right-hand side because it is where ads are," says another, and he or she does not refine the search using the facets listed on the right side.

The weakness comes out of the tension between a controlled situation and uncontrolled real life. Usability data is much easier to analyze when different participants do the same tasks and when those tasks are carefully designed to test features of the system. For example, ask participants to find a Spanish-dubbed movie version of *Gone with the Wind*. This taps into several advanced features of a catalog, but are these the tasks that those users would use frequently? Are they interested in them? Are they working harder to find "the answer" because they want to please or impress the evaluator? Or are they not trying hard because they do not care about these features? The more controlled the tasks, the easier and more consistent the results or findings; the more natural or self-selected the tasks, the more true to real life, but the harder the data is to analyze.

The main reason why usability testing is worth the effort is that it provides richer and more detailed information about important aspects of a library or information system than any other method. Surveys and interviews can catch only fleeting, large-scale, half-remembered and self-reported glimpses of what users want to tell you about using your website or your library's layout. Evaluation by observation cannot detect very small details without users' permission, and if you get that close you might as well get permission to do a form of usability testing. Logs of various types can tell you the "what," sometimes in very distinct detail, but can't show "why."

For librarians, there are two distinct challenges when you are the person conducting the usability study. The first is to assure the participants as much as possible—and it still may not be enough—that they are not wrong when they have trouble, that they can "fail" if, in real life, they would just give up. Most important, it is not they who are being tested but the system. When the person conducting the test is a librarian and is connected in the user's mind with the provider of the system, there is a natural tendency not to be too critical and to feel "they know best," and if the user has trouble, it is the user's fault.

The second challenge is complementary. The librarian/tester must avoid providing any help at all during the test. Librarians love to assist, to teach, and to help. That is not the point of the usability test. The observer is there to observe, not to change or alter the course of what would go on all those times when a librarian is not sitting beside a patron.

Librarians who select or develop systems are very familiar with them. They are invested in them in professional and emotional terms. They are expert with them in a way that no user can duplicate. But can users actually use the systems? The usability test sees how that works.

Procedure

After selecting the system to be tested, the usability test consists of five parts:

1. Identifying typical tasks and important features

2. Creating a testing protocol

3. Recruiting participants

4. Conducting tests and recording data

5. Analyzing data

Identifying Typical Tasks and Important Features

A usability test is not a place to test limits or push boundaries. It should stay squarely within the normal needed activities for particular users. Your system may have many filters, alternate pathways, and advanced features. Consider instead what most of your users should find most useful for their most important tasks.

Several sources of ideas are available for these tasks. In universities and schools, librarians know the tasks that students are assigned. What are the features that librarians believe are most helpful for those tasks? For public libraries, what questions come up? Are you considering a new feature? How does the old one work? Do not neglect tasks that you think are simple. If they really are simple, they will not take up much of your testing time.

The set of appropriate tasks is usually specific to a particular set of users. Freshmen, faculty, senior citizens, and home-schoolers all have differing needs. The ideal is to have approximately 6 to 10 testers who are all from a relatively similar group with similar needs.

If recruitment efforts give you a group that differs from what you expected, adjust the tasks as necessary.

Choose a set of tasks that you, an expert, can complete in about 10 to 15 minutes. This translates into about 20 to 60 minutes testing time per person. The testers will be slower because they are not experts. They will explain to you why they make their choices, and you should be prepared with options in cases where testers either fail at the given tasks or zoom through them unexpectedly smoothly.

Create a Testing Protocol

In research, *protocol* is the word for the exact set of procedures that will be followed. It is important to make things consistent across the individuals who are involved. The protocol includes instructions to each tester and also what the evaluators will do and what information they will gather. It includes options for situations that might arise. Ideally, the protocol can be used by any evaluator to get the same information from every participant. In research, assistants should be rigorously trained and supervised. In evaluation, consider enlisting colleagues to participate in the testing. This probably means more inconsistency because more people are involved, but the experience of watching users do something is really valuable and often more compelling than simply reading the formal report.

In the testing protocol, include the following:

- Introduction: thanks and instructions for the participant.
  - Assure the participant that this is a test of the *system*, not of the *person*. If they have frustrations or problems doing any task, they should talk about what they see as the problem.
  - Participants can *give up* if in real life they would simply stop trying.
  - Note that the evaluator watching and taking notes *will not help*. This is a test of how the system works on its own without a helpful librarian.
  - The evaluator will keep asking the participants to describe out loud why they do what they do and do not do.
  - Record simple demographic information, such as age, education, and frequency of general library or system use.

- Instructions for the evaluator
  - Record with screen capture software or take notes on the actions of the participant.
  - As feasible, take notes on the time it takes for tasks overall, for instance, 5 minutes from initial library webpage to looking at the record for a book.
  - Keep prompting the participants to verbalize their thoughts. This includes when the person is pausing without doing something visible. "Can you tell me what you are thinking about or looking for?"
  - *During* the test you *must not* ask, "Why don't you do X?" You may ask that when the test itself is over. You may ask, "Why did you do that?" in a neutral, open tone of voice.

      ◦ Follow instructions on how to change tasks depending on how the participant does.

- Tasks and options
  - ◦ Start with the core of what you are interested in. It may be something like, "Find two peer-reviewed articles on sleep disorders in the General Academic Index," or "See if your branch has a copy of a particular documentary on DVD." Consider different ways that those tasks may be done in your system.
  - ◦ Think about preliminary steps; decide where to start. Will you start with your library's webpage, Google, or another nonlibrary starting point, or start from the catalog search box or the basic search page within a database?
  - ◦ Consider additional steps in case your core tasks turn out to be very easy for some or all of your participants. The entire testing period for each person should last from 15 to 45 minutes. Less than this, and it is not worth the trouble of arranging for testers. Try for your usual test to go no more than 30 minutes, and allow for 45 minutes for people who are unusually persistent or talkative.
  - ◦ Have all of these options ready to go. Do not start creating something new for each participant.

    This is very important! The protocol absolutely needs to be pretested with one or two people who are as similar to the actual participants as possible. In some sequences of tasks, you may be interested in step C and D but people get hung up on A and B. It is hard to predict these problems. You will need to see if you should start at C to begin with, or if you have time for E and F as well. Even with pretesting, keep track of how the testing goes and change the protocol if needed. This means the first few participants are pretesters, and their data is not part of the study.

- Conclusion
  - ◦ At this point, you should ask participants follow up questions of two types. Ask for them to fill in areas where you do not have notes on why they made the choices they did: that is, times in the testing where you or they neglected to verbalize their thought processes. Second, ask for overall impressions and feedback. Besides their actions and thoughts, their judgments about the entire task are valuable.
  - ◦ Thank the participants.
  - ◦ Here and *only* here you may include some instruction or provide links or handouts. Be cautious if the participants know each other. You want each of them to go into the test as if they were the first one.

Creating the protocol is very much a team effort; work with colleagues. This is appropriate for two reasons. First, the target of testing itself is usually a team feature or function—your website or catalog or databases or tutorials as a whole. Second, testing is a labor-intensive, one-on-one process. You will usually need assistance in conducting the tests themselves. The reward is that those participating, the library team, really benefit from discussing what tasks and options are really important and should be included. Later on they will have a real stake in the results of the evaluation.

Recruiting Participants

A very commonly cited rule of thumb is that eight is the perfect and sufficient number of participants for a usability test. This can be looked at in two different ways. First, if all participants are roughly the same, such as eight college freshmen, it is very likely that by the time you get to the sixth and seventh and eighth participants, none of them is likely to discover, remark upon, or uncover new issues and problems. It is like proof-reading a paper or a webpage; by the fourth or fifth editor, virtually all of the mistakes will be caught.

On the other hand, this is not proof-reading, and the participants should not all be the same. If you have one homogenous group of eight people, then you know a lot about people like them and have no idea about the reactions of others. This is one of the most serious challenges to usability testing in a library environment. People who build commercial products select specific users whom they want to target and attract. They confine their usability testing to those users and gradually expand to others on their own schedule. Instead, most libraries have users who are defined by the parent organization: the students, faculty, and staff at a particular university and the community that a public library serves. Therefore, the key is to have participants who represent the range of users that the product, service, site, or facility is expected to serve.

Two practical ways can be used to go about recruiting testers. The first is to use all of the communication methods available: flyers, email, newsletters, webpage notices, and notices in newspapers and other publications. You then sort the respondents as they come in, including these who are youth, those who are seniors, those who are tech-savvy, and so forth. At this point it is useful to have some screening questions, such as brief demographics, broad age ranges, how familiar they are with your library and its services, or how often they use a variety of services.

The second is to decide on the particular types of users desired and go to where you can reach them. For senior citizens, you can approach people attending a program for them; for business people, contact organizations where they congregate; for children, work through their parents.

The most important consideration is to try, as much as possible, to have the recruitment not affect your results. It is very easy for it to go astray in two ways. First, people who have time and interest may be more likely to volunteer; this leads to participants consisting of retirees or young geeks. Second, when you advertise in detail about what you are testing, you may attract people who already are familiar with it. Your ideal test subject is someone who *should* be using a feature but is not already doing so.

In research situations, it is common to offer a small stipend to participants, perhaps $10 or $20 for a half an hour to an hour of time. If given, the stipend should represent simply compensation for their time, not a special bonus. Large sums can make participants less than honest about their qualifications for the study and more eager to produce the result you want. Offering compensation is very dependent on the community context. In a university where everybody is offering something for similar studies, compensation will be necessary for student participants but inappropriate for faculty or staff. In a public library, you should look to what has been done at your library before. A library is a community good, and often people simply appreciate helping the library.

Conducting Tests and Recording Data

Two types of data are involved: qualitative and quantitative. The quantitative data consists of everything that is in predefined categories and numbers. This includes demographic items such as status, for instance retired, faculty, city resident, age, and gender. It also includes success or failure at tasks, time taken to work on tasks, and number of clicks or webpages visited. The most basic information is time and steps to success. All of this numerical and category information can be recorded in a spreadsheet as shown in Table 1.16.

| | | | **Task 1: Place hold** *Start from book record display* | | | |
Person	Gender	Age	Perceived Success?	Correct?	Time Taken	Number of Pages
1	F	19–25	Y	N	1:45	2
2	F	50–64	Y	Y	2:15	6

Table 1.16 Data Example: Usability Test Tasks.

In this hypothetical case, each of the female participants believed she had finished the task correctly. Person 1 actually requested an interlibrary loan instead, not realizing that they were different processes. Person 2 understood the correct process but had to back up a couple of times to get it right. Those notes are contained in the qualitative material. From this grid, you create summaries. For example, 80% of testers completed the task correctly; 10% believed they completed it but were incorrect; 10% failed to complete it and knew they had abandoned the task.

If recording software is used, it can provide most of the above information automatically. An observer would need to indicate user perceptions. In addition, either the software automatically collects the information or an observer slowly going through the recorded screen shots and cursor movements detects, with great precision, features that are or not used.

Qualitative is the name used for unstructured textual data. In a usability study, it means the notes about people's comments and reactions. This can be audiotaped and turned into a transcript or recorded with careful notes. If a transcript is created, someone will have to create summary notes from the text. Audiotaping is therefore more accurate but adds an extra layer of time and effort. For many usability situations, simple and careful note taking will be sufficient to document basic problems and overall trends.

Notes or summaries from transcripts need to be consistent from evaluator to evaluator and at the same level of detail. The end goal is to understand reasons *why* things happen to go along with the data on *what* happened. This means a note should be made of every step taken or omitted, whether those steps are correct or not.

For an academic scenario, a transcript from an audio and screen-capturing recording, supplemented from visual notes, might look like this:

- Typed "database" into the unified search box. Hit return. List of books and articles appears.

  Q: "What were you considering when you did that?"

  Tester said, "I am trying to find this database I'm supposed to use. I wanted a list of databases. Why isn't there a list of databases? This is no good. Let me look again." Tester seems to be reading the screen.

  Q: "What are you looking at or for?"

  Tester says: "I'm reading this list of tabs across the top. Oh, right, that says 'Research.' Let me try that. I'm working on a research paper."

Notes might look like this:

- Used term "database" in USB. Got books and articles. Not happy. Q/R: said, wanted to find "database," wanted "list." Reread screen. Q/R: said, list of tabs across top; "research" key point.

A tension exists between practicality and detail even with the help of recordings. You need enough detail to detect patterns but not so much that everything becomes a blur.

Analyzing Data

A description of how to code textual (qualitative) data is given in the section on interviews. In a way, a usability test is a very focused combination of two other evaluation tools, observation and interviewing. The quantity of data from usability tests is not as much as when doing a pure observation study or conducting a series of in-depth interviews.

To analyze usability study data, the most practical and flexible approach is to draw upon the team nature of this project. At least two and up to four individuals should read the notes and look at the quantitative data from each tester. Each evaluator should independently make notes of the following:

- Where the process seemed to work smoothly as anticipated. It is important not to lose sight of what does work.

- Where there were problems, with a sense of what types of problems occurred. Some categories are as follows:
  - Physical: Tester knew what was correct but clicked wrong—a mechanical problem that might be a visual design issue.

○ Haste: Tester was hasty and clicked the first option without realizing the correct option was below.

○ Not visible: Tester did not see the correct option; option was on the screen but tester never seemed to notice it.

- When someone misinterpreted language or icons, exactly what was misinterpreted.

○ "ILL" mistaken for "Hold"

○ Book icon clicked on when the tester wanted to check on format.

- Overall themes, both those mentioned by testers and those noted by observers.

○ Tester never mentioned anything from the right side of the screen.

○ Tester said the book jackets were distracting.

The equivalent of about a paragraph about each test, task, or person is enough. Then the two evaluators should compare those notes. Are there disagreements? What problems seem to come up more often? It is at this point that the quantitative data will place this into context. Quantitative data will show how extensive a problem is, as well as if there are any commonalities among those who have problems with that issue. This helps insulate the analysts from the vividness of the testers' situations and their comments. A talkative and energetic participant may speak forcefully about a problem that only affected him or her.

A usability study report identifies areas that are of concern, that are problems for patrons. This can lead to two options: "Let us educate our users" is one, but how feasible is it to reach everyone? Instead, consider asking, "How can the resource be redesigned so that it will work with patrons as they are?" When considering changes, designers should also incorporate information about what does work so that they do not apply a fix that makes things worse.

Overall, all participants from the library side will gain a very valuable current perspective on how their library's sources and systems appear to the people they are trying to serve. It is very difficult to see these things from the insider's perspective, particularly for information technology systems that become second nature to librarians yet are used infrequently by patrons.

Study Questions/Examples

In the first study, participants were not interviewed. However, they had very detailed screen-capture behavioral information.

Imler, Bonnie, and Michelle Eichelberger. "Do They 'Get It'? Student Usage of SFX Citation Linking Software." *College & Research Libraries* 72.5 (2011): 454–63.

Fear, Kathleen. "User Understanding of Metadata in Digital Image Collections; or What Exactly Do You Mean by 'Coverage'?" *American Archivist* 73.1 (2010): 26–60.

- What was the population of users?
- Who were the participants? How many were there?
- Name one task.
- Give two findings, including if possible numeric or comment-based results.

Instructional Evaluation

Introduction

This section covers assessment of student learning after specific, intentional instruction sessions. Instruction itself takes many forms. In this case you are assessing what happens as a result of a defined instructional event: one hour or one class, or a series of classes, or an entire information literacy course. Instruction is a specialized form of library programming. In academic libraries, it is the core and primary programming so that often academic libraries do not assess any other forms of programming. In public libraries, so much other programming goes on that sometimes the instruction is overlooked or is treated like recreational or cultural programming.

Usually, there are two main targets of instructional assessment: the student and the teacher or library service. From well-designed assessments, students can learn about their own level of information literacy knowledge and behaviors. From aggregated student scores, librarians can assess if their instructional efforts are successful. The latter is truly a library service evaluation: how effective is instruction?

Most of the methods in this book can provide information relevant to assessing instruction. If librarians highlight a particular specialized database in instruction, its usage statistics ought to rise. General patron surveys can ask people if they participate and, if they do, what they perceive they got out of the experience.

This section will describe particular methods and subsets of methods that are very specific to instructional assessment. Because information literacy is so important, and because of the importance of assessment in academia, librarians are constantly using and developing more methods, so these should be seen as a few useful methods, not all the methods that exist.

Instruction involves three domains of content and three levels of measurement. The domains are cognitive, behavioral, and affective. *Cognitive* refers to specific knowledge. Do students know what a "periodical" or a "peer-reviewed article" is? The behavioral domain has to do with skills. Can a student locate a peer-reviewed article on a particular subject? The affective domain is the least well studied and is somewhat contentious. Does it matter what students feel about chemistry if they can define an organic compound or balance a chemical reaction? However, affect, which means feeling or attitude, influences how successful and persistent someone will be. Someone who sees chemistry as irrelevant and boring will learn less than someone who sees it as full of exciting challenges to be conquered. In libraries, we encourage a feeling of comfort and openness to learning in our patrons. We seek to eliminate the affect of library anxiety, or the feeling that one should not ask questions.

Generally speaking, there are three levels of measurement: nonmeasures, indirect measures, and direct measures. Nonmeasures are data that can easily be mistaken for instructional data. For example, students with a GPA of 4.0 in their major have probably mastered relevant skills and knowledge. However, if students have a GPA of 3.5, that data alone cannot reveal just what they are lacking. Perhaps the grade is low because assignments were turned in late, or they are excellent at one thing but terrible at another. The mere number of 3.5 is too blunt and provides no details for analysis.

Indirect measures are common, but like nonmeasures, they are not quite actual measures of specific knowledge or skills. A survey that asks students how confident they feel in giving presentations is an indirect measure of their actual ability. Students who report they feel they can find an article may or not be people who actually can. Research shows a distinct overconfidence on the part of many students regarding their level of information literacy, primarily because they do not know what they do not know.

Direct measures are those that capture objective, expert data that specifically targets exact knowledge, skills, or attitudes with enough detail that evaluators can discern areas of strength and weakness. When possible, assessment or evaluation of instruction should use direct measures of knowledge (cognitive), skills (behavioral), and attitude (affective).

Procedure

This section describes how to use six different methods of instructional evaluation, of varying complexity and feasibility:

1. Tests (general and local)

2. Observation

3. Projects or portfolios with rubrics

4. Citation or bibliography analysis

5. Event surveys

6. Reflections

Tests and project rubrics are direct measures for knowledge and most behaviors. Observation and citation analysis are direct measures of behavior. Event surveys and reflections are both indirect measures for cognitive and behavioral outcomes and also direct measures of affective domains.

Tests

Tests can target both cognitive and behavioral outcomes (see Table 1.17).

Test Questions	
Cognitive (Knowledge)	**Behavioral (Skills)**
Name one subject-specific database.	Select an appropriate database from a screen shot.
Name two citation styles.	Construct a correct APA-formatted citation from this information.
Define *call number*.	Given a call number, find a book on the shelf.
Who or what organization produces census data?	Read this chart and identify which program has the largest budget.
What are "controlled vocabulary" and "natural language"?	Find the appropriate PsycINFO term for gender differences.

Table 1.17   Instructional Test Questions: Cognitive or Behavioral.

Behavioral questions are somewhat harder to construct or to embed in a paper-and-pencil format than cognitive questions, so cognitive questions are more common.

Two major information literacy tests are available, SAILS and iSkills. These take different approaches. The first, Project SAILS, an initiative begun by the Association of Research Libraries in cooperation with Kent State University, is a computer-delivered multiple-choice test with questions such as the following:

You need to get information on an event that took place two days ago. Where are you most likely to find information about the event?

CHOOSE ONE ANSWER

Book

Dissertation

Journal article

Magazine

Newspaper[2]

The SAILS website (www.projectsails.org) provides extensive information on the development of the test, which is simple to use. It is often used prior to instruction in order to prime the participants to recognize that there are important parts of academic skills that they do not possess. A major one is that the academic world does not run on the level of a Google search box.

The second test was developed by the Educational Testing Service (ETS), which also creates the GRE test. Their behavioral, simulation-based test was called the Information and Communications Technology Test (ICT) in 2006, the iSkills test in 2009, the iCritical Thinking assessment in 2010, and in 2012 iSkills again. The hour-long test contains six different modules, only one of which is directly related to information literacy.

Librarians can develop their own tests. The primary advantage to doing so is that you know exactly what your instruction covers. For example, you may or may not cover citation elements or correct citation format. For one class you may emphasize the definition of primary and secondary information; for another, how to find and use controlled vocabulary. A locally developed test will be targeted, individual, and locally relevant. General tests must necessarily include only generic skills.

Developing a good test is not easy. It is not difficult for instructors to identify just what they want students to know and be able to do. It is difficult to write concrete questions in such a way as to elicit precise and gradable answers while not signaling the right answer. Multiple-choice questions are easy to grade but difficult to write. Answer alternatives need to look plausible yet be unarguably incorrect. When possible, use instructional design staff or friendly classroom teachers as collaborators in test design.

Tests that are part of required information literacy instruction, embedded in a subject course or freestanding, are part of a real, for-credit course grade. This makes students take them more seriously. It also changes librarian-instructors from research consultants to authoritative assessors. This is a change in role, and one not all librarians are comfortable with. Librarians need to continue to emphasize to students that they stand ready to assist them at any level on any occasion in the future.

Aggregated, test data is a way to assess the instruction itself. If too many students are getting the same item right, then that element is probably too simplistic for that audience. If too many students are getting the same item wrong, then there is something wrong with the material or the presentation. For assessment of instruction, conduct an item-by-item analysis of student accuracy and also their most common incorrect choices.

Examples of aggregated data include the following:

From this screen shot, name the database most relevant to this Abnormal Psychology class:

78%   PsycAbstracts

17%   Expanded Academic Index

3%   Google

Put these call numbers in the order in which the books would appear on the shelves:

55%:   correct

30%:   did not understand nondecimal initial number RA 101, RA 1015, RA 339, RA 4011.

15%:   ignored initial letters RA 47, RC 55, RA 612, RF . . .

Observation

A paper-and-pencil or screen-presented test is only a simulation of some important library behaviors. In observation, learners are posed tasks, and someone observes how they go about them. In a sense this is a specialized version of usability testing. It would be scheduled to follow an instruction session and be targeted at the exact material covered. For example, a librarian might talk with children about the parts of a book and then ask students to find the date of publication. An observer can note how many students are successful and take notes on the most common incorrect mistakes.

To conduct an observation, select tasks that instruction will cover and that you believe that the learners, *with instruction*, should be able to master. This is a big difference from general usability testing. In usability testing, the tasks are common or important things that a typical user might need or might attempt to do on his or her own.

The goal of usability testing is to determine what needs to change *in the system*. The goal of assessment of instruction by observation is to determine what needs to change *in the instruction*. These two do overlap. If students have great difficulty doing X, it is time to consider not trying to change the users and instead change the system. Consider your journal subscriptions. If students do not use the button labeled "Periodicals," maybe change the labeling to "Magazines and Journals List."

Observation in this setting is quite reactive; people know they are being observed, and it requires a lot of attention from the observer. That means it is usually not a good idea for assessment of individuals. It is too costly to try to observe closely every person receiving instruction in order to thoroughly assess their comprehension and skills.

Instead, observation is best used for aggregated assessment of instruction. In this situation, an observer does not need to observe every learner but should randomly select just a few to observe. This takes a little of the pressure off each "test" subject. You can tell students that the observer is just watching a few people to see how things are going in general, not grading them individually. Observing a few learners should yield enough information to identify, broadly, things that are being learned fairly well and areas where learners still have significant problems.

Observation is particularly useful in the lower grades when there are large-scale behaviors that librarians are teaching and that can be observed, such as identifying areas of the library and types of books or other materials, paying attention to signage, and learning the order of steps (e.g., using the catalog first, then moving to the correct shelf, then figuring out if something should be used in-library or can be checked out).

The summary of observation data is a list of the numbers of students observed who do well or poorly on particular elements (see Table 1.18).

	Yes	No	
Finding title page immediately	85%	15%	
Finding reverse of title page	55%	45%	
	Correct	**Print Date**	**No Date**
Identifying copyright date	25%	55%	20%

Table 1.18   Report Example: Observation of Skills.

Projects and Portfolios; Rubrics

Generally, the goal of information literacy instruction is to equip a user with the skills to pursue a particular goal. Project assessment examines the extent to which users have actually been able to achieve that goal. The most common example is the research or term paper with an assignment to write X pages on a particular subject using a variety of sources of appropriate quality.

Examining just the citations from a paper or project is covered next, in the "Citation or Bibliography Analysis" subsection. Project assessment examines more data than just a bibliography. It is more comprehensive, more time-consuming, and potentially more informative than a simple citation analysis. It resembles an interview while citation analysis is more like a survey: qualitative versus quantitative, deep versus concrete or limited information.

Information literacy standards at both the university and school level developed by the Association of College and Research Libraries and the American Association of School Librarians include identifying, evaluating, and incorporating new relevant information in response to an information need. These standards and faculty-specific assignment guidelines form the basis for a *rubric* with which to judge a project or portfolio.

Here the word *project* includes any final product that is the end result of information seeking. This can be a paper, a presentation, a case study, an annotated bibliography, or a series of interrelated items. In some courses, students are also expected to preserve the formative steps of their work: initial notes, rough drafts, journaling about the process and about decision points in refining and revising a topic, as well as the final product. A portfolio houses these intermediate steps as well as the end product.

When available, a process portfolio is a very rich source of data about the level of student skills in information seeking, evaluation, and use. For example, an initial bibliography may include a wide range of materials where the final project includes a very selective list. The process of refining the list of materials shows where these learners have stronger or weaker skills in information analysis. Suppose, for example, that only high-quality periodical articles, such as peer-reviewed studies, are retained, but the student does not distinguish between low- and high-quality web resources. Neither the content instructor nor the librarian may want the final product to hinge upon a Wikipedia article, but a process journal or portfolio can show students appropriately using Wikipedia to find links to resources that they examine for authenticity and quality.

You can analyze journaling-type portfolios as if they were interviews providing deep qualitative information. This information is more objective than direct librarian interviews because the students are not trying to impress or please librarians, only their instructors.

For projects and more concrete portfolios, an effective method of analyzing the data is with an information literacy *rubric*. An assessment rubric is a grid with rows and columns. Each row is a particular desired characteristic. These characteristics can target only the end product, such as "informative abstract," or it can include in-process elements, such as "initial information search." Each column represents a level of achievement from nonexistent to low, poor, or beginning; to medium or acceptable; to high, outstanding, or excellent (see Table 1.19).

Element	⊘	Low	Medium	High
Complete citations		Titles or authors are incomplete for at least 50% of citations.	Titles and authors are present for 80% of citations; date is present for at least 50%.	95% of titles, authors, and dates are present.
Quality of sources		At least half of citations are from inappropriate sources.		90% of sources are from acceptable sources.
Use of databases		Journal describes using Google or other open search engine only.	Journal describes using a general-purpose database.	Journal describes selection and justification for using an appropriate discipline-specific database.
Variety of sources		Only one medium is used (only books, or articles, or webpages).	Only two media are used (books, articles, webpages).	At least three appropriate media are used.

⊘ = Element is missing entirely.

Table 1.19 Rubric for Information Literacy.

Using a rubric has two great advantages in its construction and in consolidation of data. Powerful collaboration occurs when librarians and content instructors construct a rubric by agreeing on just what they want to see in a paper, project, or portfolio. They educate each other, and themselves, when they come up with examples of what good, better, and best student work looks like. In teaching, a rubric helps guide students as they work on projects. In grading, it is a concise and consistent way to point out weaknesses and strengths.

It is easy to summarize and use rubric data. It is best if two people are able to examine each project or portfolio, but you can get good data if two or three people split up the portfolios. If similar summaries come from those scored by each of the three, that is pretty compelling evidence. Each scorer marks each portfolio on the grid; someone then shows the overall achievement on that item (see Figure 1.1).

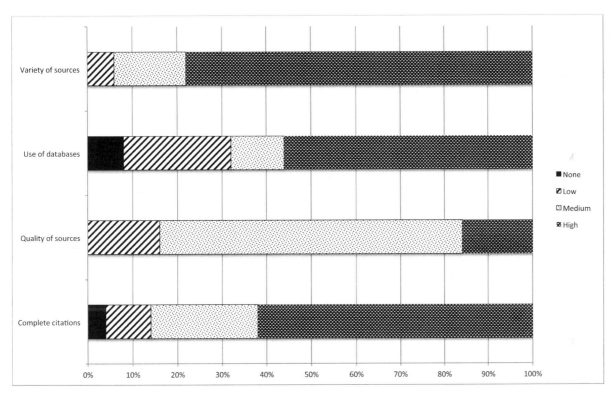

Figure 1.1 Report Example: Achievement on Information Literacy Skills.

In this way people can quickly see if there are areas that students *in general* are struggling with, patterns that go beyond individuals. Aggregated data is the key to program assessment. In this case, the "program" is the instruction itself rather than the performance of individuals.

Citation or Bibliography Analysis

Citation analysis is a very narrow and targeted form of rubric. It is quite different from analysis of citations in order to determine patterns of scholarly communication, defined as linkages between researchers, or to assess the quality—the citedness—of an article or journal. In scholarly assessment, we assume that the person citing item A does so because A is important and influential. The citation, like a use, is a measure of the quality and importance of the item cited.

In instructional assessment, we use citations as traces of the student authors' methods of information retrieval. The more skillful they are, the more appropriate the citations are.

A citation rubric is a simpler form of the portfolio or project rubric. The level of analysis is the bibliography, not the individual citation. In a bibliography analysis, judgments are made about the characteristics of the bibliography or collection of citations as a whole. This allows for scoring on the basis of enough citations, enough variety of citations, or a proper range of dates of the group of citations. Here, the unit is the bibliography; it is poor, good, or excellent on these dimensions of quality, size, and currency.

Quality: percentage of items cited that are peer-reviewed journal articles

Poor = less than 30%

Moderate = 31–70%;

Excellent = more than 70%

Just as with a portfolio assessment, librarians look to see if their instruction has really made an impact on the quality of the resources that the students use. A portfolio or project assessment can reach more deeply into how items are used. However, that is also more time consuming and definitely more subjective, so a citation analysis is generally much more feasible.

Event Surveys

The "Surveys" section above categorizes surveys into two groups: general and event or incident. In a general survey, people are asked for their input about an institution or situation in the long term. For example, public libraries survey patrons or the general public about what services and materials they value and use. Academic librarians survey faculty about the resources and services they need and need to know more about.

An event, incident, or transaction survey is a survey specifically about one instance, administered right then. You use a website and answer a survey about its navigation and your satisfaction. You attend a conference presentation and answer a survey about the program and presenters. Event surveys are especially useful when only a small number of people have experience with a particular item or service.

When a class is asked to answer questions after an instruction session, is it a survey or is it a test? In general, *survey* questions ask about opinions, attitudes, and evaluations; there are no wrong answers. *Test* questions have right or wrong answers. They are specifically designed to show evidence of learning, skills, knowledge, or facts. Using a survey after instruction may be more common than a test.

A postevent questionnaire can include both survey and test-type questions. The key lies in analysis. Some items are direct evidence of learning, some are indirect, and some are not about the learning at all. The following table gives examples of survey-type questions. Survey questions do provide valuable information for evaluating the instructional session as a whole (see Table 1.20).

Direct measure of learning	Please name two things that were new to you from this session.
	What was the most important thing you learned today?
	What still puzzles you about this topic?
	Which of these would be suitable for your class project?
Indirect measure	How confident are you that you know about X?
	How likely are you to use X in the next two months?
	How valuable was this information to you?
Assessment of other aspects of the instruction	How engaging was this speaker?
	How knowledgeable was this speaker?
	Would you recommend this program to others?
Needs assessment, not about learning or that instruction	What other topics would you like to see programs about?

Table 1.20 Direct and Indirect Assessment Examples.

Postprogram surveys such as "How was this speaker?" or "How satisfied were you?" are very common. In your organization, consider using one relatively generic outline for all events and supplement with some individual questions. Include demographic questions so that you can see if perceptions differ among groups. Filling out a quantitative-type survey as shown in the "how" questions above takes very little time. Explicitly plan on survey-answering time and announce it at the beginning: "We will stop 5 minutes before X time so that you can give us some feedback so that the next sessions will be better." In this way, people do not feel they are being kept from the next thing they want to do, and you are using time they have already budgeted for the session.

Questions that ask participants to name one thing that they learned, that was new, or that is still confusing are open ended. That makes them more difficult and time consuming for patrons to answer, especially those who have lower literacy skills. However, using one or two questions in the postevent survey, after easier scoring questions, can be very effective. This is especially true when you are trying to assess learning but you cannot really administer a test. This happens when people participate in an entirely voluntary instruction situation, such as "how to use our genealogy center." With the "name one" format, people do not feel pressure to come up with a specific correct answer, and the format implies that it is okay to still have questions. The answers help the instructors to see if what *they* thought was key was really what attracted participants' attention and interest, and to see what might be missing.

Surveys are summarized in two ways. Categories are reported as numbers and percentages, and rating questions are reported as averages, sometimes broken down by subgroups. Qualitative, open-ended questions are sorted and coded by the themes and common comments that appear.

Genealogy database session

How useful was this session? 4.6 (maximum of 5)

How soon will you use the GENEO database?

68%   Within the next month

12%   Within the next six months

30%   Not within the next six months + Never + Not sure

What was one thing that still puzzles you?

14 mentioned they needed to know how to get into the database from home.

Reflections

A reflection is similar to a single-question survey or a subset of a developmental portfolio. A one-minute essay is a form of reflection. In this format, students are asked to write down their thoughts for about a minute. If this happens right at the end of an instructional session, their thoughts will be more theoretical; that is, they are thinking about how the instruction will or could help them, not how it already has or what they have practiced or mastered or found wanting. In a one-shot library instruction session, this can be the concluding piece and will give at least some information on what students perceived as the big points covered.

If you want to know if students can apply what they have learned, then the reflection has to come after they have put their instruction into practice. A reflection can start out a second instruction session and is a good way to prime students to start thinking again about information search strategies and what they need to know. Or a librarian can ask the classroom teacher to administer the one-minute essay at a time when most students should have been working on their projects and using their skills. Lastly, the developmental portfolio could include a required reflection on the information-seeking process.

Just as in a good interview, the key to good reflection is in the prompt, defined as the directions about what to write. The reflection prompt needs to be open and encouraging, not judgmental or leading. Avoid prompts that can be answered with one-word answers. The question, "Did you use the IUCAT button on the main page?" is not a reflective question. "How did you find books on your topic?" is more reflective. "What went well about finding information on your topic?" and "What were some problems you encountered?" are more open.

Reflections are analyzed using qualitative, narrative, or text-based techniques. More detail is given in the "Interviews" section and in the review of qualitative and quantitative analysis in Chapter 3. In brief, readers isolate and code statements in categories, a sort of cataloging of the ideas that students have written. For example,

Confusion about resource type

- I don't understand why I get these weird long URLs and government stuff when I type "death penalty" into the catalog. Shouldn't I just get books?

- I tried typing "death penalty" into the box and I didn't find any articles. I know there have to be news stories somewhere.

- I want to find out how many murderers are executed, but I tried typing that in the catalog and didn't get anything.

One statement can have several codes. Perhaps several students mention wanting statistics but in different contexts such as "I'm glad I was able to find out how many people our state has executed in a news article." This would be a sort of needs assessment. It shows what students want to find as well as being an instructional assessment, if the librarian had emphasized that there are statistics on most topics they would be working on.

Each statement or section is coded with one or more categories, and then the sections are rearranged to put all of the statements for that code into one area. The idea is to see if there are common issues.

This is not an entirely mechanical process; for example, "book" is mentioned 10 times. Sometimes the *absence* of comments is important. If people keep complaining about the autocite function within the EBSCO databases, it is evidence that they actually are able to get into the databases and find things they want to cite. Evaluators should read for what is not mentioned, as well as what was mentioned.

Instructional assessment is a huge, creative, and constantly evolving area of library evaluation. All librarians want to learn if we have created outcomes and made impacts on the people we serve. Instructional assessment has one of the most direct connections between action, or instruction, and effect, or detectable skills or knowledge. However, the act of information seeking itself is so complex that all measures are only approximate, whether they are very numeric test questions or very rich and individual reflections.

Study Questions/Examples

For each of these,
- Who were the participants, and was there a control group, defined as people who did not receive instruction?
- Was the measurement required and part of a grade such as a test or a required narrative?

- Provide one specific question, prompt, or instructions used to collect data.
- Provide one summary statement or finding.

Many of the example studies used more than one method.

Tests

Sobel, Karen, and Kenneth Wolf. "Updating Your Tool Belt: Redesigning Assessments of Learning in the Library." *Reference & User Services Quarterly* 50.3 (2011): 245–58.

Observation

Cmor, Dianne, Alison Chan, and Teresa Kong. "Course-Integrated Learning Outcomes for Library Database Searching: Three Assessment Points on the Path to Evidence." *Evidence Based Library and Information Practice* 5.1 (2010): 64–81.

Projects and Portfolios with Rubrics

Sharma, Shikha. "Perspectives On: From Chaos to Clarity: Using the Research Portfolio to Teach and Assess Information Literacy Skills." *Journal of Academic Librarianship* 33.1 (2007): 127–35.

Citation (Bibliography) Analysis

Leeder, Chris, Karen Markey, and Elizabeth Yakel. "A Faceted Taxonomy for Rating Student Bibliographies in an Online Information Literacy Game." *College & Research Libraries*.2 (2011): 115–33.

Event Surveys

Figa, Elizabeth, Tonda Bone, and Janet R. MacPherson. "Faculty–Librarian Collaboration for Library Services in the Online Classroom: Student Evaluation Results and Recommended Practices for Implementation." *Journal of Library & Information Services in Distance Learning* 3.2 (2009): 67–102.

Reflections

Gilstrap, Donald L., and Jason Dupre. "Assessing Learning, Critical Reflection, and Quality Educational Outcomes: The Critical Incident Questionnaire." *College & Research Libraries* 69.6 (2008): 407–26.

Observation: Tallies

Introduction

The word *observation* has been used in library evaluation and research in several different ways. This section contains parts on tallies, on reference testing ("unobtrusive observation"), and on mystery shopping. Some librarians have organized ethnographic observation studies. That requires a level of anthropological expertise that is beyond the scope of this manual.

Behavioral tallies occur when library staff or systems note when and how patrons or staff do certain things. For example, computer reservation or log-in systems for busy computer labs record when computers are used. Reference staff members tally questions by time of day and type of question. Seat sweeps show what areas of a library are most popular and with what kinds of users. A gate counter is a very simple tallying tool used by many librarians as a by-product of their security systems.

Behavioral tallies are shallow, naturalistic data. They are shallow in that they can only record things that are consistently observable. For example, it is easy to count people in a library at one time. One can count how many are using a laptop at a given time. One cannot count how many have a laptop in their backpacks, and one cannot ask them either whether they intend to use the laptop during their visit or why they use a personal laptop rather than the library's computers.

These types of data gathering are naturalistic in that, properly done, people are not aware of being observed and will not alter their activities. This means you can capture real behavior. "How often do you visit the library?" is subject to problems with memory, with social norms such as "You should visit the library," and with interpersonal politeness when you do not want to tell the librarian you never visit.

Collecting behavioral tallies not only gives you high-quality, reality-based information, it does not depend on patron cooperation, and there are no problems with response rates. Some forms of tallying are more labor intensive than others, but many can be done within the context of normal library operations. This is a rich and inexpensive source of data.

One key opportunity to keep in mind is when there is a change to physical spaces, facilities, and staffing patterns. Changes are always done in order to provide better services or access with greater efficiency. The important thing is to gather usage data *before* a change so that the effect of the change can be seen. It is good to say "We have high use of X" but better to say "Use of X increased after the change."

Procedure: Behavioral Tallies

Behavioral tallying consists of the following steps:

1. Creating tally sheets and collecting data

2. Selecting times for tallying or sampling

3. Summarizing and analyzing the results

Creating Tally Sheets

A tally sheet is a mechanism to record behavior. In this broad sense, a gate mechanism such as an electric eye or swinging gate is a tally sheet. Forms on computers and smartphones can gather data and feed it into a database; several vendors provide reference tallying software. People can also mark paper sheets, and the subsequent data can be put into a database. The three keys to tally design are what is observable, when it will be observed, and how it will be observed.

The first key is to determine what is observable and what it means. A gap always exists between what you can count and what you want to know. We want to know about library visits, but even an automatic electric eye misses people who enter in groups or overcounts children who dash back and forth. We want to know about numbers of questions, but if the phone is ringing all the time, staff may forget to tally everything. We want to know how many books patrons check out at one time. Can a clerk count and write them down? It takes time to record all the data every time when the priority is on helping patrons check out quickly. Does a mother with two children count as three people checking out books, or just one with one stack and one library card?

For the tally, choose something that is countable, reasonably accurately and completely by either automated or human collectors, and accept some difference between what is counted and what is "really" happening. The difference is there. However, this gap is no bigger and probably somewhat smaller than the difference between a person's answers on a survey and their reality.

A second key is selecting a time period. The choices are a comprehensive stream of cumulative counting, distinct selective periods for cumulative counting, or snapshot counts at specific instances.

Consider a book owned by a library. Most systems tally how many circulations a book has had during its lifetime. This is a stream of cumulative counts. Some systems may be able to isolate how many circulations occurred during the current year or within the past year, that is, during selected periods. Or, on one particular day, is that book checked out or not? This is a snapshot of that date. Think about these potential results (see Table 1.21).

Gone with the Wind		The Hunger Games	
Circs total:	234	Circs total:	221
Circs past year:	31	Circs past year:	209
On shelf 4/1/2012:	yes	On shelf 4/1/2012:	no

Table 1.21   Data Example: Usage.

Consider reference questions at an information desk in an academic library (see Table 1.22).

How to Cite Using APA		Research Paper Assistance	
Questions total for year:	331	Questions total for year:	43
September:	11	September:	1
October:	9	October:	3
November:	43	November:	19
December:	79	December:	3

Table 1.22   Report Example: Question Type Tallies.

The three research assistance questions came in the first week of December. You can see that for the books, the overall cumulative count tells a different story than the other forms of the data. A cumulative tally of questions tells you how important the topic is but not the seasonal variations in question-needs.

Some data can really only be collected in snapshot counts. Seat sweeps are the prime example. It is not feasible, under most circumstances, to follow each person who uses a library to see where they go or how long they stay. Instead, one counts at specific times: at 10:00 am, 3 of the 10 reading lounge chairs are occupied and 6 of 12 children's desks have at least one person at them. At 2:00 pm, 1 lounge chair is used and 4 of 12 children's desks are being used. Here you do not record that one person was in a lounge chair at 10:00 am and also at 2:00 pm, while none of the children are the same. In these cases, your focus is on usage at a specified times. Video footage can capture the length of use, which can be used in some studies of the desirability for long-term use of various areas in the library.

Finally, consider your options for capturing the data. How much effort do they need?

Automatic collection systems, such as numbers of uses of a self-check machine or numbers of people passing a gate, are best for stream-of-data counting. Here, the important thing is to design useful times to note totals, such as "X time, X number of uses." If you record these totals only once a month, you will miss week-by-week variations. If you record once a day, you can see what days are busiest. If you record once an hour you may be using up too much staff time. This is the common tension in evaluation: gather enough information to be interesting and informative and not so much that it exhausts or overwhelms you and your staff. Check the automated system to see how it breaks things down and what summary reports it can provide. If it has no breakdowns by time, a human will have to make notes at the right times.

Human collection systems consist of paper sheets with tally grids, maps or diagrams, or computerized input forms—a variety of a transaction survey.

Time-oriented Grid

Think of a spreadsheet. Each row is one point or one period of time, for example, at 11:00 am exactly, or from 11:00 to noon. An at-exact-time row is a sweep-type tally sheet.

Each column is something observed. The first column is the time indication, the second is the first category, and so on. Columns and categories can be grouped. It is vital to decide when a particular behavior, tally, or item noticed is noted in more than one column. This is similar to choose-any or choose-only-one multiple choice for a survey question.

A *sweep-type* tally sheet for overall traffic in a public library is shown in Figure 1.2.

Time	Adults in Children's Area	Children in Children's Area	Adults in Adult Area	Children in Adult Area	Computers in Use
11:00	3	6	5	1	2
3:00	4	10	3	0	12

Figure 1.2 Sweep-Type Tally Sheet, Public Library.

In this sheet, each person appears as a count in only one of the first four columns; they are either adult or child and in one area and not the other. The "computers in use" category is separate. That is, an adult using a computer in the adult area would be counted in that cell as "1 of 4 at 3:00 pm" *and* in the computers-in-use column as "1 of 12 at 3:00 pm." The total number of people at 3:00 pm would be 17, of which 12 are using computers. The alternative is if there is a separate computer area and people there are not counted in the other sections. In that case, there are 29 people in the library, and the age of 12 is not noted.

A *cumulative* tally sheet for information-desk questions at a public library is shown in Figure 1.3.

Time	Directional	For Child	For Self—Adult	Policies	Tech Assistance	Other
9:00–11:00	1 1 1 1	1 1 1	1	1 1 1	1 1 1 1	1
11:00–1:00	1	1 1 1	1 1 1 1		1 1	1 1

Figure 1.3 Cumulative Tally Sheet, Questions.

Designing categories comes from a combination of previous experience and nagging questions. People who regularly work in an area or provide a service usually have a good sense of the typical types of questions or activities. They also usually want to know if their ideas about changes or developments in usage or questions or other behaviors are right. A common situation during the 1990s and beyond was the growth in demand for assistance with computers. More recently, a public library might want to document how many times staff help a child with an online homework assignment, assist someone in filing for unemployment benefits, or register someone to vote. A university librarian might want to record what questions are handled by nonprofessional staff and what are referred to specialists. Use an initial grid for about a week. Watch for too many items ending up in "other," and consider subdividing groups that seem too big.

These simple categories and sheets can be made more complex, too. For example, in academia it is often remarked that students have more group assignments or that they prefer a more social approach to studying than previous generations did. A seat sweep can record being in groups or not and also gender to see if there is a difference.

A *sweep-type* tally sheet for academic library group and individual work study is shown in Figure 1.4.

Time	Place	Solo	In Groups	Number of Groups
11:00	First-floor lounge	M M F F F	F F F M F F	1
3:00	Reference desk area	M F M M F F F F	M M F F F F M M F	2

Figure 1.4 Sweep-Type Tally Sheet, Area Usage.

Tallies made during the sweep are summarized and entered into a spreadsheet as shown in Figure 1.5.

Time	Place	Solo—M	Solo—F	Group—M	Group—F	Number of Groups
11:00	1L	2	3	1	5	1
15:00	Ref	3	5	3	5	2

Figure 1.5 Cumulative Question Tally Sheet.

Calculations on the full set of data will show, for example, the average size of groups in each area, the percentage of users who are in groups in each area, and the preferences of genders for each area. One study, for example, showed that a particular study area was almost unused by solo female students although well used by solo males and male or female students in groups. It had limited sight lines to the main areas of the library.

Map Sheet

A map or diagram makes tallying much quicker for more complex or more finely-detailed evaluations. Check for architectural floor plans, and add furniture notes. In this method, one copy of the floor plan is used for each tally period. An observer quickly notes down people and positioning, using simple marks or more complex tallies. As in the above example, perhaps an *F* is used to mark where a woman is sitting and an *M* for a man; circles can go around groups. The resulting data goes into a grid similar to the second sweep-tally sheet above, and summaries can be plotted back onto the diagram for a visual representation of usage.

Transaction Survey, Computer-Based

When each item being tallied is a separate, discrete interaction, you can design a collection instrument in the form of a small, specialized computerized survey. For each interaction, the recorder would go through a set of predefined questions including question type such as directional, policy, technology, and so forth; patron type such as faculty, staff, or student; and conditions, time and day, and by email, in person, or chat. The virtue of a computer survey of this type is that the information is automatically poured into a spreadsheet for analysis. The disadvantage is that it requires a small space of time for accurate recording at each instance. That is, after each transaction the service person needs to take the time to click through the online form or survey before helping another patron.

When humans are collecting data it is essential that all people interpret the categories consistently. What does "being in a group" mean? Does it mean a group of people sitting and talking to one another? Does it count as a group if one person, sitting, talks to another, standing? Is a young adult a "child" or an "adult" user? You do not need perfection, just an overall consistency. This is the same tension between what is useful to know and what can be recorded. It is important to know how and where senior citizens use a library's facilities. This outweighs the reality that some people are not obviously senior citizens. As long as all people who do the counting have roughly the same idea, or they use some sort of unbiased way to allocate counts, for example, every other person who seems in-between is counted as a senior and the others as adults, the data will be good enough and better than nothing.

Given these considerations, it is essential to build time in the evaluation project to create a draft, have it reviewed for content—that is, what are we interested in?—and then tried out in practice. People should discuss why they marked different categories and come to agreement on a good balance between what they want to know, what they can consistently identify, and what they have the time and opportunity to collect and not miss.

Selecting Times for Tallying

The two main alternatives for time period are whole-population evaluations and sampling. In whole-population evaluations, you set up your collection system to gather information constantly. This is how gate counters work and the way that many librarians keep track of in-house use of periodicals by reshelving counts, and it is easily managed for electronic behaviors such as chat sessions or email and instant messaging (IM) questions. When humans are doing the tallying, the advantage is that people work it into their normal behavior, and they are likely to be relatively consistent in what they record. The problem comes when some data gathering is biased. For example, the after-school rush may be the time when everybody forgets to record transactions. Or someone might be poorer at keeping records or doing the sweeps at the right time.

In sampling, a librarian would select particular times for data collection. The main advantage of only collecting data during specific sample times is that people are more mindful and are able to give special attention for a specially designated period of time. They have a heightened level of attention greater than what they can sustain over the long run. The question then is whether the sampled times can truly represent all times and behaviors.

At the least, participant responsiveness is not an issue; you do not have the bias of people neglecting to fill out surveys or not volunteering for interviews. Instead, representativeness is tied to the times selected. Here, there are two main approaches: random and purposive.

A librarian can take a truly scientific random sampling of times for sweeps. In this method, number each possible time period in a week, such as 8:00 am to 10:00 am on Monday = 1; 10:00 am to 12:00 noon = 2. Take a random sample among those, and the results will be scientifically generalizable to all the time periods. This method works best with automatic systems or with observations that can be done by existing staff because, in most libraries, some of the times selected will be only lightly staffed. For example, a simple tally of people, by gender, who enter the library each hour can usually be recorded by staff because libraries will have staff at the entrances. Sweeping all computer areas in a large library during off-peak hours may be difficult to manage. Another method for observing is to use video footage, especially when it is already in existence for security reasons; time-period observations can be managed by looking at footage without having to have a staff person actually present at each sampled time. Any random sample should consist of at least 30 sampled times.

When random sampling is not feasible, then a purposive selection is made of times of interest. For example, a library may choose a known busy week and a known slow week, for instance hours right after opening, during the middle of the afternoon, and right before closing. Some existing data can show what good times are. For example, in an urban commuter campus, other data showed that 10:00 am to 6:00 pm saw the heaviest traffic in the university's main library, so that was when the seat sweeps were scheduled.

Summarizing and Analyzing the Results

Tally data is collected in and summarized from spreadsheets. Each column represents either data or categories that can be used to sort the results.

For this type of tally sheet see Table 1.23.

Time	Directional	For Child	For Self—adult	Policies	Tech Assistance
9:00–11:00	1 1 1 1	1 1 1	1	1 1 1	1 1 1 1
11:00–1:00	1	1 1 1	1 1 1 1		1 1

Table 1.23 Data Example: Recording Cumulative Tallies.

The spreadsheet would look like this, after being sorted for time (see Table 1.24).

Time	Day	Directional	For Child	For Self	Policies	Tech
9:00–11:00	Mon	4	3	1	3	4
9:00–11:00	Tues	6	2	2	3	1
9:00–11:00	Wed	4	3	1	3	4
9:00–11:00	Thurs	4	3	1	3	4
9:00–11:00	Fri	3	1	5	3	5
9:00–11:00	Sat	4	3	1	3	4
11:00–1:00	Mon	1	3	4	0	2
11:00–1:00	Tues	1	3	4	2	2
11:00–1:00	Wed	4	6	3	3	1
11:00–1:00	Thurs	4	3	1	3	4
11:00–1:00	Fri	1	3	4	0	2
11:00–1:00	Sat	1	3	4	0	2

Table 1.24 Report Example: Tallies of Question Types.

Subtotals come from the sort. For this grid, some summaries are shown in Figure 1.6 and Tables 1.25 and 26).

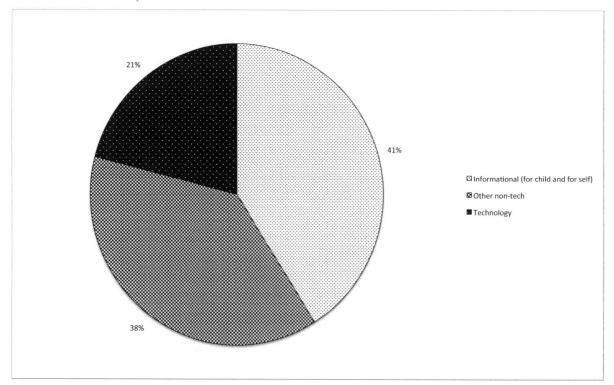

Figure 1.6 Report Example: Percentage of Question Types.

Total Questions by Type	
Directional	37
For child	36
For self	31
Policies	26
Technology	35
By Grouping of Type	
Informational (for child and for self)	67
Other nontech	63
Technology	35

Table 1.25   Report Example: Total Questions by Type.

Monday	25
Tuesday	26
Wednesday	32
Thursday	30
Friday	27
Saturday	25

Table 1.26   Report Example: Traffic by Day of Week.

For a sweep tally see Table 1.27.

Time	Place	Solo—Male	Solo—Female	Group—Male	Group—Female	Number of Groups
11:00	1L	2	3	1	5	1
15:00	Ref	3	5	3	5	2

Table 1.27   Data Example: Tallies by Sweep.

Summaries could be in the forms as shown in Table 1.28.

Usage of Areas	Male	Female
First-floor lounge:	55%	45%
Basement lounge:	85%	15%
Second-floor carrels:	30%	70%

Groups	Percent of Users in Groups
First-floor lounge:	45%
Basement lounge:	77%
Second-floor carrels:	10%

Average Use of Available Seats		N over Sampled Periods
First-floor lounge:	33%	122
Basement lounge:	13%	34
Second-floor carrels:	39%	109

Table 1.28   Report Example: Usage by Area of Library.

Please see the chapters on summarizing (3), reporting (5), and quantitative analysis (3) for more examples.

In observational tallies, it is worth trying to capture as many varied categories of information at one time as possible. If a staff member is tallying number of questions, it takes little more time to tally whether it is a technical or a directional question. The time and date of the tallying is rich data too. The resulting data can be sliced and diced enormously to provide detailed information on what goes on and when in a library.

Nevertheless, tallies miss what cannot be observed. A tally of daily traffic lists only Monday through Saturday. This library is closed on Sundays. Tallies cannot tell you what your traffic might be if you opened on Sundays. Circulation statistics cannot tell you what you do not own but should. Tallies will not tell you that people are not asking you for help in registering to vote because they have no idea that they can do that at a library. Only through more obtrusive methods, like surveys and interviews, can you find out what people are thinking about that you do not yet have.

Study Questions/Examples

Applegate, Rachel. "The Library Is for Studying: Student Preferences for Study Space." *Journal of Academic Librarianship* 33.4 (2009): 341–46.

Arnason, Holly, and Louise Reimer. "Analyzing Public Library Service Interactions to Improve Public Library Customer Service and Technology Systems." *Evidence Based Library and Information Practice* 7.1 (2012): n.p.

- What time period or type of data collection is involved: sweep, normal cumulative, or special-time cumulative?
- What were the items about which data was collected?
- Name two characteristics that were recorded.
- Describe one finding (one sentence).

Unobtrusive Observation: Reference Testing

Introduction

The term *unobtrusive observation* has a very specific meaning in the library field, and it is different from the meaning in other fields. For researchers in other fields, any capture of data about behavior where the person being studied is unaware of that capture can be called unobtrusive. A study about the reading habits of children that used circulation records conducted by education researchers was called "unobtrusive observation."

In library research, the term *unobtrusive observation* developed as an innovative way of evaluating the quality of reference service. In library unobtrusive observation, testers would pose a set of questions with predetermined correct answers to library staff. The staff would not be aware that these were tests, not real patrons, and thus it was "unobtrusive." Similar studies have been conducted of other services, such as calling the IRS help line with hypothetical taxpayer questions. Question-answering correctness is similar to but much narrower than "mystery shopper" evaluation, which is covered in its own section.

This method was a distinct improvement over the previous method of determining how well reference services were performing, which involved asking librarians. They consistently responded that they answered nearly all questions. It also has advantages over asking patrons because, by definition, patrons ask questions because they do not know what the correct answer is. However, the most famous result, the "55% rule," which reports that only 55% of questions were answered correctly and completely, has been shown to be somewhat of an artifact of the design of the tests. In most unobtrusive testing, only short-answer questions are selected, such as "Who is the president of Ghana?" not, "What caused the Civil War?" and too-hard and too-easy questions are not part of the test set.[3]

One important caution needs to be kept in mind. This book is a manual of library and information services or agency evaluation, not personnel evaluation and management. Services are provided by people. Personal differences in skill, knowledge, and attitude affect the quality of those services. However, in evaluation, the goal is an understanding of a service, not of individuals. The response to a low performance score in this context would be an examination of how to improve the service as a whole, not whether to remove a low-performing staff member. Perhaps more training is needed or better scheduling of staff to avoid congestion or distractions. It requires a systemic answer, not a personal personnel change.

The "Procedure section" describes the key steps in conducting a variety of behavioral tally observations. Then it outlines the more complicated process of creating a reasonable unobtrusive test.

Procedure: Unobtrusive Testing

The process of unobtrusive testing consists of the following steps:

1. Determining a set of test questions

2. Setting up a schedule of testing

3. Administering the questions

4. Summarizing the results

Determining a Set of Test Questions

The most important step in unobtrusive testing is to design a set of test questions that are representative and gradable. Questions should be those that are within the range of user needs at your library, and scorers should be able to determine if the answer given is correct or sufficient.

Three good sources of representative questions are described here. The first is to record actual questions for a period of time, then create questions similar or identical to them. For example, suppose a question received at a genealogy service desk is for a list of cemeteries in X county. A test question could ask about Y county, as long as that library was prepared to serve people asking about that county. The second technique is similar but speedier: ask experienced staff to give examples of typical questions. The final approach is to determine what staff *should* be able to answer, even if those questions are not particularly common. This seems artificial, but one good use of this test is after staff orientation or training. If staff members go through training on answering certain types of questions, then an unobtrusive test can check on the success of the training.

Here are some examples of these sources. Public libraries in adjoining counties kept track of questions, then swapped the lists. A Canadian library used the *Globe and Mail* national newspaper to identify news topics. After a tax law changed, questions about the change were posed to people at the IRS hotline.

All of the questions need to have appropriate answers that can be scored in terms of quality, completeness, or accuracy. This does not mean that each answer needs to be identical. An information referral question about registering to vote might reasonably have more than one answer. The format of the answer can also be part of the "rightness" of the answer. Does the librarian mention the source of each answer? Does he or she ask a follow-up or concluding question?

Some questions have more concrete answers than others. Short-answer questions, like who is the president of France, are easy to score for accuracy. However, they may fall short in terms of being representative of actual questions, particularly recently when people use Google or Wikipedia to answer bar quizzes. In the history of using unobtrusive observation for testing, short-answer questions were favored because of the consistency with which they could be judged for accuracy. However, for practical evaluation, librarians can use any question where the person posing the question can accurately record the answer, no matter whether it is short or complex. Then scorers can discuss the qualities of the various answers received.

In unobtrusive testing research, too-easy questions were not used. In evaluation, this is not necessary as long as the questions actually represent user needs. First, including them allows you to check that your staff really can handle easy questions too, and second, their success should be reflected in the data.

Setting Up a Schedule of Testing

This is not a personnel evaluation exercise or a trivia contest. The goal is not to determine which staff member wins the gold. Instead, the goal is to see how, overall, the organization functions when providing answers to questions. Because of that, it is important to select times that represent the normal rhythms of work and staffing through the day, day of week, and time of year.

Note when different levels are staffing are available. Accurate referrals are part of good reference service, so questions should be scheduled when they are likely to occur in real life.

In published library literature, the most common way to conduct unobtrusive testing is to recruit library school students to pose as regular patrons, in person, online, or by telephone. Libraries that have such a program nearby can do this. For others, the *swap* is an effective technique. Libraries join together so that their staff can contact other libraries. The "unobtrusive" part of "unobtrusive observation" means that the librarian fielding a question cannot know that it is not real, so someone unknown must do the asking. Those asking questions can be staff from a different library, friends or trustees, family, and others.

A master scheduler should organize the question times so that they fit naturally into the regular flow of questions. Space different types of questions so that staff do not detect a pattern. Double-check with questioners so that they can really commit to the given time. Here, it is less important to do a truly random sample than to have all of the questioners able to keep to the designated schedule, which will be a purposive sample of important and typical times for handling questions.

Administering the Questions

All people who will act as questioners should be trained to do so consistently. Organizers should spell out what part of the question should be presented initially and what kinds of information should be given out in response to follow-ups. The more concrete the question, the simpler this will be. For more complex tests, organizers should practice play-acting interactions so that the questioners become comfortable and the organizers have some assurance that the process will go smoothly and consistently.

If questions are posed in person or by phone, questioners should take notes immediately afterwards about the answer, follow-up questions or comments, and anything unusual. For chat or email reference, preserve the transcript.

Two sorts of information should be recorded: raw and coded. In the raw information, as much as possible of the transaction itself is recorded, along with the date, time, and circumstances.

Monday, 8:15 pm, in-person, nobody else waiting at desk

I need to know the inflation rate.

> What time period?

What is the inflation rate right now?

> The Bureau of Labor Statistics keeps the official Consumer Price Index. For July there was no change from the previous month. There was an increase of 1.4% from the previous July. Do you want the website? Try Googling "consumer price index" and look for the web address with "bls."

Summarizing the Results

Code the data into a spreadsheet. This means using shortened and consistent terms to represent what went on in the interaction; preserve the full details for qualitative analysis, if desired (see Table 1.29).

Date	Time	Line?	Question	Answer	Correct?	Interview?
Aug 10	20:15	No	Inflation	CPI from BLS	Yes	1 question
Aug 11	9:15	No	Voting	City Hall	No	0 questions

Table 1.29 Data Example: Reference Accuracy Testing.

In this example, almost all of the columns have a very concrete answer pertaining to that particular interaction. The results can be sorted and summarized, for example, 13 questions were asked during evening hours, 18:00 to 24:00, of which 10 were correct.

Use special care with the "Correct" column and the "Question" column. How "Correct" is handled depends on what the organizers wish to preserve, identify, and group. If a great deal of information is collected, such as "friendly" or "showed me how," this becomes an ethnographic observation, or mystery shopping. If too little information is collected, then managers will not know if certain key items are present. For example, how often are librarians asking follow-up questions? The more complex this is, though, the harder it is to apply these codes or scores consistently. In the above example, is asking if someone wants a link an example of citing a source, or is it providing instruction? At least two people should collaborate on how they think things can be consistently recorded and defined as "correct."

For the "Question" part, most librarians would agree that some questions are easier to answer than others. It is important therefore to preserve data on what kind of question it is so that overall success or failure can be related to type of question. The challenge is to come up with categories for the questions that are meaningful and more succinct than giving each question its own category, and not so broad that truly dissimilar questions are combined. This is where organizers should agree that there are certain groupings of the preset questions. An enormous amount of literature covers how to categorize reference questions beyond the standardized "informational" versus "directional" grouping. The most useful categories will depend on the type of library and its mission; citation help, database access, and authentication problems are common to academic libraries; school projects, employment assistance, and help with printers and computers show up in public libraries.

Data from unobtrusive testing will be mostly group percentages: Of all questions of X type, Y were successful. Of all questions at this time or of this type, Y were successful. The main groupings will be time, type of question, and type of answer or interaction.

Study Questions/Examples

Agosto, Denise, and Holly Anderton. "Whatever Happened to 'Always Cite the Source?': A Study of Source Citing and Other Issues Related to Telephone Reference." *Reference & User Services Quarterly* 43.1 (2004): 44–54.

- What types of libraries were involved?
- How were the questions chosen?
- Who posed the questions?
- Describe one finding in one sentence.

Mystery Shopping

Introduction

Mystery shopping has become well known through its use in retail establishments. It has also been used in noncommercial organizations such as churches and also can be very valuable for libraries. It is an intensive form of observation and requires significant preparation, a well-trained observer, and sufficient time to collect representative data. Little training and not much time is needed to collect data in concrete and limited tallies as described in the tally-type "Observation" section. Mystery shopping needs trained observers who devote significant time to their visits and data collection. The number of visits is necessarily limited, so a purposive selection of visit times is needed, as opposed to whole-population sampling including every visitor, every transaction at the reference desk, and every use of a lab computer, and opposed to random sampling.

Procedure

In mystery shopping, an observer makes a visit to the library or other organization and gathers data about normal, typical, and important features. This person is not a tester, as in the "unobtrusive observation or testing" described in the previous section. The goal is not to find out if staff give accurate answers to set questions. Instead, the emphasis is on the context and the delivery of services—in short, everything that makes a visit satisfactory for the patron.

Therefore the steps in designing a mystery shopping evaluation are as follows:

1. Listing the elements of a satisfactory experience

2. Determining how to consistently grade or score those elements

3. Recruiting and training one or more observers

4. Selecting specific times for observation

5. Compiling the data

"Satisfactory experience" is the overall concept. To make it concrete, start by listing everything that, when good, makes for satisfaction and, when bad, ruins the experience. Here are some elements that are common to most physical library buildings and services:

- Parking

- Initial signage, sightlines, and visual cues for various tasks, such as "Photocopiers" or "Ask Questions Here"

- Seating options and availability

- Tidiness of areas, for instance, are there many books or magazines left out? Is trash uncollected?

- Restrooms, including signage, availability, and cleanliness

Note that the observer's task is to record objective data about each of these, not opinions. For example, the observer can record how crowded a parking lot is at a particular time. With a patron survey or an interview, you can ask actual patrons to give their opinion about the closeness or convenience of parking.

Other elements have to do with the qualities of friendliness and customer appreciation:

- Greeting upon entry

- Thanks or ending greeting after checking books out

- Providing physical assistance

- Making eye contact or smiling

- Appropriate dress

On these elements, you can take either a deductive or inductive approach. You can look at how people follow existing policies or get a sense of what is currently being practiced. In a deductive or policy-down approach, a library would already have set expectations for staff in terms of whether they are expected to make eye contact, to verbally greet patrons, or to get up and show people where to go rather than describing and pointing. In this situation, the mystery shopper will determine the extent to which, on that visit, these expected behaviors are actually happening.

Many libraries do not have detailed manuals or rules. However, they may have ideas that the library staff should be "friendly." What does "friendly" mean? Does it mean making eye contact? It is sometimes easier to determine what is definitely *not* friendly, such as having to make a noise or calling out "excuse me" or waving your hand to attract a staff member's attention. The inductive approach is ground-up: observing what is actually happening. Break down the concepts of "friendly" and "responsive" into concrete, observable behaviors that would demonstrate the presence or absence of the concept. In this way you can determine what behaviors your staff is currently, on average, actually doing.

Once you have the concepts or elements and the concrete signs of those concepts, set up a scoring sheet that is similar to an instructional rubric. This is a grid that shows various levels of the signs being present or not.

Some signs will be yes or no, or present or not present: a person made eye contact or did not. You could expand this to the following:

- Made eye contact when 10+ feet away

- Made eye contact when closer than 10 feet but before 3 feet

- Made eye contact when at the desk, defined as 3 feet from edge

- Made eye contact only after shopper attracted staff member's attention

This method requires a series of these elements and how they are to be scored. It is possible to sum all the scores up into an overall average, such as "we performed at an average of 3.4 on a scale of 1 to 4." That requires making sure that all scales are either the same or are coded the same. For example, if most elements are on a 1 to 4 scale from "not at all" to "somewhat," "mostly," and "completely," and others are "yes" or "no," code "no" as 1 for "not at all" and "yes" as 4, "completely."

Some departments or areas will be scored on the same elements and scales, for example, tidiness of the young adult area, the children's area, study rooms, and magazine reading area. Another example would be information services at the genealogy desk, the government documents desk, and the checkout desk.

Some elements are not controlled by the library but should still be included. For example, a parking lot could be crowded or a computer lab deserted. Is a crowded parking lot good or bad? It will be important to know that the parking lot is crowded at the same time as, maybe, in terms of the lab, cleanliness scores are lower, or that eye contact is more common when a lab is empty. Remember not to make the noncontrollable codes or elements as part of an overall score, any more than time of day is. Instead, they are sorting mechanisms: here are scores that occur when the computer lab is or is not crowded.

The tester makes note of time, day, and date. All of this data goes into a spreadsheet as shown in Table 1.30.

Day of Week	Time	Department	Eye Contact?	Cleanliness	Seats Available
Monday	8:15 am	General		4	95%
Monday	4:00 pm	Children's		2	20%
Monday	4:00 pm	Info desk	2		

Table 1.30   Data Example: Mystery Shopping Rating Sheet.

Blank cells are characteristics that do not apply to that particular department or area.

How many visits should be made? Some mystery shopping is done with a single visit. Think about how often X element at your library changes. Room layout and the location of the parking lot do not change from month to month. The busyness of the library could be very different in summer compared to fall. Staff in the evenings might have developed different habits from those in the daytime. Your mystery shopper report will have greater credibility when you have multiple visits for items that change relatively frequently. Shorten the additional visits by leaving out observations on things that do not change.

Once in a spreadsheet, these observations can be sorted and summarized. For example, it may be that cleanliness takes a dip in midafternoon. Perhaps it is more difficult to attract a staff member's attention near closing. In a library with several departments, sorting by department might detect that each has a different practice for things like greeting patrons or staying behind a desk rather than going with patrons to find items.

The table form of the summary data is shown in Table 1.31.

Eye Contact Average Scores	
Local History room, only during staffed hours	2.4
Information	3.5
Children's Room	3.0
10 am – 12 noon	3.8
3 pm – 5 pm	2.4
7 pm – 9 pm	2.2
From 1 = "not until patron specifically attracts staff attention" to 4 = "when patron is 5 to 10 feet away"	

Table 1.31   Report Example: Mystery Shopping Ratings.

Retailers often use mystery shopping as one part of personnel evaluation. That is, any lapses the shopper observes will be used by the manager to educate, discipline, or even fire a specific clerk. Whether to use a mystery shopper for personnel or person-specific evaluation is a larger, managerial question, and many library directors or department managers would not want to do that. Rather, mystery shopping done as part of library evaluation is not personal. It is not about any single individual's habits, reactions, or performance but the performance of the library, the circulation department, or information services as a whole, in the aggregate. In addition, the response to poor scores on mystery shopping is not simply "fire poor performers." Instead, examine why staff are having difficulty achieving the desired level of performance. Perhaps areas are becoming untidy because janitorial staff has been cut—a budget issue. Perhaps staff does not make eye contact because they have never been told that that is important, and it becomes a training and expectations issue. Perhaps staff members have misdirected visitors because they have not had time to learn about changes in what different departments offer, a professional development issue.

Library evaluation is about detecting overall trends and issues so that you can design systematic responses for improvement. It is entirely true that aggregated behavior scores are affected by poor behavior by one individual. However, even in purely personnel management terms, changing one person's poor performance begins with setting and communicating achievable expectations. The process of designing a mystery shopper grading sheet itself educates those who participate in what they and their library supervisors considers important.

Study Questions/Examples

Cavanagh, Mary. "Re-Conceptualizing the Reference Transaction: The Case for Interaction and Information Relationships at the Public Library Reference Desk." *Canadian Journal of Information and Library Science* 30.1/2 (2006): 1–18.

Tesdell, Kate. "Evaluating Public Library Service—the Mystery Shopper Approach." *Public Libraries* 39.3 (2000): 145+.

- What service or area of the library was targeted or left out?
- Who carried out the data gathering?
- What was one of the concrete observations?
- What was a thematic conclusion, one supported by multiple evidence?

Notes

1. Antell, Karen. "Why Do College Students Use Public Libraries? A Phenomenological Study." *Reference & User Services Quarterly* 43.3 (2004): 227–36.

2. https://www.projectsails.org/SampleQuestions.

3. Hubbertz, Andrew. "The Design and Interpretation of Unobtrusive Evaluations." *Reference & User Services Quarterly* 44.4 (2005): 327–35.

Chapter 2

Impersonal Techniques

List-Checking

Introduction

The checklist or list-checking method is at once a very traditional, powerful, flexible, and old-fashioned way of evaluating a library's collections. Using lists is so closely related to collection development that it is sometimes difficult to distinguish using lists as buying guides from using lists as an evaluation method for collection management. Collection management turns from item-by-item buying or weeding to "how good is X collection?" In collection development you say, "This book is/is not on a quality list, I should buy or weed it." In evaluation for collection management you say, "How many of our items are on a list?" "What percent of this list do we own?"

The basic concept is to have a list of materials and to compare it to your library's collection, or to compare your library's collection to a list of materials. The two key points are selecting the comparison list and doing the checking. How useful your results are depends on the nature of the comparison list. How much you can rely on the results depends on the accuracy of the method of doing the checking. The summary finding of a list-checking evaluation is a judgment that this (part of the) collection is of X quality. A very common side benefit is that you will generate a list of books (items) that should be added or withdrawn from that collection.

Broadly, list-checking belongs in a family of methods that are used to evaluate the qualities of a particular collection unit. A collection unit is a group of materials that share some characteristics; most of the time, subjects define units, as well as format or usage policies. Several methods can be used to generate information about a collection unit:

- Usage: circulated yes, no, when; how many books, or what percentage of books, have circulated; what is the distribution of high versus no circulation; average circulations; trends over time.

- Physical condition: needs conservation or replacement, yes or no. Percentage of items needing conservation shows you how fragile the unit is.

- Age: publication date of the materials.

- Popularity: this is the White Strength test, which shows how widely owned (nationally, as recorded by OCLC), items are.

And then there is the *collection-against-list* version of list-checking:

- Quality: items are/are not on a list of recommended materials.

In each of these cases, the result is an aggregated judgment for the collection unit as a whole:

- Our fantasy section circulates at a rate of 1.13 circs per year but our cookbook section circulates at a rate of 4.55 per year; we probably need more cookbooks.

- Almost 20% of items in the Native Americans section (E99) are deteriorating while only 3% of those in the Geography (G) section are; spend time and funds on conservation and replacement in E99.

- The Careers collection at North High School has an average age of 2001 while the Careers collection at South-west High School has an average age of 1992; send a special supplement to SWHS.

- Our Peace and Justice collection aims to have scholarly-level materials, but the average OCLC holdings are so high (500+) that they are characteristic of books held by both colleges and public libraries.

- Our Business Marketing section has 6% of its items on a quality list while the Business Ethics section has none. *This is relatively rare.*

The *list-against-collection* method of list-checking, takes the opposite approach. It does not confine itself to looking at what you already own. Instead, it compares what you might own, according to your mission, to what you actually own. Circulation data is wonderful, but you cannot assess how highly circulated book X would be if only you owned it. You know what you have but not what you are missing. Surveys are one way to gather information about topics or areas you do not own, but their data provides very general directions, not analytical suggestions.

List-checking, then, is one of the only ways to get a detailed answer for the question, what *should* your collection be? This works long as the comparison list is good and the checking is careful.

In some situations list-checking is so simple it is too obvious and not of much use. That does not mean it is a simple method. For other situations, it will be difficult and sometimes impossible. The goal of the evaluator is always to keep in mind, "what can list-checking tell me, at what cost of time, effort, and sometimes processing fees, for what purpose, and in comparison to what other method?"

Consider two extremes. Librarians maintaining a collection serving American children will almost always want to include quality children's fiction. They use the Newbery winners and honors list as a collection-building tool, a way to identify items to buy. That means that there is no point in using the Newbery list for collection management. All the check would show is if the library has failed to maintain replacements for losses.

At another extreme, a small college believes it has been given the "world's best" collection of Anabaptist historical cooking books. Is there some list that can be found to see if any items are missing? Probably not: who would have compiled a list relevant to this specialty (cooking, historical, but only Anabaptist) that has never existed before?

The most useful list-checking comes in the middle. A charter school wants a strong children's science collection. A master's level university has a program in business marketing. A public library has collections on the history of its state and of an adjoining state. What is the quality of those collections right now?

The "Procedures" section describes general principles for both types: collection-against-list and list-against-collection. The two vary mainly in their interpretation, covered in the "Interpreting Results" section.

Procedure

List-checking consists of the following steps:

1. Identifying a unit
2. Selecting a list
3. Checking ownership
4. Interpreting results (comparisons; what is good?)

Identifying a Unit

Identifying a unit and selecting a list are tied together. A collection unit is a set of items that you believe has a sort of internal coherence and specific definition. You determine that specific items are part of this collection unit and identify those that are not. Consider evaluating your vampire fiction. Do we call this unit "fantasy"? If so, then an evaluation of your fantasy collection or a list of fantasy may not be detailed enough. Do we call it "supernatural"? This is probably closer. Vampires may acquire their own category, and someone may create a list specifically for it. In the end, you need a fit between your unit and a list. Different list sources match different types of units that can be assessed.

Some examples of units are as follows:

- Easy Readers

- British Literature, 1800–1914

- Ojibwa History

- Photography (art, rather than technique)

The broader the unit, the more difficult finding a list will be and the less useful the results. What can you do with the information that you own 14% of the items in the *Wilson Public Library Fiction Catalog*? The *Resources for College Libraries* database?

The "Procedures—Conspectus" section has more detail on how to divide a collection into units. The most extensive study of this has been done for academic libraries, although the principles are applicable to public library Dewey sections and genres.

Very narrow units might not have lists available.

Selecting a List

A variety of lists are available. Some are labeled lists, some are not. One thing to keep in mind is that if a list has been used to create or maintain a collection (collection development), that same list cannot be used to evaluate it (collection management). That use would be circular: you buy from a list, you own items on the list. The only thing that process measures is your buying speed and replacement efficiency for lost or stolen books. Because of that, the most obvious lists are the least useful for evaluating collections. However, some lists that may seem obvious have not been used, something you can detect quickly. Many libraries own Newbery winners; surprisingly few have complete collections of the Coretta Scott King, Schneider or Prinz award winners.

Here are sources of lists from the most specific to the most general. The more professionally produced and more specific the list, the better.

- *Articles from library periodicals.* Journals such as *Booklist, Choice,* and *Library Journal* have regularly featured best-books lists. You can use one year or compile several years of these articles into a master list for checking. The main challenge here is that because these are so well known to collection developers, it is very likely that they will have been used for buying books, so you cannot use them for evaluating the subsequent collection. Nevertheless, they are useful when identifying a beginning benchmark. Suppose you wish to improve your graphic novels (GN) collection. You have bought GNs individually for a few years; how have you done so far?

- *Book-length bibliographies* by library publishers. Many core library publishers produce bibliographies. Consider the series on U.S. presidents by Praeger. No single library would have 100% of what is listed for a president, but it could estimate how deep its collection is relative to this exhaustive listing.

- *Disciplinary (nonlibrarian) publications*, including journal articles, prizes, and websites. Researchers in a particular field may publish best-of or recommended materials, which would appear in the key journals and resources of their own field. These are especially useful to ensure you have basic core materials in a field. They can be stand-alone lists ("Best Theology Books of 2003") or a bibliographic chapter within another work. This category includes bibliographies or reading guides found in encyclopedia articles. It also includes bibliographies produced by organizations such as the National Science Teachers Association or the AAAS.

- *Citation/impact lists*. The Web of Science and other resources compile lists of journals and other items that have been cited across the scientific literature. These are quality-usage lists: items that users have found useful in their own research. Most of these lists are international in scope and geared towards academic research, so they are of limited use for nonresearch libraries. They help research libraries determine how extensive their collections are.

- *Lopez method*. This is a variation on the disciplinary bibliography idea with an important addition: iteration. In this method you begin with one high-quality book, published as recently as possible. Use the core items mentioned in its bibliography as the initial list. Then the bibliographies in each of those items are checked, and so forth. One important consideration in using this method is to decide what of the listed items to include. Many scholarly books cite both secondary and primary materials. Primary materials are often unpublished and therefore unique and unsuitable for making up a collection-checking list. The Lopez method is not good for current materials as each citing item reaches further back in time. It is not, in fact, a good first choice. It is a flexible and useful choice when there is no other alternative.

- *Exemplar/peer library*. This method uses another library's catalog as the list. The Harvard Business School at one point published its core collection in book form. The various databases published by H. W. Wilson (*Public Library Catalog*, *Children's Core Collection*, etc.) are similar: simulated ideal collections. Two variations on this include, in the first place, the consciously chosen best library available on that topic, and then measure how close you are to its holdings: the exemplar library. In the other, choose a "peer" library. This library is one that you can reasonably hope to equal in terms of size and quality. These alternatives have offsetting advantages. The exemplar library is easier to use for evaluation, as you have a good, high standard against which to measure. The peer library can give you good ideas about how to build your own collection; it is more practical for collection development and less useful for evaluation.

Some of these methods can be automated. Book vendors have incorporated existing, well-known list sources such as the Wilson catalogs and important prizes into automated matching processes. Their goal is a buying list, so this is often offered for free for smaller libraries. OCLC draws on its unmatched holdings information to provide exemplar-peer library lists: complex and very finely-detailed collection analysis, for a price. At the simplest, it can show you what you own that is unique; within various use agreements, you can compare your collections to one or more specific libraries or groups of libraries.

For checking the list against the collection, the question is, how much of the quality list do we own? The shorter the list, the more feasible it is to check. For checking the collection against the list, you need a very extensive list: something closer to the exemplar-library example. In that case, you take books from your collection and try to identify if they are part of a quality list. For example, if your list happens to be only books currently in print, then much of your collection will fail, not match, simply because the books are out of print. However, it is a little dangerous to use a very extensive exemplar library for this. Many large research libraries have never weeded particular areas, so their collections contain items of dubious quality.

Checking Ownership

This is done either manually or automatically. In each case, it is important to design and carry out consistent and meaningful rules for matching a listing with a holding. Done manually, matching is almost always meaningful but might not be consistent; automatic systems are always consistent but might not be meaningful.

Examine carefully the rules used for computerized matching of list and collection. OCLC tends to match on OCLC number; book vendors generally match on ISBN numbers. Different printings, bindings, and editions of the "same" book will have different OCLC and ISBN numbers: are they conceptually—meaningfully—a match or not? In one difficult case, a book vendor also publishes its own library-binding editions of popular or classic books, each with its particular ISBN number. When that vendor says you do not own 50% of the recommended *titles*, it is not really a *title* analysis but a binding-title/item analysis.

A 1995 printing of *Hamlet* and a 2005 printing of *Hamlet* should probably both count as "owned" if the question is, "do you own a copy of Hamlet?" If the question is, "do you own a stand-alone copy of Hamlet," then this is a title match, and for fiction works well.

For nonfiction, you need reasonable rules and a way to record exceptions. Does the 2001 edition of *Basics of Social Science Research* count as owned if the list says, "2012, ninth edition"? You can say, "editions and publication dates within three years count" or have three categories: exact edition, any edition, and not a match at all.

Ensure that people doing the checking manually follow consistent rules for noting editions and dates. They should employ a set series of search techniques, such as starting with authors or with titles, consistently.

Manual searching may seem antiquated and too labor intensive. Automated checking is the best choice if it matches the list you think is best for the purpose, if you understand and agree with the matching rules, and if you can afford the fees. Manual searching is a good fit for specialized lists. You can adjust matching rules to fit what you think are best. Finally, staffing is often "free." In many libraries, service points need to be staffed, but those staff members are not always busy with patrons. That is your labor force for list-checking.

The data from list-checking goes into a spreadsheet, whereby each row is one book or item and each column contains the data about that particular item. For list-against-collection matching, a fiction example is shown in Table 2.1.

Title/Author *from the List*	Year	Owned?
The Long Passion, Smith	2009	1
Hoping for Something Better, Jones	1998	1
Now that the Day Is Dull, Brown	1998	0
		33%

Table 2.1   Data Example: Checking List against the Collection.

For list-against-collection, a nonfiction example is shown in Table 2.2.

Title/Author *from the Collection*	Year	Exact Edition?	Other Edition (year)	None
Interviewing Techniques, third ed.	2009	1	2007	0
Fast Focus Groups, first ed.	1998	1		0
Interview Basics, second ed.	1998	0		1
		33%		

Table 2.2   Data Example: Checking Collection against List.

In the reversed collection-versus-list method, as a first step take a random sample of the particular collection unit, as long as that unit is larger than 300 items. The random sample will generate a reasonable "score" for the collection, though this will not provide title-by-title details. A collection-versus-list method can be tiered, in which books are compared to different lists (see Table 2.3).

| Title/Author | Year | Lists | | | Total |
		CoreCol	GenRefl	Awards	
The Long Passion, Smith	2009	1	1	0	2
Hoping for Something Better, Jones	1998	1	0	0	1
Now that the Day Is Dull, Brown	1998	1	1	1	3
		100%	66%	33%	2*

*Average number of lists that the collection items belong to.

Table 2.3   Data Example: Tiered Collection against List.

Interpreting Results

Except when you want to own everything on a list, which is a management, not an evaluation, decision, you need to understand or decide what the results mean. If your library owns 32% of the books on the "Core Essential Books on X Topic" list, is that bad or good? This is difficult to answer on an absolute basis. If your library wishes to be truly comprehensive on that topic, then you will be concentrating on purchasing everything available—yours will be the exemplar library for everybody else. If you consider a particular list to be truly essential, then you probably have incorporated it into your acquisition process. If you do not care about that topic, you will not be bothering with evaluation at all.

The most practical method of understanding what your data means is to get more data—comparative data. While you check *your* library, choose a *comparison* library (not a peer or exemplar, but for comparison). This should be a library that you consider to be at or slightly above your own perceived or desired level of quality and resources: one that you feel you should be equal to or better than. Your school district, city, or university may already have identified lists of peers for strategic planning and marketing purposes.

You do not need to do a comprehensive list-check of that comparison library. When you check your own library, you not only get results but also (a side-benefit) a sort of shopping list. You do not need that shopping list from another library. It is reasonable to only check a smaller, random sample from the list against comparison libraries. Here you want a rough benchmark, not precision.

In this way, you can place your results into context (see Table 2.4).

Percent Owned from 1980–2010 Best Lists	Mysteries	Romance	Suspense
My Library	32%	20%	39%
Other Town PL	12%	40%	33%
Hoity Town PL	13%	44%	41%

Table 2.4   Report Example: List Ownership.

In this case, it appears that "My Library" has comparatively few "best romance" novels. It is also clear that even good libraries do not have 100% of these best items.

Using list-checking for evaluation can look like an antiquated mechanical exercise. Instead, it is a tool that can be precisely aimed at your particular purposes for your collection. It is not simplistic: much professional judgment and adjustment is needed to identifying units for evaluation, finding appropriate lists, and designing appropriate "match" rules. List-checking results are a concise method of measuring the quality of your collection. Circulations tell you how popular what you own is, but list-checking is the only detailed way to examine what you are missing.

Study Questions

Many studies reporting collection analysis include more than one technique, as is the case with these two examples. The first article shows collection analysis applied to a specific situation, while the other is a large comprehensive project.

Crawley-Low, Jill V. "Collection Analysis Techniques Used to Evaluate a Graduate-Level Toxicology Collection." *Journal of the Medical Library Association* 90.3 (2002): 310–16.
Monroe-Gulick, Amalia, and Lea Currie. "Using the WorldCat Collection Analysis Tool: Experiences from the University of Kansas Libraries." *Collection Management* 36.4 (2011): 203–16.

- What library and what unit are studied?
- What was the list or type of list?
- What constituted a "match" or ownership?
- Name one finding.

Citation Analysis

Introduction

Citation analysis is an extremely important tool for information retrieval and for information science research. Citation analysis uses citations (bibliographic references) in articles and other scientific works as indicators of use or influence, one item or author to another. That is, author A writes an article on the effect of loud noises on cats; she cites work by author B on soft noises and cats and by author C on loud noises on dogs. Items B and C have received one "use" by author A. Ethical and publication norms in science say that the *use* of someone else's work and ideas should be reflected in explicit *citations*. Therefore, a citation is an indicator of usage. It is a "circulation" record for the article that is cited. Before mass digitization of journals, most libraries restricted circulation of journals. Most uses were in-house, not captured, in contrast to books. Citations were the best method to record at least some of the uses that an item would receive. Moreover, they contain more information than a simple circulation record: author, topic, date, and other elements.

A citation is not a perfect record of use or influence. Studies have shown that scientists may read broadly but cite only narrowly. In other cases, especially recently, important rankings may be dependent on citation counts for authors and journals; editors have been detected manipulating citations. Overall, however, the discrepancy between real usage and citing is no worse than the difference between books checked out ("used") and those actually read (really used). More importantly, a set of scientific pressures and rules governs citation behavior. This data does not depend on someone deciding to cooperate with a librarian in gathering data. They are truly unobtrusive measures, providing information that the librarian's evaluation purpose does not influence.

The use of citations for management is older than its use in information science research. Citation analysis for tracing intellectual influence exploded with the massive computerization of citation indexing undertaken by Eugene Garfield and the Institute for Scientific Information from the mid-1960s; citation for retrieval, in the form of legal case linking, goes back to the late 1800s. In 1927 and 1929, librarians proposed citation analysis for collection management. In two seminal studies, librarians counted up citations in core journals (in chemistry and in mathematics) to see which *journals* were the most-cited.[1] They proposed this as an objective indicator of which journals would be the most useful: an evaluation of journal quality based on citation.

Evaluation uses citation analysis in three main areas: general quality, local usage, and instructional evaluation. As a measure of general quality, citation analysis generates a list of the (globally) most-cited journals and other items. In that sense, it creates a list, which you then use to check how many of the top journals you subscribe to.

For local usage and instructional evaluation, you examine citation data from papers and projects by local authors. This provides very specific information about what sources your own users identify as valuable.

General quality analysis usually depends on data from international databases such as World of Science or Scopus. Google Scholar has citation data and is free, but it is formatted in a way that makes it very difficult to use for item-cited rankings. Scopus and World of Science are easy to use, but they are very expensive, approximately 10 times the cost of a topical bibliographic database such as PsycINFO or Historical Abstracts.

Local citation analysis depends on collecting and collating local information. This is a labor-intensive process.

Gathering citation analysis data is therefore expensive, in fees or labor. However, it is available. That is its great strength. It has no problem with response rates, scheduling interviews, or hoping people show up for a focus group. People will not change their citations based on what they think a librarian wants to see. Citation data is there for the taking. It includes more data than the other prime source of usage data, circulation.

Because citation analysis depends on explicit citations, it is most useful in special or academic libraries, where scholars' articles and student papers and projects provide the most raw material. In some high school situations, particularly instructional evaluation, it is also valuable. While, in concept, web linking is a form of citation, it is not easy to translate this into a usable method of evaluation. Most public libraries will not find citation analysis a good match for their users or resources.

Procedure

The three evaluation uses of citation analysis covered here have differences in their methods, so they will be discussed individually. They are as follows:

1. General quality indicators

2. Local usage

3. Instructional evaluation

Citation/bibliography analysis is also discussed in the "Instructional Evaluation" section in the context of a rubric approach to evaluating student work.

General Quality Indicators

The following is the simplest method. It creates a variety of list-checking. Use a citation index to generate a list of the most-cited journals in a particular field or topic area. For example, World of Knowledge (Thomson Reuters) has two different entry points. The standard way to identify top-rated journals is through the *Journal Citation Reports* (JCR) database, updated annually. The best indicator of top ratings is called the impact factor. This takes the number of citations that articles published in a particular journal receive (from articles in other journals and also in that journal itself) and adjusts them for the number of articles published. One journal may publish 40 articles a year, another 200. For example, in the category of Information Science and Library Science, the top three journals in terms of impact factor for 2011 were the *MIS Quarterly*, the *Journal of Informetrics*, and the *Journal of the American Medical Informatics Association*.

Two ways are used to target narrower disciplines than the large standard groupings. One is to do a keyword search on a topic ("organic farming") in the citation index and arrange the results from high to low citedness. The usefulness of keyword searching depends on how distinctive terminology is in the field you are examining. Scan the resulting citations for repetitive journals; the results are listed article by article, not journal by journal. You can order your results by the citedness of the article or by source journal, but not both.

The other way is to identify one to four journals that are most central to that particular topic or discipline: the most specialized, the most tightly-focused. Extract citations from the articles in one or more volumes. This is time consuming but is very useful for new or niche fields because it is very common for them to have one or two key journals.

The citation index or manual-extraction methods generate a list of the most-cited and therefore the most important and desirable (impactful) journals.

After generating the list, compare it to your holdings. It can also provide a shopping list, but for evaluation, determine how many or what percentage of these high-value items you already own. It is most useful to compare your findings in some way, not to take them in isolation. The comparison can be internal or external. Is your developmental psychology section stronger than your gerontology section? Is your developmental psychology section stronger than that of a peer institution? Percentages (we own X percent, they own Y percent) give you a way to get a rough idea of how you are doing without splintering into a title-by-title comparison (they have X journal, we have Y and Z but not A).

Local Usage

Analysis of citations by local users shows you what they use. It is very personal and specific in ways that circulation records usually are not. It is not as strictly a quality-oriented method as is the global impact factor data from international databases. It shows what your users find useful (because they used it). They can use something because it is familiar or available more than because it is of high quality. This is especially true with student papers.

The first step in local usage analysis is to obtain citation lists from papers or projects. The most commonly used sources are dissertations, theses, and similar capstone products, many of which are deposited in the library. Those are valuable records of how graduate students view and use your library. Obtaining faculty work is usually more labor intensive as few universities have an effective practice of identifying and depositing all faculty work in the library. This is changing as academic libraries work on digital institutional repositories. Departments and schools can also cooperate in organizing the works of their professors to showcase them. In addition, you can use citation databases or Google Scholar to search by author, a technique that does not need faculty or departmental cooperation.

The next step is to extract as much information from the citations as is desirable. Although there are page-scraping algorithms that can be devised, the general principles for manual organization are described here. Like other data methods, the result is a spreadsheet. In this grid, each row is a citation, and each column is a particular bit of data. For citation analysis, the following might be the data or columns included:

- Author's name (have some rule about how to handle multiauthor articles or books, according to standards in the discipline).

- Author's department or discipline (at that university).

- Author, other characteristics (status, years at the university, degrees, etc.).

- Original item's date of publication

- Original item's type (e.g., thesis or dissertation; class project)

- Cited item's date of publication

- Cited item's source/journal title (or book, or other)

- Cited item's ownership or access (is the item owned by the library? Where was it retrieved from?)

It is particularly important that there be some editorial control over the terms used in these columns. If journal names are abbreviated (*J of*), these need to be consistent. Author department and characteristics need to be selected from a list, a controlled vocabulary of terms. Without that, sorting and summarizing will not work out correctly.

In the analysis, data is sorted and grouped by the information in the columns. In a first pass, for example, you could sort by cited journal name, then by citing author status. Some journals may be used by graduate students but not by faculty. Use may change over the years (see Table 2.5).

	Cites by Faculty		Cites in Senior Theses	
	1950–2000	2000–Present	1950–2000	2000–2001
J. of High Energy	35	12	8	33
J. of Kansas Energy St.	15	44	5	12

Table 2.5   Report Example: Journals by Citations (Usage).

It is common to consult faculty when evaluating journals. Adding student paper citations increases your perspective on your users. Few faculty may have an overall sense of what journals are important to their students (or students from other fields). *JAMA* may be too broad and general to appeal to a specialist in gastroenterology but be important to master's students in allied health disciplines.

One important analysis is by ownership status. Are there individuals, disciplines, or other groups who cite materials that you do not own? If these are faculty, they may cite items they were already familiar with before coming to your university. That is why you should note each author's years at the university. If items are not owned, should they be? Student projects can represent very specialized one-time interest areas, whereas usage by multiple faculty over a period of time indicates items that should be owned, in the sense of having immediate access.

Sometimes it is possible to detect when some resources that are already owned are not being used as anticipated, and it is worth following up on that. At some point, citation analysis turns into an item-by-item analysis more than a collection (group) evaluation. The level of detail can be both fascinating and dangerously distracting.

Instructional Evaluation

The big change in using citation analysis for instructional evaluation is that the data do not tell you what you should own. It is not about using these citations as a measure of the quality of your collection. Instead of what you should own, the question is, "are your users accessing what is available to them?" This is determined by availability, visibility, and retrieval effectiveness. Items must be available to the users (owned/available rapidly, not checked out, not lost) and visible to the users (from shelving to website design), and those users have to have the skills to identify relevant items: information literacy instruction.

Data gathering for instructional evaluation is tied to the instruction. This technique applies to courses where a librarian gives instruction that is designed to support specific projects. The librarian already has a connection with the content instructor in order to set up the instruction. The added piece is getting permission to view completed student projects. Online course management systems can make this very easy with the right permissions. For more traditional courses, there is usually some point in time in which an instructor has a stack of projects. At this point you can swoop in and make copies of the relevant materials. Copy the list of citations but also a thesis statement, abstract, or first page. They give context to the citation list. It is important to know what students intended, as well as the resources they mustered to meet that intention.

You can conduct different levels of analysis with the bibliographies depending on time available. Use easy methods more often to keep track of trends over time. Use more extensive analysis less often or only in areas of special need.

An easy analysis is to code the items cited in broad categories such as item format or level: website, journal article, book, and so forth. Journals and other periodicals can be divided into scholarly, professional, trade, and general. These categories are based on the common requirements of student projects that they use materials of a certain level of quality. Have they done so? There are two mathematical ways to organize the data. In the first, each citation is listed and given a category. Citations across *all* users are summed up so that, for example, for Professor X's speech class, 85% of all citations were from websites and only 5% from journals. The second way is to take each individual bibliography and its percentages: person C has 45% scholarly and 55% popular materials; the average percentage of popular materials across members of the class is 59%. The second route is usually the best because the first can be skewed by extreme papers.

Another very simple but opposite technique is to scan bibliographies to see if they included particular resources. This works when students have been specifically instructed about key items. It cannot be used for intermediary tools such as subject databases but can be valuable in detecting use of unique and distinctive items such as institutional archives or important data repositories. If you have taught students about them, do students use them?

Owned/not owned analysis is much more time consuming. It should be coordinated with a look at interlibrary loan (ILL) requests, or reciprocal borrowing records for institutions located close to one another. A variant is to see how much students use materials that are available immediately and in print, by request or delayed delivery, or instantly from an online search. When libraries provide access on demand versus on site, including on a website, is it really being used?

All of these techniques give quantitative windows into what students record as they research. Students probably record more items than scholars do, as they often are reluctant to read something and *not* cite it. Manual data recording and analysis is time consuming, but it has advantages. The act of making the connection with the instructor to get the material improves liaison relations. Assessment is valued in academia, and the effort shows the content instructor that you care enough about the course and your role to gather direct evidence related to the effectiveness of the literacy instruction. Finally, looking at the bibliographies is a priceless way for you to close the loop, to see the fruit of your instruction and the library's collections and services.

Study Questions/Examples

Many examples can be found of research conducted by citation analysis. These aim to detect general trends and information, such as how "all" history students use primary materials and books.

General

Weissinger, Thomas. "The Core Journal Concept in Black Studies." *Journal of Academic Librarianship* 36.2 (2010): 119–24.

Local

Dewland, Jason C. "A Local Citation Analysis of a Business School Faculty: A Comparison of the Who, What, Where, and When of Their Citations." *Journal of Business & Finance Librarianship* 16.2 (2011): 145–58.

Instructional

Cooke, Rachel, and Danielle Rosenthal. "Students Use More Books after Library Instruction: An Analysis of Undergraduate Paper Citations." *College & Research Libraries* 72.4 (2011): 332–43.

- What collection or topic area was analyzed?
- Where did the bibliographies come from?
- What information was recorded other than the titles of journals?
- Name one finding other than a listing of journals.

Collection Mapping

Introduction

Collection mapping is a broad term. For this section, it includes four different methods that take a look at your collection with respect to all of its individual parts. Mapping reflects the reality for most libraries that you will have different goals and priorities for different segments of your collection. The process of mapping provides data to show what has been achieved and what needs attention to match your collection development plan.

This section covers these techniques:

- Conspectus

- Size (and the "Power" test)

- Overlap/unique item analysis

- Strength (Howard White technique and adaptations)

The term *conspectus* originated in important initiatives in cooperative collection development among research libraries in the latter part of the twentieth century. In one well-established example, Duke University, the University of North Carolina at Chapel Hill, and North Carolina State University divided Korean, Japanese, and Chinese expertise and collections among them, seeking to complement, not duplicate, each other. In conspectus evaluation, librarians grade each subject area, divided by Library of Congress or Dewey classification, on the extent to which it supports basic to advanced research in a field.

Overlap analysis is a variant of this that aggregates title-by-title ownership. It is an important concept for the overall strength of information providers. A network of libraries where each owns different titles is extraordinarily more valuable than one in which most of each library's collection is the same as the next.

Strength testing was developed by Howard White. It provides a reasonably objective and concrete method of numerically scoring a collection on its research depth.

The overall term *collection mapping* is used in different ways by different researchers, evaluators, and librarians. A simple way of thinking about it is as a system to match collection strengths to population needs. For example, the library at an engineering-focused university would have strong physics, technology, and engineering sections (the "engineering" aspect) but also solid collections in English, history, and cultures (the "university" aspect). A charter school of the arts would have more video materials covering dance and music than a general elementary school. In evaluation, a collection map displays the extent to which your collection management plan has resulted in a collection shaped the way you intend. This is in terms of subject and depth, not popularity, which is assessed using other methods.

The focus of this section is on a particular collection divided into separately-assessed units, a static collection that you evaluate at one point in time. This approach is most compatible with the idea of a collection as a capital asset: a fixed set of owned items, which together make up an investment in resources. Thus it is not a good match for fluid leasing or semiownership arrangements, or for collections other than books and monographs. Nor are these the only measures for books. The section on usage will be very important to most librarians.

For everything in this section, think carefully about format and unit identification. Format means that these techniques are most appropriate for traditional print books held at one physical place. They can be adapted to incorporate consortiums, remote storage, and electronic editions. In those cases, collection evaluators should make note of the format or availability for the titles being assessed.

Unit identification means, "what collection are you examining at the moment?" Agricultural technology? Persian literature? Mysteries or graphic novels? The broader the unit, the more difficult it will be to make sense of the results. Your starting point should be the library's collection management plan. What units (topics, subtopics) have you identified as being of particular importance? If there is no such plan, then map the needs of your constituents onto your collection.

Once you have identified the unit conceptually, you need a way to reliably or consistently retrieve all items, and only those items, that fit that topic or area. Moreover, if you are going to compare your collection to another, the method has to match both libraries. Using call-number ranges is the most reliable. It is flexible enough to sweep up collections in libraries that use different levels of specificity in assigning call numbers. Subject headings have more variability, especially in those more specialized items that will more often have original rather than Library of Congress cataloging.

Procedure—Conspectus

The first step in using a conspectus approach is to divide your collection into subject units. Conspectus is often used to compare your collection to those of other institutions, so it is important to use consistent categories. OCLC posts a spreadsheet that lists subject areas using DDC and LC categories, for consistency.

Each subject area is then graded on a scale. This scale is the heart of the conspectus approach. Two library consortia have developed scales, the Research Libraries Group (RLG) North American Collection Inventory Project, and the Pacific Northwest Project of the Western Libraries Network (WLN). Each scale is five points, plus a zero for "do not collect" in this area: 1 to 5 and A to E. Briefly, the levels are shown in Table 2.6.

The grade is a holistic judgment based on a number of different aspects, some of which draw upon other methods in this book. For example, you can judge a very minimal

Level	Purpose	Characteristics
Minimal (1, A)	Basic	Few items
Basic	Introductory	Up to date, basic
Instructional (basic or advanced)	Bachelors or masters level	Current and some historical, some subspecialties
Research	Doctoral level	Thorough in specialties and in historical
Comprehensive (5, E)	Everything possible	Adds out-of-print, rare, and unique items

Table 2.6 Conspectus Collection Level Categories.

collection with list-checking. At the comprehensive level, both current publishers and antique book dealers' catalogs are appropriate lists for checking, if the goal is to own everything published on a topic. For the collection goals at instructional and research levels, citation analysis shows how a local collection does or does not support local researchers, or how it matches international high usage. You can assess a comprehensive collection using overlap analysis as shown below. The White Strength method, also shown below, is another way to get a quick approximation of research level.

Expert opinion is an important element of this because these levels are so closely linked to various levels of academic use. You can ask faculty who are strong researchers at the research and comprehensive level or teachers at the instructional level with some basic research to give their opinions of the collection. This is especially useful if you have new faculty who have used libraries at other institutions. It is important for you to know how they believe your collection meets their expectations and their needs. In addition, the process of asking for their opinion and including them in the assessment and improvement of the collection is a good way to develop relationships between faculty and librarians.

The grades are summarized in a grid that provides your scoring for each collection unit or subject area. The next step is to compare the score to the library's ambitions: its collection goals and its resources and money allocated to each area. An example from a 1994 study at Montana State University is shown in Table 2.7.[2]

	Collection Level	Acquisition Commitment	Collection Goal
Agriculture	3.9	3.9	
Anthropology	1.6	1.3	2.6
Art–Architecture	2.3	2.3	3.3
Chemistry	3.3	2.6	3.9
Comp. Sci.	2.3	1.6	3.9
Geography	3.6	3.3	
History	2.3	1.3	3.3
Law	1.3	1.3	1.6
Math	3.6	2.6	3.9

Table 2.7 Report Example: Conspectus Evaluation.

You can see that in the case of history, the collection rates at between introductory and instructional level; the goal is one level up, while the resources devoted to it are one level down.

Procedure—Size (and Power)

Simple size is a very direct metric that needs supplementing with other information. Here, the technique is to conduct either a classification-code or a subject-heading search to determine how many items your library possesses on a particular topic. Done by classification code, this data becomes part of a conspectus score or metric for particular collection units.

Howard White has defined a "Power" test. Like the Strength test shown below, the goal is a numeric, concrete measurement that does not need much human expertise to provide absolute and comparative data.

To conduct a White Power test, do a classification-number search in WorldCat and in your library. Your library's score is a percentage: what percentage of the total number of items available do you own? This assumes that WorldCat represents the universe of possible items, a close approximation in most circumstances.

Procedure—Overlap or Unique Item Analysis

The goal of overlap analysis is to determine the extent to which your library provides unique materials, absolutely or within a particular network or group of peer libraries. This is useful in several ways. First, the extent to which your library's materials are unique shows that it is worthy of the "comprehensive" grade in the conspectus system. Second, you can move unique items, and collection areas with large numbers of unique items, to the top of digitization or preservation priority lists. Finally, it documents ways in which your library, and only your library, represents a valuable, special resource to your organization or community.

This analysis can be done in two different ways. The first is automatic, expensive, and thorough, and the other is manual, inexpensive, and inexact.

OCLC provides an automated overlap collection analysis in conjunction with some other collection analysis reports such as numbers of items in each subject area, their date ranges, and, if you submit your own circulation data, usage. It is a turn-key solution: you need no expertise or software design, and you get a huge amount of data easily. This type of analysis is useful for these types of libraries:

- Libraries at research-level institutions
- Libraries at institutions that are expanding their doctoral programs

- Libraries with individual topical collections that aim for national prominence *as long as those items are fully cataloged in OCLC*

- Members of interlibrary lending consortia

Two cautions are to be kept in mind in addition to the expense. First, OCLC can only measure uniqueness in terms of OCLC holdings. This limits its use with regard to rare books and manuscripts. It also is less useful when analyzing older public library materials because until the latter part of the twentieth century many public libraries did not contribute holding information to OCLC.

Second, the reason that an item is less widely held, even unique, may not be because it is rare and of high quality. A collection of how-to articles on starting up a mediated online search service using Dialog is gone from most libraries because it was weeded along with WordStar manuals and *Introduction to Biology*, 1976 edition.

Doing overlap analysis manually requires only a little staff time or the time of a student worker or careful volunteer or page. To do a manual uniqueness check, take a random sample of items from the collection you are targeting. Take at least 100 items and up to 400. As long as they are selected randomly (not, for example, because each one "looks old"), you can generalize the results of your test to the whole of the collection.

Check each book carefully in OCLC to see how many holdings it has, especially in your geographic region. This step requires some expertise in interpreting OCLC records to ensure that you are matching the correct format, date, and edition. The result gives you a reasonable idea of what percentage of your collection represents items that are not owned by other libraries in your area or consortium. For the very smallest collections, such as local autobiographies, you can check everything and the results are just as thorough as the automated OCLC process.

Procedure—Strength (White)

In his 1995 book *Brief Tests of Collection Strength*, Howard White proposed a more numerical or objective approach to determining the strength of a collection.[3] The scoring in this method points to the same five levels as in the conspectus: minimal, basic, instructional, and research, (comprehensive). Both White and other researchers have since introduced some variations, which this section discusses in turn.

This method was designed for academic libraries, and the numbers involved for scoring are based on U.S. academic library holdings. The original empirical insight was this. Books that are most basic are owned by the most libraries. For example, *Battle Cry of Freedom* is a classic, core history of the U.S. Civil War. Research libraries would own this, but they would also own more specialized and obscure books. Therefore, only the most comprehensive collections (level 5 on the conspectus scale) would own the rarest (least widely owned) materials. This is numerically expressed as numbers of OCLC holdings for a title (see Table 2.8).

Minimal	(holdings > 750)	
Basic	(400-750)	
Instructional	(150-400)	
Research	(<150)	levels

Table 2.8 Collection Strength (White) Holdings Levels.

Note that the "research" level corresponds roughly to the number of research universities and libraries in the United States and Canada: members of the American Association of Universities or the Association of Research Libraries. The scoring levels only apply to books and only to general collection books. Fewer libraries would naturally hold audiovisual items and reference books overall, so their scale would differ.

The concept can be flipped and applied to public library collection evaluation as well. For public libraries, the goal is often the opposite: to own books that are of wide interest. This reflects their size, their mission, and the idea that books need to be available for browsing at one particular library.

Below are descriptions of four variations on the Strength test. One complementary method, the White Coverage/Power Test, is described above (Size/Power).

- Strength (White) Original

- Strength (White) Lesniaski Variation

- Strength (White) Lesniaski Approximation

- Strength (White) / Flipped: Public library application

An important caution: except for the original version, each of these methods depends on accurate and consistent subject searching. This means selecting appropriate subject headings for your topic, executing exact-subject-heading searches, and relying on the catalogers of each institution to have applied headings consistent with the comparison or test lists. The more interdisciplinary, new, or idiosyncratic your chosen topic area, the more difficult it will be to ensure consistency. At some point, you will have to decide if the data you can retrieve by this method is good enough to give you confidence when you use it to evaluate your collection.

Strength (White) Original

Step one is for an expert subject bibliographer to compile a *test list* of 40 items, 10 at each level. Basic items should be owned by every (academic) library. Research items should be owned only by the most comprehensive libraries. Check each item's holdings to see that its ownership level numerically fits into the categories.

Then, check the test list against your collection. Your collection scores at the level where you own at least half of the listed books. For example, your library might own all

10 minimal, 8 basic, 4 instructional, and 2 research books. By this rule, that collection unit scores at the basic level (over half), although close to instructional (not quite half).

Once you have the test list, this is a very easy method to use. The problem is the test list. If you already know an expert subject bibliographer, you may not need a Strength test to measure your collection.

Strength (White) Lesniaski Variation

David Lesniaski proposed a variation of this that avoids the need for a human expert.[4] From a "very large list," in practice WorldCat, conduct a subject search. From the items retrieved on that topic, take a random sample of 50 to 60 items. For each item, record the number of library holdings, meaning libraries owning that title or edition. Use the edition or version with the greatest number of holdings; use only that holdings number, and do not add up holdings for different editions. Arrange the items in order of holdings (see Table 2.9).

History of Our World	556 holdings	Basic
Expectations of Our World	224 holdings	Instructional
My Own World	13 holdings	Research

Table 2.9 Data Example: Collection Strength Titles, Holdings, and Level.

The goal is to have 10 items that are in each of the levels. Continue to randomly select items from the large list, in this case OCLC's WorldCat list, until there are 10 for each level. If you have started with more than 10 in a group, randomly choose some to delete.

This becomes your *test list*, and it is then used as above. Check those particular books against your library's collection, and determine the highest level where you own at least half of the items.

Strength (White) Lesniaski Approximation

One more problem step can be avoided in this very rough but useful approximation. Do a subject search within your *own library's collection*. Then, for the results or for a random sample of at least 30 and up to 100, check each item's holdings in WorldCat. Again, this means the same item with the most widely held version of the bibliographic record. Then, average the results across those items in your collection. This average shows where your collection lands on the basic-to-comprehensive scale. For example, if the average is 122, this is below 150, and your collection for this topic is at the comprehensive level.

Strength (White) Flipped: Approximation

In all of these tests, a "strong" collection was defined as one that has more specialized materials. If you are one of only two libraries to have a particular item, then scholars must come to you in person, virtually, or through request. You are the place to be and the resource to go to. A public library, on the other hand, generally has a "strong" collection when it has what each patron wants with a minimum of waiting. A strong public library collection, then, may specifically aim to have the most basic materials, the ones most broadly desired by other libraries and patrons.

In this flipped version, a high average OCLC holdings score is good. It means that the library has fewer very obscure and perhaps outdated materials. A library has two good reasons for a book not to be widely owned. One is that it is very specialized: the ecology of specific bird species in a particular part of a state. The other is that it is obsolete: the fourth edition of *Using Your New Apple IIe*. A truly comprehensive, history-of-computing research library would want the latter, but a well-maintained public library would not.

For this test, use the approximation above by searching for items on a topic within your library. For most areas of a public library's nonfiction collection, an average holdings score in the basic area is the appropriate goal. For some areas, such as local history, greater depth is part of the library's plan.

Each of these techniques aggregates individual item information (holdings, size, quality) into a collection unit score. If you want to focus on particular segments of your collection, that is the endpoint. Another approach is to systematically cover all units or segments of your collection. If you use an automated method such as from OCLC, it makes sense to do this all at one time, every few years. If you use manual methods, you can tackle a portion of your collection every year. Reviewing all of your collection means that you can prioritize within your organization by objectively identifying what areas are weakest or most important to your library's goals.

Study Questions

The first article uses a Strength (White) test, Lesniaski approximation. The second uses automated and other systems for a holistic evaluation.

Strength (White)/Lesniaski

Lowe, M. Sara, and Sean M. Stone. "Testing Lesniaski's Revised Brief Test." *College & Undergraduate Libraries* 17 (2010): 70–78.

- What units were included (and why)?
- How was the test list generated?
- Describe one finding.

Collection Mapping/Overlap

Culbertson, Michael, and Michelle L. Wilde. "Collection Analysis to Enhance Funding for Research Materials." *Collection Building* 28.1 (2009): 9–17.

- What units were included (and why)?
- What collection-scoring techniques were used?
- Name one way in which different subjects required different techniques.
- What was the purpose of the evaluation?

Use Analysis

Introduction

Analyzing usage of library-provided materials speaks to one of the primary reasons for accumulating materials into a collection: providing what people want. Usage data shows when people have demonstrated that they want these items by actually using them. This is not the only question that librarians ask about materials and resources. Quality is important. List-checking is particularly strong about the aspect of quality. Future use is important, too. Librarians must consider future uses of materials that might be of limited popularity right now. Your mayor's autobiography may not fly off the shelf today, but if your library does not preserve it, who will? Decades to come, it will be there for historians and others to find. Usage data also cannot provide any perspective on things that you do not own or provide access to; it is confined to the resources you already manage.

Usage is not everything, but it is important. Usage data has two main benefits. First, it is a measurement of something that is very important to us. It shows some ways in which we have succeeded in meeting the needs of our patrons. Second, most library systems are set up so that they generate usage data effectively and efficiently. In many ways, libraries are engines of data generation, every day pumping out vast quantities of data about various types of usage. This information is comprehensive and valuable. It becomes raw data for other investigations, such as the reading habits of children or youth or the information needs of adults.

In research and in evaluation there is an important concept called measurement validity. "Valid" here is concerned with truth: how much does this measurement correspond to the truth that one is trying to capture? Consider the case of alcoholism. The truth you want to know is, is this person an alcoholic? That depends first on a definition of alcoholism and then on the data you can capture about that definition. If alcoholism requires drinking X amount of alcohol per Y time period—a definition—then what measures that accurately? A survey that asks someone how much they drink may be less valid—farther from the actual situation—than a series of credit card charges at a liquor store or bottles discarded in the trash. The best is probably a spycam that follows you around. We always accept some compromise between what we want to know and what we will measure.

We want to know if patrons use our items, and we speak of "usage." However, usage measures do not actually read people's minds about whether they have read, thought about, and integrated knowledge from such an item into their behavior and ideas. Instead, we can detect when people have done the following:

- Checked a book out

- Visited a web page

- Downloaded a pdf

- Left a magazine out on a library table

These are all called "uses"—not quite so, but the best we can do.

Citation analysis, discussed in another section, does go one step further. It detects when someone has incorporated a reference to X work into another work. That is a more valid measure of "usage," but it also has limitations. It fails to capture uses where someone reads X that leads them to Y, and they cite only Y. It sometimes includes inaccurate or inflated citations, such as citing X to make an impression on editors.

In the end, even though our measures are limited, we use them for two reasons. First, we care about the concept of use, and these are as close as we can get. Second, usage data are some of the easiest and most naturalistic data available. They are unobtrusive and impersonal. They capture traces as people interact naturally and normally with library systems, so they do not distort their behavior. They do not depend on cooperation or attitude; they have no problems with response rates. Generally they impose very few additional costs on the library to collect. In the physical world, we need to know where our items are anyway, whether or not we then aggregate the information for evaluation. In the digital world, "where" no longer matters much, but capturing data still costs very little.

The following sections describe four major types of usage analysis:

- Circulation

- Reshelving

- Webpages (library-generated materials)

- Electronic materials (journals, databases: commercial aggregations)

The "Procedures" section is more conceptual than in other sections of this book. The following discussions include conceptual and practical points of the process including what data are available and what you can gather using relevant tips and techniques. Implementation details depend on particular systems in existence. They will change as technology evolves, although there are still some useful manual methods.

Usage as recorded in citations in the "Citation Analysis" section feeds into a collection-mapping approach to evaluation found in the "Collection Mapping" section.

Procedure

Most usage data in a library is gathered by automated systems. Therefore, the most important sources of information on usage data for your library rest in the suppliers of a library's systems for book, item, and electronic resource management. Some vendors have made special efforts to provide comprehensive, flexible, and user-friendly data analysis tools. In open-source systems, the burden is on the user community to see the value in data analytical tools. Open-source systems often contain methods to access raw data but may initially provide very raw methods, such as SQL query modes, that are not designed for nonprogrammers. In that environment, users should collaborate to ensure that data analytic tools have a high priority for development.

Circulation

A "circulation" is a record of when patrons identify a library item that they take with them rather than using or leaving in the library. A circulation record is a link between a patron record that includes the characteristics of that patron, and an item record that provides the characteristics of that one particular physical item. For the duration of a particular circulation, there is a link between the patron record and the item record. This patron is associated with these items; this item is now "out" to this patron. For privacy reasons, particularly after the passage of the USA PATRIOT Act, after the circulation ceases, a patron record usually does not contain item history but might preserve some numeric data, such as total number of items borrowed. Similarly, the item record then usually contains information on total numbers of circulations and, usually, their dates, but not identification of the patrons. You can see how many circulations a book has had, or how many items a patron has had, but not what items a patron has had nor what patrons an item has had.

Consider what circulation data you want to extract. One is date. What do you want to include? How many years of use? It may take as many as five years for as much as half of an academic library's collection to circulate; for a public library that may be only one or two years. Exact dates of individual circulations are also important, not just aggregates. Perhaps a book has circulated five times, but the last one was four years ago; circulation ceased because there was a newer edition.

The length of the allowable borrowing period affects the numbers of circulations. This tends to be longer for academic libraries as compared with public libraries. Note the allowable length for particular formats and whether your library has changed its policies. For high-demand items, lengthening the borrowing period automatically reduces the number of circulations, artificially lowering the item's recorded usage.

Because of the difference between item and title, you must consider whether your reports aggregate by title or by item. A library with five copies of the same edition of Stephen King's *It* needs to account for an aggregate of circulations, as well as having some sense of demand for items where there is a difference in copies per title, perhaps 50 copies of *The Secret* and maybe 30 copies of *Twilight*. One way to equalize all of this is to calculate a percentage of available circulations. Three copies of *Man for All Seasons*, with a three-week borrowing period, have a rough aggregate of 52 potential circulations per year. That ignores returns prior to a due date, renewals, and overdues, so it is a rough benchmark. If these copies or items circulate 40 times, the title has achieved 77% of potential circulations.

Are these fine points beside the point? At the high end, you do not need much data to identify individual high-demand items. At the low end, aggregate circulation data for items to determine if a title is being used, should be weeded, or needs replacement.

For the purposes of collection evaluation, you calculate circulation for groups of materials, not individual items. What usage does *this* set of books achieve? For this purpose, use two main figures: percentage circulated and average circulations. For percentage circulation, each item is recorded as 1 or 0 for yes or no, respectively, if it did or did not circulate within a specified time period. This would be the past year or past two years for public libraries; it would be the past year, five years, or ten years for academic libraries. For average circulations, divide the numbers of circulations for all of the items in the collection unit by the number of items for a circulation ratio. If your collection of 120 graphic novels has 450 circulations in the last year, its circulation ratio is 3.75. You can divide by all items or only by those that have circulated at all. Consider the example shown in Table 2.10 for circulations over the past three years.

Subject	Number of Items	Percentage Circulated	Circulation Ratio *of All*	Circulation Ratio of *Used*
English History (DA)	781	32%	0.76	3.35
Native American (E99)	544	55%	1.16	5.14
American Literature (PS)	1,233	13%	0.24	0.54
Nursing (RA)	504	66%	1.98	3.01

Table 2.10   Report Example: Usage by Subject Area.

In this case, the library has an extensive American Literature collection with many classics in the field. Students tend to buy their own copies for class and do not use the secondary materials or criticism for papers. The English History section serves a small but studious group of majors and faculty. In both the Native American section and in Nursing, not all books appear to meet current needs, with a relatively low percentage of books circulating. Those that do circulate circulate heavily. The lower level of overall circulation for the E99 section can be explained by the presence of classics of historical interest in the field. The Nursing collection is intended to contain current and relevant materials, so it would aim for a higher percentage circulated.

Circulation data is some of the most feasible numeric data available to any library evaluator. Depending on the system's data search capabilities, you can generate detailed reports for nearly every user group and defined area of the collection. However, use it within an overall evaluative context that places the data in a full perspective:

- Circulation is not actually usage. It means something was checked out, which is not quite the same thing.

- Compare data for one subject unit with other subjects and with overall usage. Use of physical items is something that is rapidly changing, and some user groups and user needs may change more rapidly others.

- Circulation cannot ever measure demand for something that is not owned. Suppose five years ago someone checked out and never returned all of your books on X subject. You will not know from circulation data if there is still demand for them.

Supplement circulation data with ILL data to get around the unowned/not-circulated problem. It does have limitations. The first is on the part of users. They may not be aware that ILL exists, they may hesitate to use it because of fees, they may not want to wait, or they may change their minds about what they want, depending on what is available. In many cases, students have to write a paper and they choose a topic based on what materials are available that day instead of looking for the perfect list on a specific topic. The second limitation is in the circulation systems. Libraries sometimes use incompatible systems to route and record ILLs and circulations. The records may be joined at the patron level (this patron has these items checked out and through ILL), but not at the item or collection level recording that this ILL item is in this collection unit or Dewey range.

Reshelving

Reshelving is the broad term for techniques that seek to capture uses of library materials that do not involve circulations. In some libraries, some materials never circulate, such as reference works. In most libraries, people choose to use some materials only in the library without checking them out. You count these items before you reshelve them, providing "reshelving data."

It is important to understand user habits in a particular library setting. In a public library where many patrons come and go quickly, what sorts of books do people leave behind? These are usually the opposite of desirable; a person gathers a stack of books and then takes only some to be checked out. In an academic library with a strong study-space atmosphere, students may seldom check books out but rather use them on site. In that setting, a stack of books more clearly represents usage.

At least four ways are available to record in-house use or reshelving data. The first, and easiest, is to use the library's circulation system in a "browse use" mode. A shelving page, student worker, or volunteer gathers all books left out on shelves, tables, carts, and other areas and either uses a portable code-scanner right there or takes them to the circulation area to be recorded.

The second and third ways work with relatively low-use noncirculating collections such as reference or bound periodicals. When items are left out, a shelving staffer sweeps periodically through the area (or at the end of the day) and makes a mark on the item itself. This can be a sticker on the outside of the spine, easy to notice later, or a tick mark inside the cover. Or, the staffer makes a mark on a list of the items. This fits small collections such as some periodicals or major reference sets in a public library.

The final method is almost like spy-dust. Put small slips of paper inside the books where they will be dislodged if the item is used. The famous Kent–Pittsburgh study of academic library book use used something similar, with surveys folded around books' pages inside the covers: these were invisible until the book was actually chosen by a user.[5] This is laborious and is worth the effort mainly when you really need to determine if an item or collection is being used at all.

Do "Please do not reshelve" signs work? Yes and no. In general, researchers have found reshelving involves both undercounting and overcounting. Some people carefully replace everything they use back on the shelf; others take out items that they never really look at. The two tend to balance each other out. In general, if you have a fairly active area that you want to assess, putting up signs for a one- or two-week period requesting "PLEASE do not reshelve! We are counting!" may help people comply with what you are aiming at.

Is this an obsolete method in a virtual world? Perhaps. It does have one or two useful applications. The first is to confirm or deny that a particular item is really used or unused. The second is where you need to confirm and incorporate significant in-house use. One such situation is when children come to the library in groups. They may work with materials right there and then leave them behind as they go off to the activity. If you do not record this usage, then items that really are important may be unfairly disadvantaged. In one public library, nearby teachers brought classes in to use Native American picture books. Students were forbidden to check them out. Not counting in-house use would distort their real value.

Webpages

Webpage measurement seems simple, yet it can be endlessly complicated. On the one hand, virtual reality comes with recordability; everything that happens online emits tiny trails of data. On the other, what do those tiny traces really mean, and have they been manipulated?

For libraries, webpage evaluation mainly targets two groups of resources: (1) the library's own created webpages and (2) digitized collections. This does not include commercial databases, discussed below, but archives, image sets, and tutorials.

Four primary resources are used to collect webpage usage data: Google Analytics (GA), application logs, server data, and in-house coding. For libraries that maintain most of their own pages with in-house staff, placing GA codes on the pages of interest costs only time and attention. GA yields extensive, specific data with a user-friendly data display and user interface. It was designed primarily for commercial users and is optimized to serve their needs, but nonprofits like libraries can use much of the information relatively easily. It is important to read about current conditions and user tips. For example, there is a feature that allows you to exclude staff usage as defined by IP range so that the data reflects only truly patron usage.

The capacities of Google and its competitors are bound to evolve. Ask what exactly is being recorded and how. Stay in touch with the service as it develops so that you can make decisions about how comparable data is over time. The goal of Google and others is the same as yours: to gather reasonably accurate usage data for each page, item, or feature. For example, if you have spent much time creating extensive instructional webpages, are they used? Is a tip sheet used more than more in-depth topics? How does "How to create an MLA formatted citation" compare to "How to research term papers"?

The term *application logs* is used here to refer to data recorded by template software. Template software includes LibGuides, some archive interfaces, and some entire library website packages. These can include reporting features, such as recording popular pages or terms searched for—look for the "word cloud"! In these situations, examine just what is being recorded, in what time period, and with what comparability. A good template will show the most useful data but might not archive it. Unless the template archives data and has detailed query options as GA does, someone needs to take periodic "snapshots" of data so as to keep track of usage over time. Usage since the beginning of recorded time is not very useful, while month-by-month or even week-by-week traffic can show important patron patterns.

Server data and in-house coding refer to the fact that those who host webpages usually develop internal methods of measuring traffic. Librarians managing websites using rented servers will use the tools of those providers. Some larger libraries will run their own servers, either using packages such as templates described above or their own information technology (IT) teams. In each case, there are bit-trail crumbs to be collected. For external server companies, you will be limited to what they consider valuable to most of their clients. That is a reason to use a server company that has other libraries, cultural organizations, or nonprofits as clients so that your needs are familiar to them. You do not want to have a report all about shopping and revenue and not about page usage. When you manage data in-house, engage the IT team in understanding what you need in terms of measurement. The danger in external companies is that their standard data may not fit your needs. The danger in internal IT design is that you may create a system with such idiosyncratic data that it is not comparable to any other setting. You do not just need a count, you need a count that is meaningful. Comparisons help create meaning. Compare with yourself over time, and compare yourself to peer departments or organizations.

In all of this usage data, remember that it is very difficult to distinguish between usage information that is really about the items and information that is really about the users. Suppose you have digitized a collection of purebred llama genealogical records. Low usage figures could indicate several things. Maybe there is something missing on the item side—nobody really is interested in all things llama—or maybe there is something missing on the user side. That is, there are people who should benefit from this collection, but they have no idea it exists or how to use it. Maybe they keep typing "llama bloodlines" and not "llama genealogy." In other words, does low usage mean a truly low level of interest, or is there some barrier between real user need and effective access? Usage data of your various webpages will give some clues to this, but supplement simple usage data with surveys and interviews of those who ought to be users, as well as usability studies.

Electronic Materials (Databases, Journals, Articles)

Counting Online Usage of Networked Electronic Resources (COUNTER) is the one organization and mechanism that librarians need to know for evaluation of electronic materials. This is a major initiative organized by publishers, research libraries, and like-minded organizations to provide standardized, consistent, meaningful definitions of usage for electronic journals, databases, and other items. When a database vendor such as EBSCO, Gale, or Project Muse is "COUNTER compliant," it produces consistent and comparable usage data across time periods and across different databases.

Librarians will use COUNTER data at different levels of detail, depending on their needs. For example, there are usage data for individual journal titles as well as databases. Some librarians manage holdings on a title-by-title basis or in customized packages, and others on a simpler database-usage basis.

Some of the common COUNTER reports include

- Full text article downloads (by source title)
- Searches (by database)
- Total sessions (by database)
- Turnaways (by journal)

Like all usage measures, what these are and what they mean are slightly different. Downloading a journal article does not necessarily mean that the article was read or that it was particularly valuable, any more than checking out a book does. It does mean that someone cared enough to download it, which is the information we have and will use.

A "search" is defined as the use of a return key or submit button. This means that these count as a total of three searches:

1. "sivil war"
2. "civil war"
3. "civil war causes"

This is even though to a single user this represents one intellectual question, a search for something about the cause of the Civil War.

Pragmatically, then, electronic resource usage consists of three elements for the evaluator: (1) COUNTER data or the equivalent, (2) separate reporting by branch or individual library outlet, and (3) separation according to useful time periods.

First, each library needs COUNTER-compliant data, even when it is not provided by a particular vendor. Make every vendor aware that this is something that the library community wants. If we do not ask, our needs will not be met. Evaluators should keep non-COUNTER data separate so that managers do not mistakenly compare usage figures from COUNTER-compliant and noncompliant companies.

Second, libraries often participate in consortial leasing or purchasing of databases or database access, all the way from a simple contract for a main and branch public library system to statewide licenses. In those cases, it is important to stipulate that data be reported as close to the individual library unit as possible. In some early state licensing deals, only usage for the entire state was possible, leaving it unclear who exactly was gaining the best benefit from a particular resource.

Finally, the useful time period depends on the use to which the data will be put. As with webpage usage, some usage tells you about the resource, and some about the user. Data for a year's usage at once tells you aggregate demand for a resource: should you renew or not? Data on a weekly basis, especially in academic libraries, tells you when high patron demand occurs. COUNTER data is divided on a monthly basis, which is less detailed but still useful. For example, in some regions, summer public library patrons are distinctly different from those at the rest of the year. With limited funds, a librarian may choose to prioritize items that have a more consistent appeal throughout the year for permanent residents.

Overall, usage data is easy to gather and relatively easy to interpret. It provides direct, useful information on the popularity of library resources. It is true that a circulation, a web hit, or a download does not actually record someone's brain using the materials. However, this difference is certainly no worse than the difference between an answer on a survey asking, "I visit the library very often" and reality.

The main caution about usage data is what it does not measure. Except for ILL request data, it cannot tell you about what *would be* popular if only you had it or made it available or discoverable. For unmet needs, only surveys and interviews can show what people want but do not yet have.

Study Questions

Circulation

Jones, D. Yvonne, et al. "Simple Marketing Techniques and Space Planning to Increase Circulation." *Collection Management* 36.2 (2011): 107–18.

Reshelving and Vendor Data

Ugaz, Ana G., and Taryn Resnick. "Assessing Print and Electronic Use of Reference/Core Medical Textbooks/Brief Communications." *Journal of the Medical Library Association* 96.2 (2008): 145–47.

Webpage Usage

Brown, Christopher C. "Knowing Where They Went: Six Years of Online Access Statistics via the Online Catalog for Federal Government Information." *College & Research Libraries* 72.1 (2011): 43–61.

Database/Electronic Resource

Metz, Paul. "Two Universities in One Place: Reflections on Seasonal Variations in the Use of Library Resources." *College & Research Libraries News* (2010): 311–13.

- What tool was used?
- What data was recorded?
- What are two findings?

Availability

Introduction

Libraries have been criticized for owning materials that are seldom or never used by patrons. This looks not only inefficient but also inept, as though our selection methods are unequal to the task. However, you only need to look at the "clearance" racks in any retail store to understand that overbuying happens in all organizations that aim to have what people want, when they want it, with simple browsing and without searching, requesting, or waiting.

The goal is availability.

In information seeking, this also includes making available resources that users may not know, specifically, that they need. Someone who asks, "Do you own the US Drug Pharmacopeia?" may not realize that there are several sources that address this underlying question.

Availability of resources for your library can be assessed in four ways. Two of them are covered in separate sections. Usability studies are really essential ways to examine what barriers exist between users and the information or items they need. Process evaluation analyzes how your library handles materials, initially from request, order, reception, processing, shelving, or delivering and continuously from due dates, returns, reshelves, and on-demand or document delivery.

This section covers two specific techniques for evaluating the availability of general materials in your library. One is a collection-sampling approach that is more hypothetical but is easier to conduct and more comprehensive. The other is a patron-need approach that involves more steps but that more closely matches actual patron experiences.

Availability is a mundane but important assessment. It is an outcome-oriented, summative measure. The simple, pure "yes, you can get X item into Y patron's hand *right now*, or no, you cannot" reflects the quality of several processes and capabilities of your library. At least four main reasons explain why an item is not available. Each leads to a more specific evaluation method.

1. *Possession.* You do not own, lease, or have access to an item.
   Primarily, this is a reflection of your collection development plan, even if there is no formal plan and collection development ends up being, "buy requests as they come in until you have no more money for the year." The goal is to match your plans or intentions with patron needs. If you find high unavailability because of lack of ownership, consider more patron surveys to identify patron needs more accurately. Alternatively, revisit your collection mission or educate your staff and patrons about what they can expect from your library.
   A subset is items that are lost or missing and have not yet been replaced. This lack of possession results from a combination of policy and budget. The factors are how often lost items are noted and what lost items are replaced.

2. *Location.* You have the item, but it is not in the right place.
   This is more a matter of execution than policy. The acquisitions department is backlogged, webpage links are broken, shelvers are careless or poorly trained, or shelves are not checked, defined in library terminology as "read" for accuracy. Data from an availability study shows if this is a problem, how big it is, and where the particular problems are; this feeds into a process evaluation.

3. *Retrieval error.* You have the item, and it is in the designated place, but your patron cannot find it.
   This is usability at its core. Does your signage, classification system, or webpage design help or hinder users? When an availability study shows that you have many items, in the right place, that patrons cannot locate, it is time for a usability study. This examines in detail where problems are so that you can design different systems to decrease retrieval error.

4. *In use.* You have a certain quantity of the item and usage exceeds that quantity.
   Physical books have physical limitations; electronic items have licensing limitations. This becomes a variety of item 1, possession. Knowing the extent to

which this happens helps you adapt your collection policies to meet your desired goals; you need a policy on budgeting for multiple access or copies.

The "Procedures" section describes two methods of checking availability. Collection sampling is much easier, but it misses some data (see Table 2.11).

Detects Problems With	Collection Sampling	Patron Surveys
Possession	No	Yes
Location	Yes	Yes
Retrieval error	No	Yes
In use	Yes	Yes
Requires patron input	No	Yes

Table 2.11   Comparison of Availability Measures: Sampling versus Survey.

Both of the methods require manual processing. That is, some human being will need to check to see if an item is available. That is not a flaw but a feature of this type of study because it is designed to detect if the automated systems are actually working accurately. Are books that your system says are on the shelf actually on the shelf?

Procedure—Collection Sampling

This process has the advantage of not needing patron participation. The three steps in this process are as follows:

1. Selecting books or items randomly or purposively

2. Coding for availability

3. Analysis

First, determine your sample, a list of items whose location and availability you will check. To make this more feasible, break down your collection into coherent chunks, in which you will determine general availability of books or items *of that type*. These collection units can be groups like chapter books, science fiction, movie-tie-ins, the LC PR (British Literature) classification, or the graphic novel section. Use a random number generator to select a sufficient number, or choose every Nth item, from a list of items. The total should be at least 30 and preferably more than 100.

For each item, list its name or other identification and the appropriate code from a list (see Table 2.12).

Item Title	Availability Code (on date 01/01/...)	Notes
A Tale of Two Cities	C	
Talking about Three Cities	C	
Four Cities Makes a Quad	N	At end of next shelf
The Trail of Five Cities	X	Due nine months previous

Codes: C = Found in correct place
      N = Not on shelf/in correct place
      O = Currently checked out
      X = Overdue

Table 2.12   Data Example: Availability (Sampling).

It is important to have separate codes for items that are overdue and for those that are currently checked out but not overdue. If you combine the two into one category, you blur together several things. You might not have automated a way to follow up on long-overdue items to declare them lost. Your system would then show books that had been checked out months or years ago as still part of your collection, even though they are not in any sense available. Or there may be items that are in high demand and for which your loan period is proving to be too short for the users. Or this is a reflection of high demand and normal usage, and all available copies are in use.

The person doing this checking must be skilled and precise. Ensure that all checkers use the same rules to categorize items. For example, if a book is on the shelf and is out of place by one or two books, is it "N" or is it "C"? What if it is lying down on the end of the next shelf? When in doubt, have checkers make notes rather than simply assign a code that might be applied inconsistently.

A good list of codes reduces the need for notes. Notes slow down the process, but it is hard to get a bulletproof list of codes right at the start.

The analysis results in the number and percentage of items in each category. Examine the notes. Those will show trends for repeated types of issues. For example, if it is very common for a book to be on the same shelf but not in the right place, then shelvers are being hasty or do not understand the need for precision.

If you use a random sample to select these test items, the results are generalizable, within a certain margin of error, to your collection. Your response will depend upon the percentages found for each reason.

- High percentage of overdue: check overdue policy and item replacement rules

- High percentage of not on shelf/in correct place: revisit staff training or level of effort for shelving

It is true that usage (circulation) data can tell you with great precision checked out percentages. However, an availability study goes at this from a different direction. The number of usages or check-outs per item has a natural ceiling. People might want to check out a book more often but not be able to because it is already checked out. The availability check shows what any given patron might expect to encounter on a particular day—what is available without waiting.

You can use purposive rather than random sampling. Check items that have a certain characteristic. For example, suppose a teacher intends to give a list of recommended items to his or her class. Check this list. It will show how prepared your library is for the students' visits and also be a small, selective look at the availability of your collection. Some other examples of purposive lists are award winners, best-sellers, and recommended readings. Using these assumes that your library intends to own them, for example to own each Newbery winner published in the last 20 years. You own them, but are they available?

Procedure—Patron Surveys

This description follows conceptually in the footsteps of the Output Measures for Public Libraries developed in 1982 and 1987 by Nancy Van House and Douglas Zweizig for the American Library Association.[6] Their book, now out of print, has extraordinarily useful forms and summation and analysis guides.

The patron survey approach to availability asks actual patrons what they are looking for and whether they have found it. Currently many retail stores have adopted this as a sort of automated mantra: "Have you found what you are looking for?"

People are generally looking for one of two types of books in a library: (1) a specific, known item by title or author, or (2) a topic or area—the latest novel by John Grisham or cookbooks for diabetics.

You can do this specialized survey using paper or a computer at check-out. In paper on a clipboard, ask people as they enter the library to quickly jot down one or two items that they are looking for that day. At check-out, patrons note with Y or N that they have or have not found the item or area and then leave the piece of paper with the clerk. Although this seems cumbersome with a two-step process, people have a little more time when they enter a library but are in some haste as they exit the library. You catch them to give you the most important information, what they are looking for, as they enter and only need a single yes or no at the end.

To do this solely during the check-out process, the clerk or a popup screen on a self-check machine asks patrons what author or title or subject they were looking for and if they found it. It is simpler to ask what they have *not* found, but if you only ask that, then you do not find out how big the not-found issue is in relation to all of what they want, some of which they did find. Someone then takes the surveys where patrons have said no, they have not found what they are looking for, and searches them as above.

Analysis of the requests, found or not found, and availability codes generates two lists, one of specific items or authors and another of subjects, and whether they were found or the reasons they were not found (see Table 2.13).

Subject	Patron	Staff	Staff Reason	Unit Type
Diabetes cookbooks	Y			NF-600s
Judo contest rules	N	Y	C—correct place, correct book	NF-700s
Leaf identification	N	N	U—In use	NF-500s
Biography of Neville Chamberlain	N	N	O—Not owned	Bio

Table 2.13   Data Example: Availability (Surveys).

This method requires patron cooperation and more staff effort. Results reflect just those patrons at those times you can target for the survey. However, it has three great advantages. It has more of what is called external validity, or a match to the real world. It is a reflection of the real experiences of your patrons. Even more important, it can tell you what they are looking for that your collection does not have. You cannot examine this with the collection approach. That is based on your existing collection. Finally, it identifies cases where your systems seem to show something is available, owned, and in the right place. It really is not available, if the patron is unable to find it.

Some published articles imply that some libraries expect a loss rate of 5% of their collection a year. Some library budgets seem to assume that nothing will ever be lost, not having a specific budget for replacements. Replacements are obviously desirable books. They were bought because they fit collection goals of the library, and they have vanished because they were popular with at least one patron.

Availability studies are time consuming. They can be carried out little by little, on a small scale, as you assess what the overall level of presence is for your items. If you find that 99% or more of the sought items are indeed available, then you have little to worry about, except that you are not circulating very many books.

This method, in its variations, is clearly most suitable for circulating book-like collections, particularly in public and school libraries. Circulating DVDs, books on CD, games, and so forth all can be examined in this way.

In an academic library, this could be done as well, especially the patron-survey type. This study would also include a notation about the format desired, such as books or journal articles. Some of this information, in terms of topics desired, can be gotten from transaction log analysis.

The patron-survey availability study captures the actual experiences of individuals. Or to put it another way, it does not matter if you have 16 copies of Hamlet if John just wants one book on legal aspects of parodies and the one you had was checked out two years ago and never came back.

Study Questions

Availability is most useful for public libraries. Some colleges use ILL requests as a proxy for a survey of unmet needs. This requires patrons to feel very free to enter the ILL system: to make demands for specific items and to wait for results. Public library evaluators seldom publish their results; most published studies have been about academic libraries.

This article is a scholarly analysis of availability studies in general:

Nisonger, Thomas E. "A Review and Analysis of Library Availability Studies." *Library Resources and Technical Services* 51.1 (2007): 30–49.

- What kinds of libraries have conducted availability studies?
- What are two reasons for nonavailability?

This article has a specific focus on public libraries:

Senkevitch, Judith J., and James H. Sweetland. "Evaluating Adult Fiction in the Smaller Public Library." *RQ* 34.1 (1994): 78–89.

- What methods are used to evaluate the collections?

Process Evaluation

Introduction

In a library, a "process" is anything that involves more than one step. Answering a person's question is not a process. Sitting with children in a story group is not a process. Selecting, preparing, digitizing, cataloging or tagging, and uploading an image is a process. Interlibrary loan, from receiving a request to getting the item back to the lending library, is a process. Organizing several story groups across several branches might be a process. The process includes managing room reservations, travel for the staff, and publicity, not actually conducting the groups.

We generally know when a process has been successful and often have some record of how long the whole process takes from start to finish. The goal in full-fledged process evaluation is to identify the strong and weak parts of the process. This involves understanding the steps involved and, for each, measuring time, volume, and quality.

All three elements of time, volume, and quality are important. There's a possibly apocryphal story of a large research library that had a backlog of two to three years in processing monographs, defined as single books. A new director insisted that catalogers process them using a less complex level of cataloging rather than full detail. Catalogers protested that the quality of their records was part of the high standards of the institution. The director countered that books that could not be accessed at all because nobody knew they were there for years on end was a worse outcome than somewhat less detail in the cataloging record. This represents a clash between values of speed and quality. A third option would be to increase staffing. Any request for staffing, in any organization, begins with a consideration of volume: no volume, no staffing. Thus all three, time, volume, and quality, are the measurements that managers use to figure out the most feasible solution at that particular time for a given need.

The "Procedures" section describes the essential steps in organizing a process evaluation. Some of the techniques in other chapters and sections will be relevant here, such as conducting interviews and collecting tallies of observations. The steps involved in process evaluation are relatively simple. The most challenging part is to put together an evaluation so that it takes the least amount of effort yet yields high-quality data. An evaluation has no point if it is more cumbersome than the process it is evaluating.

Procedure

A process evaluation has two dimensions. One is the process itself, and the other is the selection of the items whose process will be captured. The steps are as follows:

1. Understanding the process and its components
   - Identifying distinct steps
   - Choosing measurements of quality

2. Selecting items for measurement

3. Reporting quality, volume, and time

Understanding the Process

The first step is to thoroughly understand the process itself. To do this, interview people involved in the steps. This works best when done by someone who is not already familiar with the process. That person can ask many questions and make full notes about everything without seeming to question in a criticizing way and also without missing steps that a more experienced person might simply ignore as being too familiar.

Key questions to use and points to notice include the following:

- What do you do with this one?

- *Are there exceptions? How frequent are exceptions? Are they in a few large categories, or are there a wide variety of particular exceptions?

- Do you do a group of items all at once in batches, or do you handle them one at a time as they come in?

- From whom do you get the previous step? To whom do you send the item next?

- When does each item physically or virtually move? Does the cart go across the hall and then the item is uploaded?

- What checkpoints already exist for accuracy or quality?

- *How often do items return to a previous step? Are they returned individually or in batches?

At this stage in developing the evaluation, the questions with asterisks (*) are not an attempt to measure quality. Instead, you are getting a sense of what volume is involved in exceptions or in redoing steps in order to set up the evaluation data collection efficiently. An experienced worker's rough estimate is sufficient.

Create a flowchart from the answers. This lays out the path of each item with decision points and routing. You can use specialized workflow or diagramming software or a simple hand drawing.

The next step is to determine where in the process quality can be measured or is an issue. One easy place to note is where your interviewees have noticed items returned to previous steps, or loops. How do you determine whether an item should be sent back? That is a quality check. At those loops, note how many items proceed and how many need to be sent back. Determine what categories of reasons there are for a return. The definition and measurement of quality depends on the process being evaluated. For example, digitized images need to meet image-quality standards. Broadly speaking, though, most people can identify what an error looks like, and the overall goal is to show where errors occur and under what circumstances.

Not every step needs a quality check. Many steps will involve only time and volume data.

It is important to go back to the managers and workers in this process with the full flowchart. To manage the evaluation, you need a correct description. It is possible that in documenting each part of a complex process, managers and librarians may notice not just that you have missed a step here or there but sometimes that there are already duplications and unneeded branches. An example of this is where a university graduate office realized that two different staffers were hand-calculating specialized GPAs.

Finally, determine what you need to record about the item or issue itself, separate from the process. An ILL request may be for a returnable book, which is a physical item, or a duplicate, which would be a journal article. An information literacy request comes from this faculty member in one department or from a faculty member in another department. Books are ordered from this vendor or from that vendor, from a standing order or individually. An important category is staffing. If staffing will vary over the course of the evaluation, you need to record available staffing resources. Perhaps there were two interns at the beginning of the semester but only one in the last month.

Preparation for evaluation data-gathering includes creating a log in spreadsheet form. It seems somewhat counterintuitive to take a graphic, dimensional flowchart and reduce it to one line per item that goes through, but when you flatten the data like this you can summarize it. The summary shows where there are problems in the process. For real data, this line-per-item would be a horizontal row in a spreadsheet. The following example shows it in a vertical line for readability.

This example describes the process by which faculty request a library instruction session for their classes. In this particular setting, this process happens centrally, not by individual faculty contacting individual librarians. That would be a different and more difficult process to assess. The logging aspect is similar to a call-center log or tagging system. It also includes an after-session evaluation form used by both students and the faculty member (see Table 2.14).

For each IL request		
Step	*Example*	Note
Time—day request arrives	9/1/12	
Method of request	Email	
Session date requested	10/5/12	
Time—day sent to librarian	9/3/12	
Time—day librarian contacts faculty	9/5/12	
Number of faculty contacts	2	*Interviewees have noted that many contacts are often needed*
Name of faculty	Smith	
Department of faculty	Economics	
Date of session	10/5/12	
Time—date faculty session evaluation sent	10/5/12	*Assumes sending a link to a quick survey*
Time—date faculty session evaluation received	10/30/12	
Number of reminders for evaluation	1	
Student evaluation score	3.4	*Student evals conducted at time of the session, so no time-date is needed.*
Faculty evaluation score	4.3	
Days from request to session date desired	34	
		This is data calculated from other information.
Days from request to contact	4	
Time requested is time conducted?	Yes	

Table 2.14 Data Example: Process Flow for Instruction Session Requests.

The reason to lay out the data like this is to sort it in order to identify correlations between elements. For example, you can sort by faculty member or by department. Perhaps the Economics Department averages four weeks' notice for a session, but faculty in the Arts Department tend to make a request one day in advance. When there are many requests on one day, perhaps it takes librarians more time to get back to faculty—a volume issue. Maybe faculty from one department are less satisfied with sessions than others are; perhaps they tend to request sessions too close to the desired date and hence have fewer sessions scheduled when they want them. This is a quality—volume—time issue.

Each grid will be unique to the processes in place at your library using and embedded in your services, facilities, and collections. Listen to those involved in the process to capture anecdotal clues as to where to look. If catalogers complain that Romanian books are the hardest to catalog, then it will be important to include a note in the process about the language or subject area of the books that are being tracked. If acquisitions specialists enthuse about how easy some publishers are to deal with, then "publisher" is an important data element.

This evaluation identifies areas that are causing problems in the process. The spreadsheet full of data goes beyond anecdotes and is where you start to measure and confirm the existence of particular problems. You show that they exist, to what extent they exist, and, hopefully, when they disappear. It may be the case that it was only a single batch of Romanian books five years ago that caused all the problems. It could be that one branch in the system consistently seems to have too few people to reshelve books, and their reshelving distinctly slowed down a year ago when the budget for pages was cut and that branch did not happen to recruit volunteers.

Selecting Items

Sometimes it is not too much trouble to track data on every item in the process, each step of the process. In processing books, for example, workflow software built into many commercial integrated library systems will automatically note days and times for many of the steps involved. IT centers often have call ticketing systems for capturing issue and time information. However, there are some steps even in those types of tracked processes that are not captured, and there are some processes where there are almost no automated step captures.

The more steps for each item that need to be logged manually, or the more items that are being processed, that is, the greater the volume of manual logging involved, the more likely it is that a sampling rather than a "census" of data is appropriate. A census approach gathers data about everything. A sampling gathers data only about some things. A section in Chapter 3 explains about sampling.

The three basic choices in selection of items include the following:

- Census: capture information about all items for all steps
- Tracing: select specific items and trace their progress through the system

- Snapshot: at designated, specific points in time, capture information about all items currently in the system

The above example for information literacy sessions used a census approach. The volume is not very large, and the people involved could relatively easily keep track without it interfering with their normal work.

The tracing option is most appropriate for processes with larger volumes, at least 20 a day. Prepare a log sheet for each selected item: it shows a simple grid taken from the spreadsheet and made as concise as possible. The easiest method is to put the sheet with every 10th, 20th, or 100th item, depending on volume. The goal is a sample of about 100 items. As the item+log passes through the process, each person makes notes about time and events, including quality checks or step re-dos, on the sheet.

It is important to have this sample tracing be considered entirely routine and noncontroversial. Your goal is not to evaluate individual workers on their own personal performances. Your results are not, "Sally simply is slower than Dan." The goal is to identify bottlenecks and problem areas. When you identify those areas, the response is not to replace problem workers. Except in exceptional circumstances where there are real problem employees, something that normal personnel evaluation should detect, the problem is in the system, not the people. Something needs adjusting—worker time or training or the quality and quantity standards involved.

With a nonpersonal, nonpersonnel approach, staff will cooperate in gathering information. It is to their benefit to note where there are problems and get them corrected. This is part of what happens in total quality management (TQM), where all workers involve themselves in identifying good quality and needed levels of quantity. They work with management to smooth out problems that lie in the way and eliminate unnecessary steps.

However, there is a danger that the existence of a tracing sheet will mean that workers will treat those items differently such as doing them first, better, or more carefully. It is a "reactive" measure, in that people, human beings, notice that this is being measured. A census avoids this because people cannot treat everything specially. Snapshot data gathering also avoids this. It is cumbersome and more difficult to carry out, so it is useful only when tracing or census will not work.

In snapshot data gathering, data is gathered at a particular time for each step of the process. Consider the process of digitizing photographs in a historical society collection. This example assumes that a particular group of photos, 5,000 in all, has been identified, and it does not include technical details. The last two rows are quality checks. One already exists, the quality-check queue. This form gathers the results of the assessment into the whole process evaluation. The other means that someone at this day and time, September 1, 2012, 10:00 am, takes the scanning out-tray contents and checks on quality (see Table 2.15).

Location of photographs		9/1/2012 10:00 am
Yet to be scanned	1899	
Scanning room in-tray	23	
Scanning room out-tray	34	(to be filed in physical archives)
In-tray for metadata application	86	
Quality check queue	54	
Digitized photos completed in collection	2805	
Unknown	100	
Spot-check scan out-tray: error %		Number needing to be redone vs. total
	13%	number in out-tray
Quality check results for queue: error %		Number failing metadata quality control vs.
	2%	total in quality check queue.

Table 2.15 Data Example: Snapshot for Digitization Processing.

The "Unknown" line shows the strength and limitations of this version of evaluation. In real life, there are often unknowns. What is really important is to figure out how big the unknown area is and whether it needs additional attention. Evaluation is often most helpful when it shows managers things that were invisible before.

The snapshot system is less precise than tracing. The biggest advantage is that it cannot be gamed if the times for taking the snapshot are reasonably randomly selected and not announced in advance. In this system, simple counting is done quickly. The quality checks are more time consuming. Managers should determine just how much checking is necessary. It is possible to perform more detailed quality checks every so often, and more limited ones for each snapshot, but it is important to have some assessment of quality. Not only does time equal money, but quality equals time equals money. We all can produce excellent material given unlimited time.

Reporting Quality, Volume, and Time

The result of a process evaluation is a comprehensive look at the entire process. In many cases, staff already has measurements of quantity, quality, and even time for individual parts of the process. The process evaluation plan pulls all of these together so as not to duplicate effort. You will add in some measures to cover sections that have not been measured yet. The result shows the entire process.

There are two types of summarizing and reporting the data. The first is an individual look at each step. This is a relatively simple description. You can present it in a table or as visual graphs superimposed upon the process flowchart (see Figure 2.1).

Another approach is to analyze data in combination. This is feasible with the item-tracing or census selection systems more than the snapshot systems. The aim is to identify when condition X most often occurs with condition Y. Is faculty satisfaction with

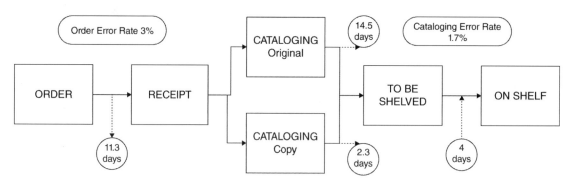

Figure 2.1 Report Example: Flow Chart Time and Error Rate.

information literacy sessions correlated with the time it took librarians to contact them to arrange it? How much does staffing levels affect volume? Does it have an effect on quality, for example number of errors, too?

When a process is so short that one person knows about and performs all steps, then it is not worth a formal process evaluation. It is sufficient to monitor counts of volume, time, and errors. The value of full process evaluation is that it shows managers and all those involved exactly what is going on with the process as a whole. Managers are responsible for prioritizing, and they can prioritize effort and training on the most important and problematic parts of the process.

Study Questions

The Murphy study was based within the context of Six Sigma quality management, although its host site had not formally adopted this as an overall style of management. The Piorun study is a more conventional time-cost study; in both cases the framework of process evaluation is visible.

Murphy, Sarah Anne. "Leveraging Lean Six Sigma to Culture, Nurture, and Sustain Assessment and Change in the Academic Library Environment." *College & Research Libraries* 70.3 (2009): 215–25.
Piorun, Mary, and Lisa A. Palmer. "Digitizing Dissertations for an Institutional Repository: A Process and Cost Analysis." *Journal of the Medical Library Association* 96.3 (2008): 223–29.

- What process was examined?
- Who conducted the evaluation?
- Name a measure of:
  - Time
  - Quality
  - Quantity

Transaction Log Analysis

Introduction

Technologically speaking, the modern library is a living breathing data-generating organism. The library's integrated library system (ILS) holds warehouses full of data about library collections or items, patrons, and uses. These are static, dynamic, and also transactional. The static data, its catalog, contains a reflection and representation of what "is" the library. The dynamic data, its circulation and acquisitions systems, record what is going on at a particular moment, what is checked out and what is being purchased or processed. Transactional data is a record of what requests are made of the system.

Part of an ILS is the online public access (OPAC) computer. Early library automation was often for staff use only and not for the public or was used in a batch-processing mode and was not online; hence the acronym OPAC names things that today seem obvious but that developed over time.

Transaction log analysis examines captured transactions in the forms of queries or commands submitted to the system. These are not like oral words which, once spoken, simply vanish. Most systems are designed to record each transaction, and these logs then are the verbatim, exact replica of everything submitted to and through this system.

On a very large scale, current studies of web transactions such as Google queries, Twitter trends, and memes use the same type of data. They use vast computational power, some manual analysis, and natural-language processing algorithms to produce summaries such as word clouds and hot topics for each day.

On the local level, within a particular library system, transaction logs are an extensive raw record of how your patrons interact with your systems and collections. They can yield important information even with relatively low-tech tools for analysis. At least three areas can provide evaluation information:

- Chronology or timing

- Command preference

- Topical requests

Consider the individual unit within a transaction log. Typically it consists of a time stamp, a type of query, and the query itself. With the time stamp, you can analyze the high-demand times for your system, detecting the rhythms of your particular community of users. If, for example, you do not want to provide 24/7 reference, when are your users least likely to be using your systems? Using command preference or type of query, you can detect if and when people use techniques more complex than the basic search box. Finally, you can examine exactly what they want or at least are typing in. You can conduct a patron-request availability study as described in the "Availability" section to ask people what they want when they "come" to the library. Transaction logs capture this information without effort or patron cooperation.

The great benefit of transaction log analysis is that the data is there for the taking. There is no question about having to seek out or create data. The question is how to make sense of it.

Procedure

Using transaction logs for evaluation involves three steps:

1. Extracting/downloading data for a sample of time frames

2. Sorting and filtering the data

3. Summarizing results

Downloading Data

All transactions download into a spreadsheet or database format, where each row is one particular transaction and each column is a data element, such as date, originating IP address, and wording used. Exact techniques for extraction and analysis depend on the software and expertise you have available to handle the data. For example,

- *Date/time stamp*: If it downloads into one column or field, use string commands to store date, day of week or convert, and time separately. Then you can compile aggregates over hours, days, weeks, and months.

- *Type of query codes*: If your system generates these automatically, all you need to do is to sort and summarize. Even a simple pivot-table pass will generate a summary table.

- *Typed inputs such as "the beatles"*: You can use qualitative text analysis software to create word clouds or manually examine series of queries to trace patterns.

How much data you download depends on the capacity of your software or staffing, the question you want to explore, and the typical number of transactions. Consider if you can download and deal with one entire week of transactions. If you can, download entire weeks at representative times of the year. If that is too much, try a day. If you can handle a day, take a random sample of days for a representative period. This could be one month during the summer and one during the fall for a public library. If not a day, choose an hour. Again, take multiple days or hours so as to represent more of the range of activity at your library.

The section in Chapter 3 on sampling discusses how to take random and purposive samplings. With transaction log data, if you have too much data to begin with, you cannot take a transaction-based random sample. That is, most systems will not allow you to download *only* a random sample of transactions. You have to specify a particular time period.

You can choose those times randomly or purposively. For example, you may choose 1:00–2:00 pm and 7:00–8:00 pm on a Tuesday and a Thursday.

Sorting or Filtering Data; Summarizing Results

The following describes some overall considerations for sorting and reporting results based on three common purposes of transaction analysis. The more complex the purpose, the less data you will be able to organize usefully.

Chronological Analysis

The goal of this kind of analysis is to track periods of heavy and light usage. Researchers have done extensive time-variable analysis. For example, one study in the 1980s determined that subject searches were more frequent during semester breaks than during the semester; that is, subject searching was a higher, though still low, percentage of all requests during those times. They speculated that graduate students or faculty were responsible for more complex and subject-oriented searches and were present more on a year-round basis than the undergraduates who generated the bulk of transactions.

Report a chronological analysis in tables and graphs that visually depict high and low usage. This analysis of peaks and valleys helps library management gain a picture of virtual visiting. With this you can time automation events such as upgrades. Public service librarians can ensure coverage for the most intensive times of the year or at least an estimate, as this year's peak is predicted on the basis of last year's peak. Public librarians often adjust their open hours in a constant balance between budget and patron demand. This objective virtual-visit data shows demand for the library's services outside of physical visits, especially as you cannot measure the trips people would have taken if only the library had been open. That does assume at least some correlation between physical visits and virtual activity.

Command Preference

If the OPAC or other library system offers a variety of methods of searching, you can examine the transaction log to see if those methods are actually being used. You might find, for example, that methods on an "advanced" screen are almost never used, which may indicate that users do not think to page to an advanced screen. This type of analysis is most useful to librarians who have control over either screen design or user instruction, or both. That is, if you find that people are not using a particular feature, you can seek to change the feature or to change your users' habits through instruction. Changing the screen is more effective than trying to change people, but only if you have control over or input into screen design.

Visually tie a report of command preference to the patron interface. That is, from *this* particular screen, *these* are the most commonly used features. This is similar to a website use report.

If your patrons change substantially during different time periods, break down the data accordingly. Before and after school, daytime and evening, exam time and beginning of semester—when are people using the most powerful features?

Topical Requests

This is the most difficult and rewarding area of assessment. This is a record of what exactly your patrons have typed into your system, not, exactly, what they have requested from your system. Perhaps people keep typing into the search box, "English database." That is a resource they want to use, not a subject they want to examine, but it is very close. "Trees," "Hanukkah cookbook," or "suicide prevention" help determine what your users want.

A section in Chapter 4 on software describes qualitative analysis. *Qualitative* is the name for data that is generally textual or narrative in nature or uses words in natural form, not predetermined lists or categories. Reading these is easy; summarizing them adequately is hard.

Qualitative software can perform some automatic analysis of text data, in this case, summarizing the frequency with which terms are used. Depending on the power of the software and the settings used, this can include multiple endings such as *dog* and *dogs* but not *dogmatic*, and synonyms—*cats, dogs, pets*.

If you are working with a small amount of data, less than 400 queries and less than 10 pages, you can manage a human-powered and insightful analysis. First, because your goal is to understand what people are looking for and how, examine the queries in their naturally occurring order. You can detect when people are trying several ways to get at the same thing. In one copy of the data, simplify typos and false starts into one line to represent the one intellectual query the person is after:

Replace this:

Ciivl war

Thecivil war

The civil war

With this: Civil War

The idea is that if you see two or three items in a row and can reasonably interpret them as simple typing errors, it is more realistic to count them as one conceptual search.

Then, check for initial stop-words like *a* and *the*. Delete these so that a search on "The Alamo" will show up right alongside "Alamo."

Then sort the edited queries alphabetically. The result is an alphabetic listing of terms. It gives you an idea of the topics or authors that your users are interested in. Look for repeated topics and map them to your collection's strengths and weaknesses. Consider adding a column to the spreadsheet and entering classification codes corresponding to the topic searched. That allows you to quantify what areas of your collection are most in demand, at least through OPAC searches.

See if people are using the search box appropriately. If they are typing "how do I get a card?" into a catalog search box, that means that the website design does not alert would-be patrons as to where they should go for library card information. If they are typing topics that are more appropriate to journal articles, then they may not realize that the search box will not get into those resources.

What do patrons actually do? What do they want? Transaction log analysis is a huge, rich resource to answer those questions. These are actual transactions, mostly about actual needs. They do not require someone to remember, to be honest, or to cooperate. They are not what the library thinks people want. Transaction log analysis is a fire hose of information, well worth looking at even in relatively raw shape. Summaries are difficult because of the variability of the data, but in this case the raw material is worth a lot itself. But few people take the time for it.

Report the summary in two ways. Quantitatively, list the most-used terms and classification areas. Qualitatively, ask two or three librarians to scan through representative days or weeks of material. Each lists four to five observations. Discuss, then report what they collectively see as the themes and important points raised by this observation of actual patron behavior.

Study Questions

The first article thoroughly describes how GA code was used to capture search strings; the GA dashboard depicted a chronological analysis—traffic patterns—and the researchers hand-coded search terms to detect patterns of inquiry.

The second is a more classic example of transaction log analysis examining a very specific resource.

Chen, Hsin-Liang, et al. "Analyzing Users' Retrieval Behaviours and Image Queries of a Photojournalism Image Database." *Canadian Journal of Information and Library Science* 34.3 (2010): 249–70.

Mardis, Marcia A. "Classroom Information Needs: Search Analysis from a Digital Library for Educators." *D-Lib Magazine* 15.1/2 (2009).

- What was the setting?
- What kind of search system was involved?
- How much data was analyzed?
- Describe two findings or results.

Notes

1. Gross, P. L. K, and E.M. Gross. "College Libraries and Chemical Education." *Science*, New Series, 66.1713 (1927): 385–89; Allen, Edward S. "Periodicals for Mathematicians." *Science* 70.1825 (1929): 592–94.

2. Olson, Georgine, and Barbara McFadden Allen. "Cooperative Collection Management: The Conspectus Approach." *Collection Building* 13.2–3 (1994): 5–103.

3. White, Howard D. *Brief Tests of Collection Strength: A Methodology for All Libraries*. Contributions in Library and Information Science, 88. Westport, CT: Greenwood Press, 1995.

4. Lesniaski, David. "Evaluating Collections: A Discussion and Extension of *Brief Tests of Collection Strength*." *College & Undergraduate Libraries* 11.1 (2004): 11–24.

5. Kent, Allen, et al. *Use of Library Materials: The University of Pittsburgh Study*. New York: Marcel Dekker, 1979.

6. Van House, Nancy, and Douglas Zweizig. *Output Measures for Public Libraries: A Manual of Standardized Procedures*, 2nd ed. Chicago: American Library Association, 1987.

Chapter 3

Technique Selection and Sampling

When evaluation is the gathering of data for managerial decision making, from *whom* or *what* is the data gathered? Data, analysis, and conclusions are all dependent upon the source of the information. *Sampling* is a broad term that includes all methods of identifying, selecting, soliciting, or including particular data sources in a particular study or evaluation. The key considerations are how large the population is; how much data is needed from each unit, person, or item in the population; and how much labor is involved in both gathering the data and making sense of it. These considerations weigh against each other. The more information, and the more complex the information, you need to gather from each unit, the fewer units you can gather it from. The fewer the units, the more specialized the selection or sampling techniques.

In each technique section in chapters 1 and 2 such as interviewing, there is a brief discussion of how to recruit participants for that technique. The goal in this chapter is to discuss general considerations all in one place. Choosing the best evaluation technique means balancing between feasibility and quality of data. You need a minimum level of quality and strive for the richest and most realistic data, but resources are necessarily limited. Rich data is not abundant, and shallow data is not informative. For each evaluation situation there is a good-enough middle ground.

You select from options based on your own resources and priorities. This section covers the following topics:

- Decision factors

- Population and sample sizes

- Types of sampling
  - Population
  - Selective—random
  - Selective—nonrandom
  - Purposive

Decision Factors

The following considerations affect the selection of an evaluation method. They are based on the complexity of the question and of the available data. They include the amount of human judgment and hence effort; the amount of data available or desired from each item examined or included; and how much effort is required to solicit or include items or people.

Amount of Human Judgment

This applies specifically to the transition between observation and data. That is, how can you make a record of X, which exists in the real world, so that it is represented within a spreadsheet, analysis, and report? For example, you may wish to know whether your graphic novels are being used more by young adults or by adult patrons. This requires you to capture "use," "graphic novel" as item category, and "patron type." This is further divided between what is difficult to collect or easy to collect. If you have your graphic novels separately catalogued or marked, then this aspect is easy. If not, and you need to look at your shelves to identify titles individually, that is truly difficult. *Use* usually means circulations recorded by the integrated library system and is easy. If you want to count in-house use, it is difficult, and you will not know whether the item has been used by a young adult or an adult patron. Using different patron classes is easy; if you have recorded birth year in a part of the patron record that is not usually queried, it is difficult.

The more concrete you make the definition of the data, the less you need human judgment. A "use" equals one circulation. This definition avoids any judgments about whether the person who checked a book out actually read it. We accept this limitation because it makes counting usage much more feasible. On the other side of this spectrum, the more detailed and individual the data, the more human judgment is needed to record or summarize it and to analyze it. *Why* does someone choose or not choose a particular graphic novel?

Some items that seem complex can be treated in a simple and concrete way. For example, suppose you want to know how people value the library. You can ask open-ended questions, or you can simply ask, "Do you value the library for yourself and your family?" and provide a scale of "not at all," "somewhat," and "essential." The result is concrete; it is treated as definite and unambiguous in that format; the score is 1, 2, or 3. Asking the question in a more open fashion is more respectful of varieties of valuing, but will you be able to summarize the results? Will your report after 20 interviews end up as a listing of each individual answer? In a way, this tension is the same as the one catalogers face when deciding how detailed they should be in applying levels of subject classification. A classification that, however accurate, leaves each individual term assigned only to one item is of very limited utility. Classifications must provide some level of groupings, even though every item is unique in some way.

Coding is the process of summarizing variable input into categories. "I like the library," "We always want to visit," and "My study group chooses the library first" can all be coded as "positive" library comments. Coding can be done by humans or by machines with natural-language processing. Human coding involves a high level of human judgment but is currently more sensitive to language's inherent complexity, context, and nuance. For example, irony is very difficult for an algorithm to process properly. Machine coding is consistent in its own way but requires certain levels of simplification. Machine coding reduces the level of human judgment involved and thus allows processing of much more data.

Amount of Data from Each

This is the data from each item or each person. On this spectrum, the more data each item provides, generally, the fewer items you will select to provide that data. A webpage or e-journal has a use or not; this can be collected comprehensively. Surveys fall somewhat into the middle. For most closed-ended questions, survey respondents can answer quickly, and the analysis is also rapid. Surveys usually target relatively large numbers of people (up to about 400 in most cases). The more quantitative and concrete the data, the more is collected.

On the other end, human beings as interviewees or focus group members are capable of providing enormous amounts of textual data with little effort on their part. That is qualitative data. This volume of text requires a lot of effort on the part of the researcher. Multimethod approaches are rich, variable, and challenging to summarize and categorize. Recording equipment does not solve this challenge but compounds it. Someone still has to summarize the data. In usability studies, not only are concrete data such as clicks, time spent, and click paths recorded, but participants comment on their thought processes, providing much richer data. For these reasons, usability studies generally involve some of the smallest samples among evaluation methodologies.

Solicitation Effort

This refers to how easy it is to capture the data that you want. This book groups methods into two categories: personal methods (Chapter 1) and impersonal methods (Chapter 2). Most impersonal methods are used for resource (collection) evaluation, and most personal methods for services evaluation, but there is also overlap.

Impersonal methods are very popular for library evaluation and for library and information science researchers. They take advantage of already existing data; they are nonreactive; and they do not depend upon the cooperation of humans. There are no response-rate worries, and nobody is trying to influence you, the evaluator.

Existing information systems already capture a large part of the processes of scholarly communication and library use, such as citations, hits or downloads, and circulations. A scientist and a freshman create bibliographies for their papers—citation analysis for their own reasons, not to influence the librarian-evaluator. They do not react to the act of recording this data. These traces are either public (citations) or exist within librarian-controlled systems (circulations, checklists, availability, transactions). This data is ready for the taking.

Personal methods can be interactive or unobtrusive. Surveys, interviews, focus groups, and usability studies are interactive. Specific participants or respondents knowingly provide data. These people must be solicited and persuaded to take part. To get good data, respondents must be able and willing to provide relatively honest information. For methods such as usability studies, focus groups, in-person interviews, or oral surveys, they also have to be available at a specific time and location.

Some personal methods are unobtrusive. Observation tallies and unobtrusive testing do not require cooperation; they are nonreactive in that the people observed go about their normal activities and do not need to actively consent to provide information.

Instructional evaluation is somewhat of a hybrid. In an educational setting like a school or college, librarian-provided information literacy often looks like any other kind of teaching. It has defined learning objectives, and people take required tests. However, in public or special libraries or in some forms of information literacy instruction, people must be solicited to participate in the program and in the evaluation. The evaluation part of the program needs to be enticing; people do not have to provide their feedback (see Tables 3.1 and 3.2).

Population and Sample Size

While the tool or method itself affects how many items, participants, or respondents you will include, another consideration is the size of the target population. This is also affected by the difference between evaluation and research.

Research, generally speaking, involves the creation of generalizable information, while evaluation is an exploration of local conditions. Each has its own focus, although the results tend to have overlapping areas of interest. Here are some examples of research studies compared to evaluation studies:

Research: How do mathematicians use preprint articles?

Evaluation: Do the mathematicians at our university use the library's portals for preprint access?

Research: What kinds of graphic novels appeal to low-skilled readers?

Amount of Machine $\longleftrightarrow$ Human Processing		
None	Some	Every item
Amount of Data from Each		
Brief, numeric, concrete	Brief, codes and categories	Deep, rich, narrative, textual
Solicitation Effort		
None: Existing data	Some: Captive audiences	Large: Strangers
Sample Size		
All	Some	Very few
Population	*Random* *With replacement* *Without* *replacement* *Sequential*	*Nonrandom* *Unrelated* *convenience* *Available* *Snowball* *Biased*	*Purposive* *Maximum variety* *Extreme case* *Intensity*

Table 3.1 Processing Data: Human versus Machine.

Evaluation: Is the location of our graphic novel collection affecting how it is used?

Research: What are effective methods of storytelling to enhance early literacy?

Evaluation: Is our Story Hour appealing and effective?

Research: How do new lawyers compare with established attorneys in their legal information seeking?

Evaluation: What services do newer and more experienced staff at our law firm use and need?

Whenever a study is done at a local level, it may be of generalized interest to others, even for a local design. If you study your financial literacy workshops and report on what you found to be effective and satisfactory for participants, other librarians will usually find this interesting. It will give them ideas for their own libraries. On the other hand, precisely because the study was confined to one locality, its results are very dependent upon the particulars of that situation. Something that works or does not work in one setting may not generalize to many settings.

Serious research studies are designed from the outset to consider this, which is called external validity. This means the degree to which findings or results can be considered broadly applicable. For example, one study examined not-born-digital (received MLS before 1995) librarians' attitudes towards learning about digital advances. Because of feasibility issues, it only surveyed librarians belonging to one state's professional organization. This was not a national population, and it was biased towards people interested in professional development, so it cannot be generalized to all librarians. However, it would be much more expensive and difficult to target a national sample.

	General Guide *Effort and Choices*	
Easy/feasible		Difficult/complex
Machine processing		Human processing
Existing data		Solicited data
Nonreactive		Reactive (bias?)
Requires no cooperation		Needs cooperation
Concrete/numeric (quantitative)		(qualitative) textual, needs coding
Shallow and easy		**Rich and difficult**
	Checklists[1]	
	Availability	
	Process evaluation	
Circulation/usage[2]	Surveys	Interviews
Citation analysis	Instructional assessment	Focus groups
Transaction logs	Observation tallies	Usability studies
Collection mapping	Unobtrusive testing	Mystery shopping

[1]Some checklists can be programmed; others need hand selection and checking.
[2]Most elements.

Table 3.2   Techniques by Data Complexity and Processing Effort.

Evaluation studies, strictly speaking, are on a local level and hence have target populations that are much smaller than research studies. They look at this school's students, this university's staff, this town's population, or this library's books and electronic resources. In this situation it is a matter of matching the evaluation questions, the population size, and the technique chosen to achieve the most effective and efficient combination. Choose the method that gets the best data with the least amount of effort, where the balance between effort and result is feasible for that library, question, and situation.

In terms of methods of collecting data, consider interviewing compared to surveying. Both involve asking people questions. Interviewing is one on one, personal, interactive, and detailed: it requires much effort for the evaluator and much cooperation from the respondent. Surveys are massive and shallow: they involve much more limited and efficient use of the evaluator's time and effort, and less extensive effort and cooperation from the respondents. Generally speaking, though, if your target population is small, it is worth the additional effort to interview people rather than to do a very small survey. In evaluation settings, where you are working with one library's staff and users, you can use the evaluation process to build bonds with key users. Interviewing does have a major drawback in a lack of anonymity, but in small-scale operations, that is a problem that simply cannot be avoided (see Table 3.3).

Types of Sampling

There are four types of sampling for choosing your participants. One is population, census, or all. The others are selective–random, selective–nonrandom, or purposive samples. All of these can be seen in published articles and in in-house studies. Some are more scientific or externally valid than others. However, even the weakest can

Population Size	Technique
1–10	Interview all
10–30	Interview or survey all
*30–100	Survey all
*100–2,000 (if email)	Survey all
*200+	Survey random sample

*or purposively selected interviewees

Table 3.3   Population Size: Survey versus Interview.

be usable as long as the evaluators and the readers of studies admit and understand their limitations.

Population

In population selection, you intend to include everything or everyone in your defined target population. When your study involves inanimate objects, this is relatively easy. You include all webpages and hits, all electronic journal articles and downloads, all books and circulations, all passes of the electronic gate count. The technique sections discuss limitations in the practical application of these counting mechanisms. For example, not all books checked out actually make it into the integrated library system; system errors can wipe out download data; playing children can multiply gate counts.

When using *population selection* it is important to avoid mistaking the population you include for a larger or different population. Overgeneralization is common, but undergeneralization also occurs. For overgeneralization, a classic error is to hand out surveys to all library patrons for a couple of weeks, then to consider that you have surveyed your service population. This is not correct. You have only included those who visit the library and are oversurveying those who visit frequently and undersurveying those who visit less frequently. This is not an error in method so much as in interpretation. Reaching people who have already volunteered, in a sense, to be present in your library is obviously much more feasible than those who have no detectable interest in the library. As long as the results and reporting of this study continually use as a subject word *library visitors during these weeks* rather than *citizens* or *the community*, people will not mistake it for a more comprehensive study.

Undergeneralization also occurs. This is when you intend to target a population but the method you use includes others. For example, some instructors or other academic staff will receive and respond to notices sent to students.

Listservs present one of the most common and tricky issues in population surveying. Most of the time, an evaluator does not know exactly who is a member of a listserv. Even when there is a roster, some of those members may not pay any attention to any listserv postings and others will forward postings to others. Using a listserv to reach a population of interest is more like a purposive selective sampling than population selection. It is very feasible in terms of time and effort and can yield interesting and important results, but the reporting needs to be careful. For example, the wording should not be *students* or even *new-media students* but *respondents to a survey posted on a new-media interest listserv maintained by the university for students.*

Some evaluation situations have easily accessible, functional listings and contact information for exactly defined populations. This would include faculty or teachers, students in various categories, parent or household contacts, or participants in a specific program. In these cases, evaluators can feasibly solicit each of them individually and even follow up with reminders when there is no response. Whole-population surveys with individual solicitations can be stretched to include up to a maximum of about 2,000 individuals.

It may seem just as feasible to send out a survey solicitation to 10,000 students as to 2,000 students rather than taking a random sample out of the 10,000. However, this is usually not a good idea, for two reasons. The first is that some effort should be expended on emphasizing the importance of the survey and sending reminders to increase the response rate; this is more difficult the more people are involved. The second reason has to do with the ecology of surveying. That is, yours is not the only survey that these people will receive. It is important to coordinate, prioritize, and, usually, be selective when considering surveys of a specific target population. Survey fatigue is an increasing and worrisome development. In this light, it is far more important to randomly survey 300 people for the library survey, a different 300 people for the student support services survey, and another 300 for the National Survey of Student Engagement (NSSE) than to exhaust 10,000 students with three different surveys.

Selective-Random

Random sampling is the gold standard of scientific selection. In truly random selection, there are mathematical ways of translating the data from those selected into conclusions about the larger population from which they were selected to a reasonably accepted degree of certainty. Random samples are generalizable, meaning data from some can apply to the whole.

It is sometimes hard to think that a random sample can be as informative as selecting the entire population, but it really does work. The key is that the selection is random and unconnected to the issue of interest. That is, people or items are selected to be included based only on randomness and with no consideration at all of the characteristic of interest to the evaluator. That characteristic will be present in the sample in the same way that it is present in the population.

For example, consider library cardholders and a survey of their use and satisfaction with the current physical building. From a list of cardholders, a random sample (either every Nth or using random numbers) can be sent a survey (and reminders). These people are selected because they are included on the list, with no knowledge beforehand of their current usage or opinions about the building.

If this survey were to target people visiting the library, it would necessarily miss those who avoid the library because they dislike or do not need the physical premises.

The larger a sample size, the more it will tend to match the population from which it comes. If you toss a coin (fairly) only 10 times, you are not shocked that it would come up heads 2 or 3 times in a row, as opposed to head, tail, head, tail exactly. Variations happen. If you toss it 100 times, you would expect the tally to be fairly close to 50 heads, 50 tails. If you tossed it 1,000 times, and it was 700 times heads, you should be suspicious that there was something wrong with the coin. The smaller the sample size, the more natural variation affects it. This can be seen in political polling by reputable, scientific organizations. Generally speaking, there is a fuzz-factor (margin of error) of $\pm 4\%$ for a sample size of 600, and 3% for a sample size of 1,000. You can see that to achieve a small increase in precision (from 4% to 3%), you need more than twice the number of respondents.

The two different types of random selection are sequential and set-group. In sequential selection, people or items are solicited or selected one after another, with each next item chosen randomly, until the desired number of people respond or items qualify. For phone surveys, the most common technique is random-digit dialing (RDD). For example, these may be the numbers generated randomly:

723–1178

998–1277

212–5348

Generally area codes and prefixes are preselected so as to target particular geographic areas, and then the last four digits are randomized. Contact is attempted with each number. That contact results in a nonexistent number, a company, no answer, or possibly, about 4% of the time, someone who can and will answer questions. These types of surveys generally do not report response rates, as in set-group sampling, but report, in the technical section, how many items or people were contacted before achieving the final result.

In set-group random sampling, contact information for the whole population is known. Each person or item is numbered, and random numbers are generated that select from within that range of numbers, for instance student number 1 to number 425, or book number 00023156 through number 00129098. Spreadsheets have functions for random number generation; older studies used tables of random numbers. Using every Nth—10th, 20th, and so forth—is not really random selection, but its results are close enough for many purposes.

Those items or individuals are solicited, and they do or do not respond. The evaluator starts with a number large enough to yield the desired number of respondents given expected response rates. For example, for a physical-inventory sample for preservation purposes, some items, perhaps 2%, may be missing but none will be uncooperative, a 98% "response rate." For humans, a 30% response rate to an emailed survey is pretty good (see Table 3.4).

Response Rate	Initial Sample Group Size *Target: 300 responsive,* *present, cooperative*
95% 0–5% missing	316
80% captive audience	375
50% cooperative audience	600
30% most emailed and paper surveys	1,000
4% phone dialing	7,500
Divide final number desired by the percentage response rate	

Table 3.4 Response Rates and Sample Sizes.

A high response rate is always good, but a low response rate is not necessarily devastating for an evaluation study. The real question is whether lack of response is tied to the evaluation or to the topic itself. If people are *in general* not inclined to answer surveys, simply because they are surveys, then the *library* aspect is not involved. It is true that survey-answerers may be subtly biased; they may be more cooperative people, better educated, or more tech-savvy. This is not something that can be entirely controlled.

Two small notes are needed here: First, the most mathematically sound version of random sampling is done *with replacement*. That is, for each selection or sampling, each member of the entire population is available to be sampled even when the item or person has been selected once already. That is, the item or person is replaced in the population and available to be chosen again rather than removed once selected This is generally not done with human respondents, but it should be done when one is sampling inanimate objects. That is, if a book's number shows up in the random sample two or more times, its data should be entered into the evaluation just that many times.

Second, using every Nth—10th, 20th, and so forth.—item or person is not really random selection, but its results are close enough for many purposes. It is particularly useful in sequential random sampling when you cannot number the population at the beginning. For example, you may want to ask people in your reading room for interviews. You cannot interview everybody, but you should not interview just those who seem friendly. A practical technique is to approach every 5th or 10th person.

Selective—Nonrandom

In this form of sampling, you are aware that you have not reached your entire population. However, you wish to extrapolate from those you have contacted to that larger group.

All of these are examples of selective but nonrandom sampling:

- Visitors to the library on X days or times
- Freshmen in large basic courses such as the introduction courses to biology, psychology, and so forth.
- Parents at a swim meet, when asked about library services
- Attendees at a Kiwanis or Chamber of Commerce meeting

In each case, these people have not been randomly selected from among people in the library's service area, from among all freshmen, from all parents of children, or from among all community leaders or businesspeople. Just as in not-quite-population sampling, one important key is to understand and acknowledge what distinguishes the people you have contacted from the larger group you are making inferences about. People at a Chamber meeting, for example, are businesspeople who are more connected to community groups than businesspeople who do not belong to the Chamber or attend meetings.

Selective nonrandom sampling is used when it is the best practical way to reach more than other methods can. The most valuable use is when you are trying to reach library non-users. You want to know what all teenagers think; asking the Library's Teen Board is one approach. Reaching out to community teen organizations is better; it still will not reach all teenagers, but it is a step in an inclusive direction.

Purposive Sampling

Purposive sampling is used with the smallest samples. In these small groups of respondents or participants, you realize that they cannot be randomly representative of a population. Instead, you seek a greater depth of information from fewer people and are more cautious about drawing broad conclusions. This is the type of sampling used with what in research are called qualitative methods. These include interviewing, some focus groups, usability studies, and some aspects of mystery shopping. The goal is richer data from fewer participants.

The four primary types of purposive sampling are maximum variety, extreme case, intensity, and snowball. Saturation is a concept that guides you as to when you can stop sampling and gathering data.

In *maximum-variety sampling*, your goal is to include one, two, or three reasonably representative people from each of the subgroups you believe exist in your population. Consider a library's webpage. The users of the webpage for a public library include senior citizens, professionals, parents, and teenagers. You begin with an idea that they might have different views of how user-friendly the site design is and then ensure that you include at least some people from each of these groups. This builds upon your professional, day-to day-knowledge of your population. Unlike what is called convenience sampling, or sampling people who happen to show up, it is more inclusive. People who volunteer for computer-use studies, for example, may already be more computer savvy and engaged than others. The main weakness is that you may not correctly predict which subgroups exist. For example, academic librarians are beginning to realize that international students, although fully qualified to be students at their university, have different perspectives on library usage and services.

Extreme-case sampling is a subset of maximum variety sampling. For example, in a high school library setting, you have experienced, tech-savvy teachers, new teachers, freshmen, and seniors. In maximum variety you would try to include each of these. In extreme case, you would identify the characteristic with the most importance to you and the most extreme situation, for example, the freshman from the far side of the digital divide and the info-geek science teacher. By including both ends of this spectrum, you can explore two things. If things are common between them such as they both find X easy, then it is relatively sound to conclude that X works for most people. If things differ, such as when freshmen are baffled and the teacher is adept, that starts your exploration into where the middle is and what is important about that characteristic. An extreme case can be a very economical way to start an evaluation because it quickly identifies things that always or never work.

In *intensity sampling*, you deliberately choose participants who have a great depth of knowledge. The disadvantage is that these people by definition are not typical. The advantage is the level and detail of information that they can provide. This is especially valuable for services or features that are not known to many people but that are nevertheless very important for your library or to key individuals. Key individuals also influence other users, so involving them serves many purposes.

Snowball is the name used when one participant leads the evaluator to another participant. This is particularly valuable for self-organized social groups without a formal structure. For example, if one wishes to know how students from certain backgrounds perceive the library's services, finding one person and asking him or her to suggest friends or others is very valuable. A formal group such as the University Latina Club might work, but members of that club may not be as representative of other Hispanic students as you would like. Snowball sampling has problems in that selection is subject not only to the evaluator's own biases or ignorance but also those of each person in the referral chain, but it is useful when it reaches some people that no other method will.

When can you stop? When you keep hearing the same thing over and over *and* you have included the right groups, you have queried enough people. Learning nothing new means you have reached *saturation*. Consider a usability study. If five of the first six participants have trouble distinguishing how to click from "Find Articles" to "Databases by

Alphabet," you probably do not need 10 more testers to tell you the same thing. Instead, in sampling for usability studies, it is important to make sure that you have not overlooked types of users who can show you different perspectives.

For small, concrete bits of information, try for large numbers. Random sampling really does reflect what a larger population is like. For in-depth information, be very thoughtful about choosing participants. Try beginning with extreme cases and proceeding to include all useful subgroups. In all cases, be conscious of the difference between the population that you are actually able to include and the population you are thinking about.

Author's Note—Research and Nonrepresentative Sampling

A great deal of psychological and sociological research is based upon a classic nonrepresentative population: university undergraduates enrolled in courses in psychology, management, or other subjects. A professor will do a study, for example, on attitudes towards savings or sharing, then report that "people" prefer X or Y. Similarly, medical studies that test X drug against Y drug usually do not solicit people randomly from the population at large but take volunteers. Their studies are based on a different set of research parameters and almost always are experimental in design. In an experimental study, it is *random assignment* to different groups, to this drug or that, this procedure or that, that is the most important and makes the conclusions sound and valid. Library evaluation almost never uses an experimental design, so it is important that it is based on a random or consciously purposive *selection*.

Summarizing and Analyzing Data

This section describes basic elements of concepts and procedures for handling both qualitative and quantitative data.

- *Qualitative* is the name for data that usually comes in the form of words. It can include photos or video for some types of observation. The key is that it is unstructured, open-ended, and variable.

- *Quantitative* is the name for data that comes in a predefined shape, usually categories (is this person male or female?) or numbers (how did this person rate his or her satisfaction?)

Sections in Chapter 1, "Personal Techniques," and Chapter 2, "Impersonal Techniques," also describe what kind of data each method produces and outline some specific ways of handling it. The sections on interviews and surveys have the most detail. Here is an overview of concepts and some very simple, direct tools that apply to a wide variety of situations.

Analysis is the process of summarizing and making sense out of the information that you have gathered. Here is what you want to do in your data analysis:

- Detect and describe what is there

- Avoid mental errors

- Separate natural variation or noise from something important

Detect and Describe

Imagine a series of interviews about how or when students decide to ask a librarian for assistance. One person says, "Oh yeah, my grandma, she babysits us, and she always pokes at me to go ask the librarian so I kind of had to." Another says, "My brother said he did that project last year and he didn't need any help. I just did what he said worked." Two others do not mention any family-member input, and five do.

What is there? What have you detected? Maybe you have found out that one important source of advice about whether to ask the librarian or not is family members. *Detecting* is the process of deciding that something is an actual theme present in the data, and *describing* it means coming up with summarizing wording that is more concise than, "Let me read you these five statements about family members." In other words, your report will list the main themes that you have detected in the comments and other material.

Keep an eye out for absences and for exceptions. An absence is where you might expect to see something and do not. For example, imagine third graders often mention their parents when discussing the library. However, no sixth graders do. The absence of a parent mention, if they generally are discussing similar situations, is itself a theme. This information would lead you to involve parents in programs for third graders but not so much for sixth graders. Exceptions are important to note, too. Because qualitative data analysis is not concrete and unambiguous, it is possible for you to unconsciously ignore data that goes against what you expect to find.

Summaries of qualitative data take these forms:

- For interviews and open-ended questions on surveys, the number of participants who mentioned something. For focus groups, do not report the number of individuals but the number of different groups.

- Descriptions of the different ways people expressed what you have organized as one theme.

- Vivid, informative extracts from the source material.

The way to be really confident in your analysis is to involve more than one person in this detection and description of themes. If two or three or more readers consistently identify a particular theme, then you and your audience will have much more confidence in your reporting.

Quantitative data normally resides in a spreadsheet or similar data structure. There are three components to each tiny bit of data:

1. The item or unit of analysis is the person or thing about which you have data. For example, surveys have survey respondents. One survey respondent has an answer to the question, "what is your status?" A book has a publication date. A journal has a number of downloads or citations.

2. The variable or characteristic is the quality about which you have information. For a person, the variable is gender, age, or satisfaction with interlibrary lending. For a book, it could be age, number of circulations, or subject classification. The variable is the *category*, not the particular values, that is, "gender" rather than "male," "female," or "other."

3. The actual value that that one item or unit has on that variable or characteristic. This describes the way that particular unit exists: *this* book has 23 circulations: unit, book; category, circulations; value, 23.

In a spreadsheet, the *rows* are *units*, the *columns* are *variables*, and inside the *cells* are the individual *values*.

An example from a survey is shown in Table 3.5.

Respondent	Gender	Status	Satisfaction with Study Space	Satisfaction with Library Hours
1	Male	Sophomore	4	5
2	Male	Senior	4	3

Table 3.5   Data Example: Survey Response.

Example from citation analysis is shown in Table 3.6.

Citation	Source Type	Source Name	Year	Number of Authors
1	Journal	C&RL	2009	4
2	Book		2005	1

Table 3.6   Data Example: Citation Analysis.

In the second table, nothing is entered for "source name" for citation 2. In this spreadsheet's data, we have decided not to report the names of individual books because they are likely to be very different. While there will not be any summarizing of books, for journals you can report summaries such as "12% of citations are from *College & Research Libraries*." You always summarize down a column, not across.

Values come in two forms: categories and scores. In formal research design these are called nominal and ratio or scale data; this is a simplified version. Categories can be two—for instance, a patron is a card-holder or is not—or several possibilities—the person is faculty, staff, or student. See the "Surveys" section in Chapter 1 for more details. Each category is a named quality—faculty, staff, card-holder. Notice that some numbers are actually named categories: age 18–24, 25–50, 51–64, and 65+. Scores are numeric. These can come in specific ranges or in absolute open-ended numbers. Someone's GPA is measured on a scale of 0 to 4.0; a survey asks about satisfaction on a scale of 1 to 5; a book has circulations of 0 or 38 or 310.

Summaries of quantitative data are shown in Table 3.7.

Used with Categories	**Numbers (quantity)**	Out of all of your units, how many have X characteristic?	Of 112 total citations, 44 are to books.	Of 39 respondents, 11 were freshmen.
	Percentages	Of all of your units, what percentage have X characteristic?	37% of all citations are to books.	28% of all respondents were freshmen.
Used with Scores/Numeric	**Averages**	*Measure the "center" of the data*	*Line up data in a spreadsheet and use a function [Excel: = average(B1:B55)]*	
	Mean	Add up the scores for all units and divide by number of units.	The average date of publication is 2004.	Respondents had a high average confidence in their retrieval skills: 4.2 on a scale of 1 to 5 (very confident).
	Median	Line up all scores from lowest to highest; this is the middle score.	The median date of publication is 2006.	The median salary of respondents was $42,000.
	Mode	Find the most common score.	The mode was 2004; more books were published in that year than any other.	More respondents were in the seventh grade than any other.
	Spread/ Standard Deviation (SD)	How spread out are the scores around the average—Tight/ consistent or wide/ scattered?	The standard deviation for the age of books cited by historians was 30 years; they cited both very old and very new materials.	Most people consistently liked the genealogy workshops (average 4.8, SD of 0.2), but there was a wider spread of opinions about the cemetery-hunting workshop (average 4.5, SD of .5).

Table 3.7 Summarizing Quantitative Data.

Avoid Mental Errors

Speaking very broadly, human beings love noticing patterns and get excited at exceptions. This can lead us to cognitive biases where we see things that are not there and ignore important things that are not exciting. To end up with robust, reliable analysis, take the time for a few steps to avoid some common analysis and reporting errors.

In qualitative data analysis, here are some common errors. First is not coding things that are so familiar you do not notice them: "I went to the second floor lab because the first was full." Did you code that with "availability" or "congestion" or just nod your head and look for something more interesting, something you did not know? Second is noticing more of what you want to hear and less of what is painful to hear. Did you code "the librarian who came to my class never looked up" for "teaching style," or did you try to pass quickly by? Third, do you as an insider know what is really new or different for an outsider?

Consider this exchange in an interview:

Librarian: What do you think about our ask-a-librarian service?

Interviewee: Um, I don't know what you mean.

Librarian: If you click the "Ask a Librarian" button on the webpage, you can chat or email a librarian right then.

Interviewee: Oh, that's cool. I like that.

In this interchange it is easy to notice and to like the "cool" remark. But if your summary is only "positive" because of the "cool" attitude towards Ask-a-Librarian, you have over-looked the fact that the person did not know what it was.

The three powerful weapons against cognitive bias in qualitative coding and summary are multiple coders, outsider coders or readers, and member checks. It is essential to have more than one person independently code and summarize themes from your materials. Generally, each person should work on a set amount of material, less than 20% of the whole. Then the coders should compare their results and discuss any discrepancies. Each needs to be working with the same set of concepts and at the same level of detail. This initial test coding sets the full coding up for success.

Then, it is very valuable for at least one coder or an additional analyst to be someone who is familiar with coding but not familiar with the topic or area that the text is about. This person's reactions and questions will help you come up with an analysis that is robust enough to be understandable by everyone, not just the people closest to the evaluation project. Did you code a comment about librarians being "shy" as a "positive" comment? Not everyone thinks so!

The member-check process used in serious qualitative research consists of going back to interviewees or participants who are the members for the study and asking them to check if your summaries and theme identification are accurate. A brief form of this is useful at the end of focus group sessions and can also be used in interviews: "I hear you saying that this and that are problems. Is that right?" "Is there anything else?" The main drawback is that people may seek to change what they first said to please you or to make themselves look better. However, the great advantage is that you are not interpreting them on your own. Their voices can be truer to themselves and what they want to say.

For quantitative data analysis, there are at least three ways in which simple data can become misleading: sampling, misleading precision, and ratios.

Sampling is a problem in quantitative summarization because it is one thing to say that *out of the data you have* these are the percentages or averages. You always have to remember that the data you have is usually a subset of the data that exists. Keep a firm grasp on the relation between your data and the world's data. The section above on sampling describes ways in which a sample can correspond to a larger population. One can make a mistake in each direction. In overgeneralization, you inflate the importance or generalizability of your data without considering how limited it is with respect to the whole population. If five of six teenagers interviewed said they loved Harry Potter, can you say "teens love Harry Potter?" Maybe not. Skeptics tend to undergeneralize, or not believe that a sample that was "only 300 out of 5,000 students!" can really tell about the larger population.

Misleading precision occurs when your mathematical formula arrives at a long string of numbers. Consider that four out of seven dentists recommend X. That means that 57.12287% of dentists recommend that. However, your instrument, your measurement, is in no way capable of defining the recommending population so precisely; it is a mathematical figment. For almost all evaluation purposes, two decimal places is the limit, and consider using only one.

The ratio problem is what occurs when you fail to consider the relation or ratio of one part of the data to another. For example, your finding is that 50% of graphic novels have circulated in the last month, but only 5% of your mysteries. This ratio is meaningless when your collection has only 20 graphic novels but 2,000 mysteries. In another example, suppose that at one point in time you have 2,000 students and 3 librarians. Five years later, you still have 3 librarians; but if you now have 3,000 students, your staffing actually has changed from a ratio of 667 students to 1 librarian to a ratio of 1,000 to 1. If your library's program attendance increases 15% over five years but your service population increases 25%, you are actually falling behind. Both absolute numbers and ratios are essential for full understanding of a situation.

Separate Natural Variation or Noise from Something Important

In qualitative analysis, the best defense against mistaking something that is a one-off, or unusual, unrepeatable instance, is to have multiple observations checked against as many sources of data as possible. You can think of this as a forensic method where a defense attorney carefully scrutinizes every piece of evidence and questions it. In this case, an evaluator also needs to keep in mind the possibility that the bits of observations are not evidence at all but just "noise," unimportant comments. One person in one focus group mentions rude patrons; nobody else does. One interviewee seems very exercised over clerk rudeness; nobody else mentions it. Something that appears in only one form or format should be moved to the "to check" pile but not included in the main report. The strongest evaluations incorporate multiple sources of information.

For numeric, quantitative information, this is the realm of statistical tests. If you flip a coin 10 times, and then 10 times, and then 10 times, it is unlikely that each time there are exactly 5 heads and 5 tails, head-tail-head-tail exactly. If you give a library skills test to a group of students and the same test to another group of students, or even the same test to the same group of students, it is highly unlikely that the class averages will end up *exactly* the same, such as 85.6% correct, even if the real abilities of each group are the same. Scoring is not that exact, and people vary on any given day.

Suppose you flip a coin 10 times, and 10 more times, and 10 more times. The first time it falls heads three times, the second two times, and the third three times. You flip another coin and it falls heads five times, four times, and five times. Nothing is wrong with the first coin.

Suppose you give an information literacy test to three classes before instruction. The class averages are 75%, 78%, and 72%. Then you give the same test after instruction; averages are 79%, 81%, and 92%. Is instruction the reason for the rise?

Statistics generally means making numeric summaries of data, and *statistical testing* is a way to detect a difference between natural variation and a real difference. The formulas for specific statistical tests compare natural variation to what you have observed. If what you have observed is *consistently quite different* from the type of variation one would see normally, then you can have some confidence that what you have is changed or different in some way. You improved students' information literacy skills.

Library research employs a wide range of statistical tests and modeling. These equations and models incorporate a number of variables and measure the effect of each. For example, is students' likelihood to use the library associated with or able to be predicted by their reading scores, their parent's level of education, or their grade in school?

In library evaluation, the main goal is to detect real differences that are not the result of natural variation. If high school seniors rate the friendliness of your service at 4.5 while sophomores and juniors rate it at 4.3, does that mean you are pleasing seniors more than younger students or not? This is similar to taking a political poll with a margin of error of 3%. If candidate preferences come out 51–49, that is within the margin of error, and thus the poll has not detected a real preference difference.

Statistical tests incorporate three factors. The first is the size of your population. The more data you have collected from participants, either human or units, the more confident you can be about it and the less likely it is that a small natural variation will have an outsize impact. This is like having more pixels in a picture: It makes it sharper.

The second factor is the variation within each group as you compare it to the variation between groups. If *all* seniors rate friendliness very close to 4.5, with scores of 4, 4, 5, 5, 4, 4, 5, and 5, and *all* underclassmen rate friendliness very close to 3.5, with their individual scores being 3, 3, 4, 4, 3, and 4—that is, they are consistent within each group—it is more likely that the difference between the two groups' averages reflects a real difference between groups. Similarity within groups, differences between groups.

The last factor is the absolute difference between the group averages or scores. A difference of 4.5 to 4.6 is more likely to be mere chance than a difference of 2.5 to 4.1.

As this discussion moves into the application of statistical tests to data, the need for more in-depth understanding becomes imperative. Most librarians have not had the privilege of studying statistical analysis, and even when they have, unless they work with statistics constantly, it is always wise to ask for help from persons who are statisticians. The next information presented is a very simple verbal, non-mathematical explanation. Reading this section will help you design your data gathering and summary so that a statistician can review it for testing.

The three powerful and simple statistical tests that fit most evaluation data are the t-test, test of proportions, and chi-square, pronounced *kai* as in Cairo and written χ^2. A "Student's t-test" is used for score or numeric data, and a test of proportions and chi-square are applied to category data. These tests can be performed using spreadsheet calculations, which are applications of formulas. Statistical software, as described in the "Using Technology" section can do them easily and can perform more advanced variations than spreadsheets.

T-Test

In a t-test, you have *groups* and a *score* for each member of the group. Groups are formed by categorical variables or characteristics, such as grade level of students or LC classification of books. You can also change a score variable to a categorical variable, such as "all those who scored our graphic novel collection as 4 or 5 on the scale of 'not to very important'" and "all who scored it 1 to 3" (see Table 3.8).

Method	Groups	Score
Survey	Status: faculty, graduate student, staff, undergraduate	Satisfaction with library collections (scale of 1 to 5)
Survey	Usage: frequent + very frequent visitors; medium + seldom + never visitors	Usage of library services (total number of items used in the past year)
Citation analysis	Discipline (English, engineering, history, sociology, political science)	Age of items cited in thesis bibliography
Tallies	Time of day (afternoons, evenings, weekends)	Number of people in the Teen Zone

Table 3.8 Group Comparisons: T-Test.

In a spreadsheet, form the scores into a column under each appropriate group name. Use the spreadsheet program's functions to calculate averages and standard deviations. The average is a way of saying where the center of the group of data is. The standard deviation is a measure of how spread out the scores are around that data. Consider asking people how often they visited the library during the last month. One group of retired people had these numbers: 2, 12, 3, 11, and 6 visits. A group of mothers had these numbers: 8, 6, 7, 8, 6. Both groups had an average of 7 visits, but the second group was more consistent. This is what a standard deviation measures. Without that knowledge, you would overlook the variety in the first group: Not all retirees have the same library visiting habits (see Table 3.9).

Retirees	Mothers
2	8
12	6
3	7
11	8
7	6
Average	
7	7
Standard Deviation	
4.05	0.89

Table 3.9   Group Comparisons: Averaging Scores.

With this test you can say statements such as the following:

- Statistically, men were significantly more satisfied with the nonfiction collection than women respondents, scoring it on average at 4.5 out of 5.0, compared to 4.1.

- There was no statistically significant difference in the information literacy test scores between the group of students who had an online module compared to the group with an in-person lecture (average of 78% correct versus 82%, difference not statistically significant).

Test of Proportions

In this situation, you have a group of items or participants, each of which has a particular characteristic. It could be "male" or "female," "has-circulated" or "has-not-circulated," or "lives-in-service-area" or "lives outside." The test is whether what you have observed is different from what you expect and more greatly different than natural variation.

Consider respondents to a survey on a college campus. You receive surveys from 34 male students and 32 female students. Now, the student body at your campus is almost

65% female. Your observed group is 48.5% female, not the expected 65% (43). Is that really different, or is it just chance? It might differ if for some reason male students had a greater opportunity to answer the survey, or it could differ just by chance. To test your survey, in a spreadsheet, organize your numbers in two rows. One has the totals in each category that you actually observed, and one has the numbers that you would expect, with the same overall total, divided among the categories according to X. You have to decide where your expectations come from. They may come from underlying data such as the percentage of female students, general rules of thumb, or predictions you hope will come true. The test is called a chi-square or a chi.sq. function (see Table 3.10).

With this test you can say statements such as the following:

- During academic year X, out of all books circulated, 45% were nonfiction and 55% were fiction. After a year of working on Common Core Standards, the proportion of circulations that were nonfiction changed to 51%, which is a statistically significant increase.

- The survey's respondents were demographically the same as the underlying population: 12% of respondents were faculty, 6% graduate students, and the rest (82%) undergraduates.

- Young people were statistically underrepresented among survey respondents. Only 12% of respondents were under 18, while by library card membership, almost 16% of card holders are under 18.

Chi-Square Test

This test is similar to the test of proportions, but in this case there are two grids. The observed and the expected are divided into at least 2×2 categories rather than into just one row each.

This test answers the question of whether two variables or characteristics are related to each other. Consider the frequency of visiting your library and the areas where your patrons live. Suppose your library is nearer the west side of your county. A question on your patron survey asks how often people visit the library:

___At least 1x/week __Between 1x/week and 1x/month __Less than 1x/month

You can sort the data so as to arrive at this sort of grid or summary (see Table 3.11).

Here, it is clear that more people from the west visit the library. Also, it looks like not many people from the east visit the library often—only 39. Look for the ratio problem: overall, fewer people from the east visit at all, so their numbers for visits at least once a month and less than once a month will naturally be less in each case. A chi-square test shows that there is in fact no real difference in whether they visit more or less than once

Survey respondents		Male	Female	Overall total
	Actual	34	32	66
	Expected	23.1	42.9	66
		35% of total	65% of total	

"Expected" comes from the proportions in the population you are trying to survey.

Books in a college collection		Circulated	Have not	Overall total
	Actual	6,589	3,465	10,234
	Expected	5,629	4,605	10,234
		55% of total	45% of total	

"Expected" comes from the Kent-Pittsburgh study showing that only 55% of books in a research library had ever circulated.

Attendance at programs		Create-a necklace	Face painting	Build a birds nest	Overall total
	Actual	11	34	12	57
	Expected	12.3	12.3	12.3	57
			Each is 33% of the total		

If the programs are equally attractive, then the numbers of people attending will be the same: 3 programs, 33.3% of the people at each program.

Table 3.10   Test of Proportion: Chi-Square.

Lives In	Visits at Least 1x/ month	Visits Less than 1x/ Month	Total
West	145	88	233
East	71	39	110
Total	184	159	343

Table 3.11   Data Example: Grid-Association Testing: Chi-Square.

a month. If the numbers for "west" people were the opposite, that is, 39 visit more than once per month and 71 visit less, the result would show that there is a relation between where you live and how often you visit—that there is a difference between these two groups based on where they live. Some math is required to calculate the observed values. An appendix gives the formulas.

With a chi-square test you can say statements such as the following:

- Biology majors are more likely to use the library primarily for studying than English majors (see Table 3.12).

- Women aged 35 to 45 are statistically significantly more likely to use the children's literature section than men in that age group (see Table 3.13).

- Seniors are no more likely to know about the interlibrary loan/deliver-a-book feature than freshmen (see Table 3.14).

Major	Primary Reason for Last Visit	
	Studying	Researching Information
Biology	33	12
English	13	11
Total	46	33

Table 3.12   Data Example: College Major and Reason for Library Visit.

Gender (all are 35–45)	Have Used Children's Collection in Last Six Months	
	Yes	No
Men	7	18
Women	13	11

Table 3.13   Data Example: Gender and Children's Collection Usage.

Student Year	Know about the ILL/Delivery System	
	Yes	No
Seniors	11	43
First year	9	45

Table 3.14 Data Example: Student Class Standing and Knowledge of ILL.

Appendix B shows examples of how to set up t-tests, proportion tests, and chi-square tests.

The term *margin of error* is often reported for large random-sample polls, as are common in social science research. It can be used when you have data on at least 100 items, such as respondents to a survey or books sampled from a collection. For example, suppose that a random sample of 400 items in your collection shows that 8% of them need immediate preservation work. The margin of error for a random sample of 300 is 5%, so you can say that probably between 3% and 13% of your collection needs such work. Or, perhaps 30% of 400 survey respondents said they wanted a coffee shop. That would be 30% ± 5%, or estimate that between 25% and 35% of your total population have this desire. There are specific scientific formulas to calculate this, and statistical software quickly reports it.

All of this is a lot of detail, but the conceptual steps are relatively simple. Summarize your data; see Chapter 5 on effective reporting. Double-check your data to see that you are not making some easy mental errors. Then, if you believe you see a difference, and either the numbers involved are small or the difference involved is small, use a test to see if what looks like a difference is only natural variation. For qualitative or textual data, increase your confidence by using multiple coders and summarizers. Finally, with your results, something that makes sense to all readers generally is sensible enough to report.

Using Technology

I have a stack of surveys—now what? I have an online web survey—now what? I have papers with tallies—now what?

Right at the beginning, the design phase of an evaluation project, run through all the steps of the process, from deciding what to focus on to the best methods, on to the report you hope to present. You do not want to get to the final step, the report, and discover that the data you have gathered, the format it is stored in, and the summary that you have prepared do not answer your questions.

The individual technique chapters (1 and 2) review what data looks like for each method. This section discusses how to use technology in three areas: data gathering, quantitative data analysis, and qualitative data analysis. Overall, the goal is the best quality and quantity of data for the most efficient use of time and money. In different libraries, staff expertise, time, and money are available in different quantities, so you adjust your methods to your resources.

A web-based survey tool is an excellent example of the decision points involved. What functionality is free? What requires a separate payment? How extensive will your data gathering be, and how intensive will your analysis be?

The very first question is whether to use a computerized survey form or not: delivered via email, presented as a link, or available on a kiosk. The goal is not the technology but the greatest number of respondents providing the appropriate amount of information. That means that a paper survey could be the best choice. For a captive audience, a paper survey is easy for the participants and gets a very high response rate. When respondents are not captive, as when you send people the survey, there are pros and cons to both paper and web-based methods. Some people will consider paper clumsy and awkward and not really be familiar with their post office box; others think that a real paper survey implies importance and serious purpose. Some people are very technologically adept; others find paper easier to deal with. Match your method to the particular audience because your respondents will; that is, people who dislike your method will not be represented as much.

At this point, do not consider your own ease of use. Do not choose web-based methods for your own convenience. It is true that with paper surveys you need to budget an extra step to enter the data, but you can use a web survey template, and once entered, the data set is the same as if it had been born digital. It means labor, but it is worth it when paper gets you more and better responses.

Free survey websites have limitations: a limit on the number of respondents, a limit on the number of questions, and a limit on the types of analysis available. Typically, analysis is confined to question-by-question reporting. For example, it may tell you that the average satisfaction score for your library's children's services is 4.5 out of 5. It will tell you that 30% of respondents are parents and 11% are teens. It may not tell you that the average score for children's services from parents is 4.7 while the score provided by teens is 3.2.

Subgroup and comparative analysis is often called cross-tabbing. Consider whether the survey site can provide cross-tabs and for what kind of fee. Or see if the data can be downloaded into a spreadsheet such as Excel or a statistical package such as SPSS or SAS.

If you have quantitative data from at least 100 respondents, it is worthwhile either to pay the fees for cross-tab analysis and customized reporting from a website or to download the data and spend time developing some expertise using Excel. Patient sorting and subtotaling in basic Excel can yield extensive detailed information. Or, again with an investment in time and training, Excel pivot tables are a powerful tool for summarizing and reporting.

A librarian responsible for assessment for a public library system or larger academic library would benefit from acquiring knowledge of a standard statistical package. Once the basics are mastered, these programs are flexible, powerful, and quick. They repay the time devoted to training with very quick analysis. When people ask questions about the data, the SPSS-savvy librarian can quickly run additional analyses.

Another form of data gathering happens with tallies. Tallies can be recorded using literal tally marks on paper grids that you then transfer to a spreadsheet. Or you can set up a spreadsheet with a data-entry interface on staff computers so that the tallies go directly into the repository spreadsheet. The trade-offs are almost the same as for paper versus web surveys. Are those making tallies computer literate? Maybe they are not if you are using volunteers. Is getting into and out of the spreadsheet so easy that it will not interfere with normal work? Use whatever works to most easily capture reliable data. It is like exercise: the best exercise is the one you do, and the best tally mechanism is the one that people will actually use, one that does not slow them down or interrupt their real work, and one that they will keep on using. It is true that paper tally sheets mean extra time and labor to enter their data into a spreadsheet. It is worth the effort if the data is of greater quality.

The following table shows where features such as speed of analysis match technology options for survey data. Statistical software means high cost and high expertise; free web surveys need little expertise but provide a limited amount of reporting (see Table 3.15).

High Cost, High Expertise	Low Cost, Medium to High Expertise	Low to High Cost, Low Expertise	Feature
		Web—basic/free	Limited questions
		Web—basic/free	Limited respondents
		Web—basic/free	Single-question summaries
		Web—paid	Unlimited respondents
		Web—paid	Downloading data
	Excel (slow)	Web—paid (quick)	Cross-tabs/comparing subgroups
	Excel pivot		
	Excel	Web—paid	Graphing
	Excel pivot		Extensive group reporting
Stat s. (fast)	Excel (slow)		Basic statistical testing
Stat software (fast)			Extensive group reporting

Table 3.15   Technology for Quantitative Analysis.

Qualitative data is textual: answers to open-ended survey questions, responses in interviews, or transcripts of focus groups. The sections on these tools describe how to use a word processor or a spreadsheet to collect, code, sort, and analyze the data.

Specific software programs are designed to work with qualitative data. They can include automatic coding, or mechanical processing of verbal data, such as finding all instances of the word *librarian* or *research*. This sort of automated processing is usually only needed with very large quantities of information. It is more concrete and more consistent, according to its rules, than human coding, but it will miss nuances and synonyms that humans can catch. The goal here is to match your questions to the type of automated processing that a software tool makes available.

For smaller sets of data, human coding is very feasible. In these situations, the software tool speeds the process. Coding material will be as easy as highlighting text and dragging it to a tag or typing a tag for it. The software can retrieve coded data quickly and flexibly: all text coded with "e-books" or all text with "female respondent" *and* "e-books." Some of these packages are very powerful and flexible, enabling you to combine qualitative and quantitative data, as well as coding pictures and segments of videos (see Table 3.16).

	Qualitative Software	Excel	Word
Cost	High	Low	Low
Expertise needed	High	Medium	Low
Automated coding?	Yes	Yes/no (sorting)	No
Speed of coding	Quick	Medium	Slow
Speed of sorting	Quick	Quick	Slow (cut and paste)
Cross-group analysis	Easy	Medium	Hard

Table 3.16   Technology for Qualitative Analysis.

Here are decision factors for using technology to support assessment, both in gathering data and analyzing it.

- *Gathering data.* Choose computer platforms to make data entry easier and more efficient *except* when
  - ○ It is easier or quicker for respondents or staff to use a piece of paper.
  - ○ Respondents are an in-person, captive audience.
  - ○ You need to reach and include people who are not computer owners or computer comfortable.

- *Analyzing and reporting data*
  - ○ Free websites provide basic summaries.
  - ○ Assuming you use an office suite, any word-processing program and spreadsheet program can handle qualitative and quantitative data.
  - ○ Using an office software suite requires patience or expertise (pivots) for sorting; some expertise is needed for subgroup processing (Excel) or statistical analysis.
  - ○ For text data such as long interviews, word processing is better than a spreadsheet. Attach tags or codes, then copy and paste to gather together like-tagged segments.
  - ○ Relatively brief (less than one sentence) comments can be quickly coded, sorted, and analyzed with a spreadsheet program. Put codes in columns next to the original comment, which is best for one code per comment.
  - ○ Qualitative software can be expensive but handles large amounts of text easily and quickly.
  - ○ Quantitative software or statistical packages are expensive but when loaded with properly formatted data provide quick and flexible analysis. More costly web survey engines download data in statistical software format.

Someone who has a formal assessment librarian position first should determine what software for surveys or other data entry and for analysis exists within the library or the parent organization, school, university, company. Then, it is a worthwhile investment to lease or purchase high quality survey, quantitative analysis, and qualitative analysis software and to spend time learning to use it. Having someone with those skills will make the process of analysis so much easier and more effective that people will have a much more positive attitude towards assessment itself.

For smaller libraries, where assessment is more broadly shared and evaluation projects are less frequent, you can still do high-quality analysis with ordinary software. Each time, it will take more time than with the more powerful software and more advanced skills, but that is the trade-off: if you do not anticipate needing that level of power very often, be prepared to spend more time in analysis.

Using Consultants

This book describes techniques for evaluation that professional librarians can master on their own. With a few local adjustments, librarians can apply all of the methods using their own staff and resources.

The three main reasons to employ outside consultants or experts are as follows:

1. Expertise or tools

2. Time and cost

3. Context and comparisons

Expertise or Tools

In some cases, outside consultants have expertise and tools that your organization lacks or has at a much lower level. For example, sophisticated software for qualitative analysis is expensive and has a significant learning curve. An in-house team can run basic focus groups, but experts can do it more easily and effectively. Doing data mining on transaction log analysis is possible using only Excel but is much swifter and more reliable with specialized systems. OCLC itself is a prime example of an outside source of expertise and tools. Much of the data for its collection and circulation analysis comes directly from your organization's integrated library system, but OCLC has designed tools that automate the process for analysis and detailed reporting. Duplicating this is unnecessary and inefficient, even if OCLC fees are significant.

Use experts, when using experts will improve the effectiveness or efficiency of your method without compromising the quality or quantity of your data. Using an expert, an outsider, will involve a compromise between his or her generic skills and your specific needs. It is expensive and sometimes not even possible to customize a method for your very particular circumstances. An example of this is the LibQUAL™ + survey and other standardized surveys. They come as preexisting packages with entirely automated reporting. This is quick and easy on your part, but it may omit the areas you are most interested in.

Time and Cost

The more you do something, the better you get at it. Your organization may devote someone to assessment, in which case you will develop on-site expertise. For others, it can be a struggle to retain everything you learned doing *this* survey for when the *next* survey comes around. An expert, by definition, is someone who is able to design and implement a method of evaluation much more quickly than someone learning to do so for the first time.

Time is money; money saves time. Spending some money to get high quantities of data and high quality of analysis can even encourage the greater use of evaluation, as people can see its benefits more quickly and clearly.

Here the question is, "how often *should* you be doing a particular type of evaluation?" If it is often, build that expertise within your own staff. If it is seldom, meaning less than once a year, consider contracting at those times.

Comparisons

One of the most important reasons to go with an outside consultant or organization is that when they have been in business in an area long enough, they can compare your data to those of similar libraries or organizations. This is easily seen in standardized surveys such as the NSSE. Participating universities can get extensive comparisons with peer and aspirational institutions. The same happens with LibQUAL™+. With other consultants, ask if they can compare you to industry or organizational benchmarks.

This is not strictly applicable to some qualitative methods such as interviews or focus groups. However, even with these more ambiguous tools, experienced experts should be able to tell you in an informal way how your experiences gathering data, such as "it's hard to get focus groups going," can be more effective. They may tell you, "22% is not that bad a response rate for that group" or that your results compare with what they have experienced.

Therefore, use consultants when they can be easier, faster, or better: easier because you do not have to teach yourself, and faster because you are new at it and they are not. They are better especially when you have no access, on your own, to comparative data.

To help you in your consideration, here are some potential costs. In 2012, $100 per survey question or $100 per hour of consultant time were not unusual rates. Another way to compensate experts is access. Academics in library and information science, nonprofit management, and in other disciplines may be very interested in using your library as a site for their own research or teaching such as case studies. Public and school librarians should consider contacting universities to see if you can design a project that will serve your evaluation needs and their research goals.

The best way to be economical with outside consultants is to use them for the most high-level tasks, such as designing an instrument—a survey or a set of interview questions—or analyzing a data dump, and using volunteers or lower-paid workers to gather carefully specified data. It is true that when using volunteers you need to be very careful in describing just how they should collect data, but that very precision pays off in the quality of the data and the ease of analysis.

Chapter 4

Planning for Evaluation

You want to evaluate and now you know how to evaluate collections, services, and facilities, with impersonal and personal methods as discussed in Chapters 1 and 2. You are now ready to put all this into a plan.

Why do you need to plan for evaluation? Evaluation takes extra time and effort. Librarians are already doing their main jobs: managing collections, designing systems, assisting and educating users. Why add on a layer for evaluation? The plan answers the "why" question. The plan helps with motivation, feasibility, and perspective.

In terms of motivation, an evaluation plan provides everybody involved with an overview of the various evaluation activities that exist. They are not just interesting or boring or tedious pieces of individual work. Instead, they add up to an overall sense of how your organization is doing. People are more motivated when they can see the big picture, understand their own part in it, and see how all parts of the organization are involved in evaluation and what could happen as a result of this evaluation that will make the library staff, services, and collection more useful and effective for library patrons.

Feasibility means that a plan prioritizes evaluation activities. Many evaluations are possible, but only some of them will be really valuable for assessing your most important features and functions. More importantly, in an age of overmeasurement, the need is to prevent evaluation activities from bumping into each other. Survey fatigue means that a body of people will quickly lose interest in any particular survey if there are too many surveys. The planning process lays out just a few carefully timed surveys, and the process points out the best way to accomplish your collection of the information you need. If you can determine journal usage from electronic systems, consider not asking people directly. The plan selects not only what to do but what not to do.

Perspective means that an evaluation plan links the combined data it generates for internal managerial decision making to the goals and roles and plans of the organization as a whole and its overall context. A plan brings everything in the library into a coherent whole and then reaches outward to link to the larger world. For example, a public library evaluation plan should measure how the strategic plan is being followed. Because the strategic plan is tied to the development and possibilities of its community, assessing the success of the plan can help determine if changes are needed or if what is in the plan is meeting goals and objectives.

An academic library exists within institutions that are called to have assessment cultures, with periodic accreditation visits to ensure that every part of the university or college unites mission, planning, and assessment for the purpose of student learning, discovery of knowledge, and service to community. Special libraries need to demonstrate how they are advancing their company's goals.

School librarians are in critical need of ways to demonstrate their role in the education of their students. While many studies of the effectiveness of school librarians and their libraries exist, school administrators, teachers, parents, and the community must be shown local results. Results of research done in another state or even within their own states are never perceived as quite as important as a local study done within the local school.

The following describes how to create a simple, basic library operations evaluation plan (LOEP). The next parts cover three special cases: school / academic / special library strategic planning, academic library continuous assessment, and outcomes-based evaluation plans for grant proposals.

Library Operations Evaluation Plans (LOEPs)

In this term, the word *operations* means the normal daily, weekly, and yearly life of a library. It means the story hour, the database lesson, the question answered, the electronic resource licensed, paid for and used—the things that make up the normal and defining activities and resources of that library. It does not include major capital projects, such as new buildings or renovations, or separate programs, defined as activities that come and then go, such as grant-funded projects. The word *operations* means everything that is considered permanent, ongoing, and normal.

The steps in an LOEP are as follows:

1. List everything that can be evaluated: services, facilities, and collections.

2. Prioritize all these items according to one of these overall schemas:
   - Mission statement
   - Strategic plan
   - A "balanced scorecard"
   - A dashboard

3. Match each item to be evaluated with a potential method of evaluation.
   - Note when some methods can cover multiple items.
   - Note which methods are more laborious than others.
   - Note a reasonable frequency for evaluation—every year? Every five years?

4. Select evaluation methods: the combination that covers the most important items, often enough, with the least amount of effort.

5. Make a calendar of activities indicating what is to be evaluated, when, and why, and their linkage to mission, planning, scorecard, or dashboard.

This is based on all of the individual techniques described earlier in the book. In order to choose the best methods, you need to know what is involved in each, the "how." Then you need to know what is most important to your own library, the "why," Only then can you design an efficient plan, the "what."

List Everything

You can generate lists in several different ways. A traditional list is oriented around functional personnel departments and grouped into collections, services, and facilities. In larger libraries, the organizational chart shows what the different departments are responsible for. In smaller ones, review the tasks that are listed in job descriptions. Or, think about your typical patrons: what do they see and experience when they visit your library, physically or virtually?

Some items cross between the traditional divisions. One example is access to digital collections. The collections themselves are collections or resources. How do people access them? What is the overall marketing plan so patrons know about them? What is the user interface, how they search the collections, and other forms of services? This affects the data, too. If a digital collection is underused, it may be because the images are of poor quality, the items themselves are not of much interest, or people simply cannot navigate themselves to the collection.

Prioritize

Here are four ways to organize your lists in a way that will make it easier to pick the most important things to focus on and to create a report for your internal and external stakeholders:

mission, strategic plan, balanced scorecard, and dashboard. In each case, reorganize your initial list of services, facilities, and collections so that the items are related to the important goals of your organization. You will prioritize by noticing areas of the mission statement, strategic plan, scorecard, and dashboard that look too crowded or too empty.

Mission

Your mission statement shows why you exist: the mission of X is to ___. Every time you ask yourself, "why do we exist?" Every time you make a statement about why your organization needs support, you are making a case framed around your mission. Having an evaluation plan organized around your mission gives you data to back up your statements.

For the mission LOEP, break down the mission statement into clauses and tie items from your list of what you have and do to each part of the mission statement. You want each clause to have some items or evaluations and for items or evaluations to be tied to clauses. If you are evaluating something that can't be tied to your mission, either the item or the mission needs to change!

Example Mission Statement

The mission of River City Public Library is to provide educational and recreational information services and resources to engage citizens and enhance the quality of life.

Educational

    Collections: Children's materials organized by reading level

    Services: Homeschooling Outreach

    Facilities: Study rooms

Recreational

    Collections: Adult and juvenile fiction

    Services: Community programming (e.g., Family Film Night)

    Facilities: Art displays, meeting rooms

Information Services

    Collections: Business, genealogy, and academic databases

    Services: Reference, Small Business Question Center

    Facilities: Computer lab

Strategic Plan

General management books show how to create a strategic plan. A basic format is to list a set of five to ten large-scale "goals" and then, for each goal, two to five very specific "objectives" or ways to accomplish or advance the goals. The key for a LOEP is to devise concrete measurements for the goals. It is relatively common in strategic plans for objectives to simply list *what* will be done, not specific measurements.

Example—Strategic Plan with Actions

Goal: Diversify funding sources

Objective 1: Hire a development officer

Measure: Development officer hired

Example—Strategic Plan with Evaluation

Goal: Diversify funding sources

    Measure G1: By 20xx at least 20% of overall funding will come from individual and foundation donations

    Measure G2: By 20xx overall income from all sources will rise 5%.

Objective 1: Hire a development officer

    Measure O1: Development officer will make 20 contacts per month with individual donors and 2 grant proposals per year

    Measure O2: At least 30% of grant proposals during X years will be successful

---

This type of LOEP starts as a strategic plan embedded with measurements and then becomes an *evaluation* plan when you pull out all the measurements to list them separately. You do that so you can keep track of what you need to measure and when.

Balanced Scorecard

Kaplan and Norton from the Harvard Business School developed the balanced score-card[1]: notice the business origin. Their insight was that business "score-keeping" had been too focused on money, defined as income, profit, stock price, and size. They designed something that was broader, more balanced, and reflective of issues important to company success. Fiscal issues still appear in the scorecard but they are "balanced" by other angles. The scorecard as shown graphically below typically has four parts: fiscal, customers, innovation, and efficiency. *Fiscal* is the cost per use; the *customer* area includes customer satisfaction. *Innovation* is seen as employee turnover and grants received. It includes motivated and creative employees, so this usually uses measures of employee satisfaction. *Efficiency* is how well products and services are created and delivered at the desired combination of cost and quality (see Figure 4.1).

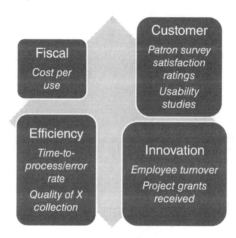

Figure 4.1 Balanced Scorecard Example: Public Library.

Using a balanced scorecard has at least two attractions as the framework for an LOEP. First, some of your external constituencies—a parent company, donors, and trustees—may be from the business world and value this kind of approach. The "balance" part here is good to broaden a strictly bottom-line business perspective. Speaking their language, literally, by using a business-created model is an effective way to explain your organization to them. The second reason is internal. Scoring means accountability. Do you have numbers to back up what you think you are accomplishing? Balance means that you can look outside your own comfort zone. Often libraries focus exclusively on the customer experience, which can be as unbalanced as the business-dollar approach. Balancing your evaluation means also looking at how employees feel, what your fiscal situation is, and whether your processes are as efficient and effective as they should be.

Dashboard

Dashboards are also from the business world; they have spread into libraries, particularly academic libraries, more than the balanced scorecard approach. A dashboard is a visual display of numeric information about an organization based on the metaphor of a car's dashboard. Indicators concern quantity, such as fuel and speedometer, and quality, such as the need for an oil change, an ATS system on or off, and check-engine lights. One limitation is that it is very oriented towards daily, ongoing items. This includes things like numbers of visits, hits, or questions; evaluations of presentations or programs; and current usage of computer workstations. It is weakest on quality and collections. It is hard to summarize quality measures, and overall collection characteristics just do not change as often as numbers of hits on a webpage.

A practical approach to creating a dashboard is for every department or general function in the library to think about its most easily gathered quantitative data, such as the number of journal issues, or books processed as well as what is most important, the key performance indicators (KPI). Take a large whiteboard. On a grid, nominate candidates for the library-wide dashboard (see Figure 4.2).

WestLaw	Main LL Web Page	Combined LL Web Pages
Number of Uses per Day	Number of Hits, In-State	Number of Hits, All Sources
Average This Month	Average This Month	Total Today
Number of Requests Received	Number of Requests Received	Number of Inquiries Received
External–Legal	Internal	External
	(Staff attorneys)	Nonlawyer
	Response time	
	Average Last Month	

Figure 4.2   Dashboard Example: Government Law Library.

Most dashboards are intended for use by external audiences, so select items that are most interesting and most easily understood.

Match Each Item with Evaluation Techniques

This stage of the process has two important parts. Your goal is to have a measure for everything that is important and to check all measures so that they work harmoniously and effectively together: coverage and efficiency.

One important consideration is when a given measure covers more than one aspect. Many of the measures in the personal methods covered in Chapter 1 are like this, including surveys, interviews, and focus groups. An annual survey of patrons can have questions on existing services, collections, and facilities, as well as asking about things that you do not already offer but might. One survey, in other words, can address several sections of your mission, strategic plan, and balanced scorecard. On the other hand, surveys notoriously do not include everyone. You depend on response rates.

You have already organized your plan to tell you what is important to measure. For example, your mission or your strategic plan lists support for information literacy; your balanced scorecard considers this part of "efficiency," defined as the effective delivery of needed services; and you can easily slot how-many-sessions into a dashboard.

In the match or select step, check to see what is the best way to get information about these key functions or items. You can interview a few students about their information-seeking habits; you can survey teachers about what they observe in student papers; and you can test every class you give a presentation to. What should you do and when? (See Table 4.1.)

To Provide Educational Resources and Services	
Collections: Children's materials organized by reading level	List-checking (quality)
	Usage (popularity)
	Comments from parent interviews
Services: Homeschooling Outreach	General patron survey (measure extent of need)
	Special survey to Outreach users (satisfaction, needs)
Facilities: Study rooms	Usage tallies (observation, reservation data)

Table 4.1   Mission-Grid Evaluation Plan: Public Library.

Calendar

The two most important parts of this whole process are the *priorities* and the *calendar*. Priorities, established by your mission statement, strategic goals, or scorecard areas, show *why* you are doing evaluation at all, and the calendar shows *what* you can actually accomplish.

From your chosen schema, pull out everything that you listed as a measurement and figure out exactly when and how you will collect, and analyze, the data. Collecting and analyzing often are two separate steps. Most usage data is collected continuously, but you would only analyze it periodically.

Check two things as you create a calendar. The most important is to pace yourself and the library's staff. You need to put evaluation measures where they make sense in the seasonal rhythms of your library: for example, many advanced information literacy sessions in an academic or school library occur in the spring, not the fall, and not in the summer, either. Things not season dependent, like conducting list-checking or strength evaluations, can be scheduled during slower periods.

The second is to check back with your mission and strategic plan to ensure that you have not left out important areas of your library. Spend your limited time and energy on what is most important.

Full LOEP Example

Generic high school library

Nightingale High School

List things to be evaluated

Collections

    Fiction, nonfiction, graphic novels, career collection, reference, paperback exchange

Activities and services

    Student groups (book clubs, poetry slams)

    Library skills instruction

    Individual research assistance to students

    Collaboration with teachers (individual planning sessions, workshops)

    Parent Night

Facilities

    Open computer lab, lab assistance

    Before- and after-school open library hours

Prioritize

Mission statement:

    The Nightingale High School Library exists to develop students' personal and academic skills through vibrant collections, collaboration with classroom teachers, and facilities and programs that enrich student lives.

Most important:

    Academic skill development

    Teacher collaboration

    Enriching programs

    Vibrant collections

Strategic Plan:

a) By 20xx all English and Social Studies teachers will have received refresher training on state databases for student research

b) Collections: By 20xx the career collection, science, and medical sections of the collection will be completely up to date with quality materials.

c) By 20xx students will find the recreational reading resources to help them develop higher reading ability.

Balanced Scorecard (one or two items per quadrant):

Fiscal: Cost-per-use of magazines, journals and locally-funded databases

Process: Downtime for lab computers; fulfillment rate for class visits

Innovation: Training of teachers in new databases

Customer: Satisfaction of students

Dashboard:

Ongoing indicators of library quality and use:

Visits by individual students, teachers, and classes

Circulation rates for different segments of the collection

Hits on library databases

Satisfaction scores from parent, student, and teacher surveys

Match each item; select best methods

Mission:

Academic skill development

Test for ninth graders after each library session (instructional evaluation)

Citation analysis of twelfth-grade History papers (instructional evaluation)

Teacher collaboration

Teacher satisfaction survey: every 2 years, all teachers

Teacher interviews: each year two departments

Enriching programs

Focus group of students, every fall and (different students) spring

Vibrant collections

Circulation data

List-checking

Calendar:

After every library session: test for students.

September

Focus group of students (freshmen)

October

Circulation data for each collection area

Each year pick two areas to list-check (using student aides)

November

Teacher interviews: one experienced and one new teacher each year

December

Analyze aggregated library session test data

February

Focus group of students (seniors)

May

Analyze aggregated library session test data

Citation analysis of random sample of History projects (both AP and regular)

Teacher satisfaction survey—*every 2 years, all teachers*

All of this data then goes into a report that says, in brief, "Our mission is to do X. We are doing well with Xa and Xb as shown by Y data. The Xc and Xd areas are weak, and we intend to work on them; these other areas are particularly strong or have improved from last time."

Specific Cases

The previous section covered a stand-alone evaluation plan. This section describes how to use evaluation planning in three embedded situations:

1. School, academic and special libraries: strategic planning for the larger organization

2. Academic libraries: assessment for accreditation

3. Outcomes-based evaluation for (grant-funded) project planning

Strategic and Organizational Planning

The section on LOEP, or stand-alone evaluation plans, described how to go through a library's strategic plan and incorporate measurements for most or all objectives. This case is where you have a strategic plan that has been devised for a larger organization of which the library is only a part. Larger libraries might have their own strategic plans, but smaller ones may do planning only as a part of the larger organizational effort. Planning along with the parent organization has several advantages. Participating in the development of the overall strategic plan lets others in the organization see how the library serves everyone's mission and goals. It enhances coordination; that is, it avoids having the library come up with goals and objectives that are not in sync with what the larger organization will value. It maximizes efficiency so that library staff members are not doubling their planning efforts. The main disadvantage is that librarians always need to ensure that their issues are suitably represented and that nothing that they need to know is neglected.

Libraries are for service. They serve individual users, and most of the time they also serve a parent organization. What measurements will demonstrate the value of the library in relation to overall goals and objectives? Here are some examples of goals and actions in different types of libraries:

School

General public elementary school:

- Goal: raise reading scores.
- Objective: increase silent sustained reading times.
  - Library: match reluctant readers with engaging hi-lo materials.

Charter school:

- Goal: science-themed curriculum
- Objective: create inquiry-based lessons on local ecological issue of air pollution.
  - Library: provide teachers with in-service workshop on state-provided children's-science databases.
  - Library: conduct searches of ERIC for curriculum specialists to find research and examples of comparable programs.

Academic

Community college:

- Goal: increase success rate for transfer curriculum.
- Objective: embed writing tutors into second-level English course.
  - Library: create complementary in-person and online tutorials for citation formatting and plagiarism in collaboration with course instructors; provide training for tutors.

Special

Association support library

- Goal: increase satisfaction of volunteers running affiliate locations across X state.

- Objective: provide customizable resources for affiliates to use.
  - Library: create generic web-formatted resource listings; have a two-day turn-around time for requests for customization per location.

Creating a library evaluation plan from these embedded goals and actions involves four steps. First, ensure that the library is a part of the overall plan, at an appropriate and visible level—a presence. Second, choose suitable measures for the library-specific objectives. Third, incorporate the library into any existing measures in the overall plan that are appropriate. Fourth, look at the sum of library measures in the strategic plan, specific and general, and see if there are important elements that have not been included.

That third point is about general measures. Look to see what people outside the library are planning to use for evaluation. General patron or customer or student surveys are very common. Examine these to identify what in the existing survey is relevant to the library. Then see if you can add library-related questions. For example, the National Survey of Student Engagement includes questions on students' study habits and assignments such as short and long papers or research opportunities. A student satisfaction survey often covers food service, facilities, academics, counseling—and the library. A company's employee satisfaction survey covers human resources, teamwork, communication, and information services. Many standardized surveys can add a small number of questions to the general survey.

The fourth point means that an organization's overall strategic plan may not be specific enough for library purposes. Librarians need to consider what they need to know for their own internal uses. This can include immediate things like internal process efficiency or long-term collections issues. The point is this: piggy-back on other efforts when you can, and then add just exactly, and only, what you need to fill in for the best library-specific picture.

Assessment for Accreditation

Academic libraries are necessarily part of a culture of assessment that is becoming pervasive in colleges and universities. A strong regulatory chain not only encourages but enforces it. The federal government recognizes accrediting organizations such as the regional or institution-wide accrediting bodies like the Higher Learning Commission. Those accreditors certify that a college or university as a whole is eligible for federal funding including financial aid (grants and loans) and research grants. The federal government insists that accredited colleges show accountability for student learning. It relies on the accreditors to enforce this. Therefore, all institutions of higher learning that receive any kind of federal funds must document what they accomplish, specifically for student learning and generally in terms of using assessment to advance their mission.

The bottom line of academic assessment is this:

- Are students learning?

- At what level are they learning?

- When and how successful are they (completion percentages and times)?

Detailed data is used to identify strengths and weaknesses in order to improve.

Libraries contribute to student learning. However, their contribution is only one part of the learning ecosystem. Libraries are never the sole cause of student success or retention. This book cannot lay out a plan to show a solid, unambiguous link between A, the library feature or function, and B, student receiving a diploma in X period of time. Too much else is involved.

However, libraries can take part in the whole assessment culture. While effective information literacy instruction or strong, up-to-date collections are never the sole cause of student success, they are an essential part of the picture.

A widely used academic assessment framework is relatively simple. It was designed primarily for academic departments such as English or Biology. Libraries fit it more awkwardly. It is worth using this particular model, even awkwardly, to show that the library is part of the academic enterprise.

The sequence of the framework is mission, goal, measurement, result, and use of results. The first three are the plan; the last two are the assessment loop: using results to make managerial decisions to improve. Note that the goal and the use of results are actions; measurement and results are data (see Table 4.2).

Mission	Goal	Measurement	Result	Use of Results
Support faculty research	Provide orientation on new databases to department groups	• Participation rate • Satisfaction of attendees	• 40% of departments scheduled a session in 20xx	• Interview non-responding departments to see what their needs are
Advance undergraduate information literacy	Provide IL sessions to every COM 101 course	• Post-test	• 85% of students achieved an overall passing score • 55% of students missed identifying X type of plagiarism	• Coordinate with COM instructors about X plagiarism issue to reinforce in the nonlibrary portion of the course

Table 4.2   Mission-Goal Assessment Plan: Academic Library.

This framework is used for consistent reporting across academic units. In order to make it a practical evaluation plan, pull out the measurement indications and organize a calendar or event schedule such as "interview selected faculty every May" and "use tests for each instruction session giving results to coordinator."

Outcomes-Based Planning and Evaluation

The old-fashioned model of grant funding was that somebody said, "there is X need, and we promise to do Y." A philanthropic organization or a public agency would provide funds, and accountability would focus on "doing Y." The funds and items purchased by them are inputs, and the record of the quantity of "do Y" reported are outputs: "we hired staff and provided lunches (inputs) to a group of people; X meals were provided (outputs)."

This type of accounting is certainly necessary: describe what you get for what you pay. It is not sufficient, however, to demonstrate that the original *need* has been addressed. That is an *outcome*. Outcome measures are much more challenging, though. Outputs and inputs happen within the program itself. Outcomes are not about what happens specifically inside or during the program. The program could really be anything: pumpkin-smashing or face-painting, story time or acrobatics. It is not about how happy participants are during the program, although they will not come back if they are not. It is about how they are *changed by* the program. An outcome is an enduring difference in a participant.

The classic outcomes approach encompasses five broad types of outcomes. Here is an example based on a personal financial literacy program, something that a public, academic, or school library might provide.

- Knowledge: compounding interest increases debt over time unless payments exceed interest and reduce principle owed.

- Skills: how to design a monthly budget

- Attitudes: comfort level with talking about finances with one's family

- Behavior: regularly checking one's credit report

- Status/life condition: not being delinquent on any loan for one year

It is much easier to measure knowledge, skills, and attitudes because you can do so at the conclusion of a program before people leave. To capture behavior and status, you need to contact people at some point afterwards. This is hard, but to demonstrate the effectiveness of your program as a whole, it is not necessary to contact every single participant. Just as when using surveys, the idea is to contact enough people in an unbiased way. That will give you confidence that the results from a few people indicate what the program has accomplished with most people.

This grid shows suitable techniques for each of these types of outcomes. By far the most common type of library programming is instructional of some sort, so refer to the section on instructional evaluation in Chapter 1 for more detailed guidance (see Table 4.3).

Knowledge	Test
	Survey
Skills	Observation
	Interviews
Attitudes	Survey
Behavior	Postprogram survey
	Postprogram interview
Status/Life Condition	Survey
	Institutional records

Table 4.3 Program Outcomes and Evaluation Techniques.

Evaluation provides good-enough data for managerial decision making. In that light, it is not necessary to use a research-oriented, experimental design to really test outcomes. It is inevitably true that it is not entirely *your* program that has achieved or not achieved these outcomes. People may already know how to balance their checkbooks; people already comfortable with budgeting may be the majority of people who have chosen to come to such a program. In research, a control group assesses the special value that your program has achieved. For most library programming, control groups are not ethical or feasible. Two partial solutions are a pretest or survey as well as posttests; another is to use a waiting list to capture information from people who are indeed interested in a program and are on waitlist and have not experienced it yet. However limited or extensive you are able to manage, at least some outcome data is far preferable to having only input and output data.

Most grant guidelines ask for an evaluation plan to be part of the project proposal. Here is a generic outline for a plan that includes inputs, outputs, and outcomes. This particular plan describes a program with specific, identifiable participants.

X Day for Teens

Problem: Teens have no idea about X. It is important that they know X.

Program purpose statement: _____ (participants) will achieve _____.

Inputs:

    Staff time (salary/time spent on the X Day)

    Paid consultant time (anyone not already on staff)

    Marketing

    Materials

Outputs:

> Number of attendees
>
> Satisfaction with program
>
> Parental satisfaction

Outcomes:

> End-of-program survey: satisfaction of teens
>
> One month later: phone interview. Name one thing you remember about X. Name one thing that you still wonder about. Have you changed your plans or behavior because of the program?

Summative program evaluation:

> This program is a success because X number and percent of participants could name at least two things that they learned because of this program.

In this *plan* there are three basic groups of measurements:

1. Costs: time contributed by library staff
   Stipends for consultants
   Direct expenses for materials and other items

2. Immediate surveys: of parents and of participants

3. Long-term follow-up interviews: of participants

The whole *project plan* needs to spell out who will collect what data and when, so as to have it ready for reporting to the project's funders.

Libraries often have projects that do not have an identifiable group of participants. Digitization projects are one example, and so are exhibits. It is still important to think about who will benefit from this project. "The library" is not the right answer. Libraries do things for people, not for themselves. "Hired more staff" is not an audience-oriented outcome, it is simply a means to an end. "Hired more staff to provide open labs on Saturdays" is better. "Hired more staff so that students studying for college entrance exams could use the lab on Saturdays" is best. The final, best formulation is, "We know the number of students who used the lab on Saturdays to study for college entrance exams."

Sometimes it is simply not feasible to collect outcome data from an audience. A local-history preservation and digitization project has audiences that exist both now and in the far future. Even today's audiences are hard to contact for evaluation: how valuable was this digitized project for you? Who can you ask? Why would they answer? The more tightly focused a potential audience, the more successful you can be in targeting specific people for interviews or surveys to get their perspective. Consider identifying people who are likely to be the most enthusiastic users: members of local genealogy clubs, professors in that area of history, and so forth. Their input will show at least some outcomes—whether they know about it and use it. If they do not, then you have either a marketing or a product problem.

In the end,

- Some data is better than none; some systematic effort is better than collections of anecdotes, which are better than never listening to your users at all.

- Organize your program proposal around audiences, not the library.

- Consider what small bit of data will tell you if your project is a success—is worth your time, money, and effort—and seek to collect that specific bit.

If even 3 out of 10 children in this program come up to a librarian

in the weeks ahead and ask questions

then this program was worth our time and expense

Note

1. Kaplan, Robert S., and David P. Norton. *The Balanced Scorecard: Translating Strategy into Action*. Boston: Harvard Business School Press, 1996.

Chapter 5

Reporting about Evaluation

The whole of evaluation is a four-step process:

1. Understand what you are doing.

2. Pick suitable methods of gathering data about what you have and offer.

3. Organize data collection for single-purpose evaluations and overall for your organization.

4. Report your findings to your organization and stakeholders.

This chapter describes succinct ways to organize two types of evaluation reports. Then there is a section on overall considerations in communicating about evaluation and your organization. An afterword lists tips for handling numeric data.

When you design evaluation, it is very useful to think all the way through from initial questions such as "how are we or how is X doing?" to the eventual report and its readers. By imagining how it all ends up, you will avoid getting to the end without the data that you want.

So, first of all, begin by imagining a short elevator speech for your board, president, or director.

Ms. Smith, I am so happy to be able to tell you about our X. We just finished an evaluation and found out that Y. This conclusion is based on Z sources of data. I propose we:
*gather more data to confirm/support this

OR *change or maintain X because we are doing poorly or well

Stop right now! You need to go back and review data options. If you do not think you will have sufficient information to have sufficient confidence to make intelligent recommendations, you need to decide what to do so that you are confident.

The following describes useful report formats for two types of reports: targeted evaluations and periodic organizational reports. Grant reports follow the structure outlined in the section in Chapter 4 about organizing for grant evaluation: purpose or audience, inputs, outputs, and outcomes.

Targeted Evaluation Reports

Most reports have two sections, an executive summary and details. The first part is called an "executive" summary because executives seldom have time for the details. They want the bottom line and to be able to choose to read more details or not. As an evaluator, assume that your audiences are more interested in summaries and conclusions than in the supporting data. For the executive summary, a good communication framework is *name*, *explain*, *support*, and *conclude*.

For *name*, succinctly state your topic, the focus of the evaluation, and its results. The topic includes the target of the evaluation and the overall conclusion about how the target of the evaluation is doing: "Our tiered reference service has reached 10% of undergraduates." "Almost 20 people a week take part in our caregiver early literacy outreach." "Our scientist-liaison librarians have had 15 contacts per week with their business side departments."

The *explain* part expands on the terms used in the summary to describe it for a specific audience. You know what you are talking about; here, put it in terms that the audience will understand.

This tiered reference service involves having a trained student employee field all initial questions and then refer informational questions to the on-call librarian. Jones Library moved from librarian-staffing to tiered reference service in January of last year.

For an evaluation report, the *support* section is a summary of the data. Briefly state how the data was collected: "We conducted interviews with two or three patrons on each of eight different days." Then report what the results were: "Of the 19 interviewees, none mentioned experiencing any delays in receiving assistance. However, three did mention wanting to spend more time with the librarian and felt that the librarian was rushing them along."

A *conclusion* can take one of two forms. It is possible that the evaluation report just does not have enough data for real confidence in the next step; your conclusion will then be to describe what data would be sufficient.

> Three interviewees reported feeling that the librarians were rushing through their encounter. We suggest having librarians keep track of how long each encounter is taking.

This should be rare, but before embarking on evaluation, it is important to imagine the final report. In particular, imagine finding out something negative. If you find something negative, would the evaluation you have planned collect enough data to have confidence that it is not a fluke? For example, suppose a negative finding is that "interviewees said that staff was rude near closing time." How many interviews would this have to appear in for you to report it? Would you need to conduct an overall evaluation in order for you not to dismiss this? Would you say, "unfortunately, we hit only cranky people in our interviews"? If you only plan to interview three people, that may be what you will end up with. If you plan to interview 10, then you are in more confident territory.

The more common conclusion is a recommendation based on solid, sufficient data: "Tiered reference appears to be a success right now, from the point of view of interviewees, although relatively few library visitors even approach the information desk. Liaisons tally only three visits per day while there is an average gate-count of 800 per day."

That is the executive summary.

In the full report with details, summarize all of the available data. Most evaluation methods are set up according to the questions you have. Use this to organize the results. For example, a survey often starts out with demographic questions. The first section of a full evaluation report shows the results: X number and percent of female or male student, staff, faculty; county resident versus nonresident; and so on.

Go through each main topic of the evaluation method. Check themes from interviews and focus groups, numbers and categories from survey questions, and data details from tallies and electronic data.

Whenever relevant, report on cross-tabs or subgroup data as described in the summarizing and analyzing data section of Chapter 3. For most reports, include only data from subgroups when differences are of sufficient size. If 75% of respondents from X county are satisfied or highly satisfied but only 50% of those from Y county are, that is significant, and not only in statistical analytical terms. If the difference is 70% versus 75%, it is harder to imagine any managerial conclusions to draw.

For textual data, while you should primarily report on themes, be sure to illustrate those themes with specific quotes. This anchors your reporting and makes it much more interesting for the reader: "Most interviewees were happy with the tiered service; one said,

'I was less nervous about asking the student, but then I was surprised when he explained just what the librarian could do for me.' "

When writing each section, draw out one or two highlights for each topic in bullet points. When you are done, go through and gather those highlights and place them at the beginning of the details.

Sample Report Evaluation of Tiered Reference Service

Executive Report

    One page

    Tiered reference is/is not a success, mostly with freshmen and to a lesser extent with graduate students.

    Tiered reference is X and started at Y.

    We gathered data from 14 interviews and 121 transactional surveys. Most interviewees mentioned positive themes; people responding to rating questions rated X and Y highest and no rating was below Z.

    Tiered reference should continue, but we need more data about how graduate students learn about and use reference services

Full Report

    Paragraph repeating the main conclusion

    Bullet points extracted from subsections

    Demographics of survey respondents and interview participants

    Theme A: approachability

        Bullet points

        Data from survey: tables/graphs

        Data from interviews: key themes and illustrative quotes

    Theme B: instruction need

        Bullet points

        Data from survey: tables/graphs

        Data from interviews: key themes and illustrative quotes

Theme C: overall satisfaction

    Bullet points

    Data from survey: tables/graphs

    Data from interviews: key themes and illustrative quotes

Methodology

    How interviewees were solicited; who conducted the interviews; analysis

    Blank survey; how respondents were solicited, overall numbers, and refusals; notes on statistical testing

Periodic Organizational Reports

This type of report is used when an entire organization such as a library is reporting on how it is doing. It is a systematic reporting on everything but includes an introduction with specific highlights.

The Planning for Evaluation chapter, Chapter 4, lists several ways to organize an evaluation plan, and these plans lead into reports. You can have a mission-oriented report; dashboards or balanced scorecards are themselves report formats.

Strategic plans are typically designed to span three to five years at a time. However, they also need annual reporting. For a strategic-plan-organized evaluation, report on what has been measured during that specific year. Use comments to highlight where things are on track or are ahead of or behind schedule.

Another, simpler way to organize the report is according to your organizational structure, that is, department by department. Many librarians use this method, often by having department heads write each section. This is very feasible, with two cautions. First, if this report will be read outside the library, have some one person exercise overall editorial control so that the final product has a similar tone and level of detail, with coordination between sections to avoid duplication or missing information. Second, just as in some strategic plans, some department heads tend to write more about action than evaluation. They may produce reports that are mainly "We did X" rather than "X was measured as Y" Have a consistent level of data and evaluation in different sections.

Some libraries use the format of their parent organization, university, school, company, or agency. This has the usual challenges of fitting library-specific information into what is usually a personnel-oriented schema.

Some school libraries, all public libraries annually, and all academic libraries annually or biennially participate in a national reporting format: the quantitative surveys conducted by the National Center for Educational Statistics and supported by the Institute for Library and Museum Services's Public Library Data Service. These quantitative measures are not as sensitive or as informative as the whole range of evaluation techniques described in this book. You can use their framework as your starting point, adding local evaluation data. When you include your own survey data, also include comparisons from prior years and from peer libraries.

Sample Periodic Organizational Evaluation Report

Introduction: Highlights of this year; general trends

Service Department A

    Bullet points

    Changes in the department, facilities, staffing, and services

    Quantitative data from national survey, last five years

    Special evaluations conducted that year

    Plans for change and evaluations for next year

Service Department B

    Bullet points

    Changes in the department, facilities, staffing, and services

    Quantitative data from national survey, last five years

    Special evaluations conducted that year

    Plans for change and evaluations for next year

Collections *unless reported in another department, such as Archives*

    Bullet points

    Quantitative data; national survey of holdings, additions, and fiscal information

        Subdivide data according to local areas of interest.

        Supplement with additional fiscal data.

    Special evaluations conducted that year

    Plans for next year

Facilities *unless reported elsewhere*

    Bullet points

    Changes completed, in progress, or planned

    Any evaluation data or an indication of the next evaluation point

Reporting and Organizational Communication

An evaluator writes a report for at least three different purposes. The first is for external audiences, for marketing or accountability or both. The second is for internal managerial use. The last is for the future.

For external audiences, the first guideline is to follow the practice of your parent organization. If you are new to writing reports, look at reports from parallel departments or agencies, especially initially, because you want yours to fit in. Incorporate what your readers expect to see, and choose a style that positions the library as part of the larger organization or community while highlighting its special contribution. It is especially important to show that the library is a player in the future of the organization to bend people away from negative "warehouse" stereotypes.

A blurry line exists between candor and marketing in terms of reports for external audiences. For external audiences, honesty is needed, but whether you choose to describe all your weaknesses at a particular point to a given audience depends on their needs and your situation. This is an important reason to consult peers writing reports for other departments or agencies. You do not want your report to be gloomy while others are writing glossy marketing copy or to be cheery and superficial when they look honest and analytic.

Internally, for managerial purposes, it is vital that people understand everything in detail—strengths and weaknesses both. Internal management is the most important audience for evaluation. Because evaluation serves the needs of management, it should have begun with management's blessing, approval, and eager anticipation of results. The goal for the report is to present a succinct and thoughtful summary of what you found out, with thorough, solid details for anyone interested.

Also, consider the future. As the planning chapter notes, every evaluation takes place in a sort of ecosystem where you are trying to gain confidence in your observations and conclusions by using multiple sources of information without wearing out either your evaluators or your targets. Every evaluation also occurs in a chronological series. Once you have gone to the trouble of gathering data, be sure to preserve both the raw data and the summaries in formats that can be used for comparative purposes down the line. It is true that an evaluation that is a perfect fit at one point in time may become less and less a good fit as things change, but that is much better than no comparative data at all.

Libraries always change—always, always, always. Over and over, in many ways, for many reasons and with many results, libraries change. A good evaluation plan and good evaluation reports give you the ability to determine the success and accomplishments of your change; without a "before" measurement, the "after" is much less meaningful.

Afterword: How to Handle Numbers

Numerical findings from your evaluation should be shown in three ways: sentences or bullet points, graphs, and tables. These include words, visuals, and details. For example,

- Almost all (95%) students reported that they had made a classroom visit to the school library in the last month, but only 15% said they had visited on their own before or after school (see Figure 5.1 and Table 5.1).

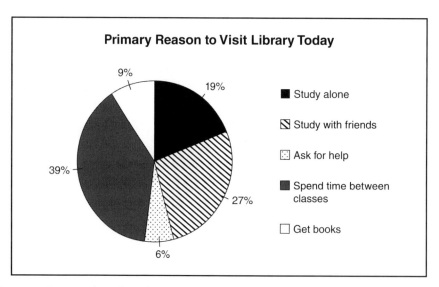

Figure 5.1 Report Example: Pie Chart for Library Visit Reason.

Satisfaction Ratings 5 = *highest*	Faculty	Graduate Students	Undergraduates
Collections	4.6	4.3	3.7
Services	4.8	4.1	4.5
Facilities	3.5	4.8	4.2

Table 5.1 Report Example: Table of Satisfaction Ratings.

Different people have different learning styles and reading preferences. This applies to the librarian writing the report and also the audience. Therefore, even if you prefer one style and think that it is sufficient, use all three types in both the executive summary and the details. It is highly likely that there are some people in the audience who prefer each of the three and who have difficulty reading or interpreting the other types.

Not everything needs to be presented three ways, but the most important points should have at least a bullet point and either a table or a graph. As a rule of thumb, each of the styles fits a particular type of data, from the least to the most detailed (see Table 5.2).

Format	Guideline	Example
Bullet points	Single-issue overall findings	The features with the highest and lowest satisfaction scores
Graphs	Rough groupings of overall data	Average attendance per month for the last year
Tables	Detailed findings for every specific item	Satisfaction scores for every item on a survey

Table 5.2   Guide to Numeric Reporting Formats.

The following are tips for professional presentation of data. The goal here is to keep the readers' attention on the findings, presenting them in a clear and informative appearance. Format inconsistencies and errors act as potholes, annoying, distracting, and even misleading readers.

Check the report as a whole for consistent formatting. Fonts in graphs and tables should be at least 10 point for readability. The same font should be used for all graphs and all tables and if possible should be consistent with the text. Although bullet points and tables can be in a serif font such as Georgia, Garamond, or Time Roman, a graph might use a sans serif font such as Ariel or Calibri.

For Bullet Points

- As far as possible, create parallel grammatical forms for each bullet point in a group.
  - Knowing...
  - Learning...
  - Accepting...
- Put a common "stem" or introduction into a header so that it is not repeated in each point. A common stem
  - Avoids wasted language.
  - Shortens a report.
  - Helps readers see how the points relate to each other.

- If you are pulling out one point from a detailed table to highlight, consider using formatting, such as shading, in the table itself to link the highlighted point to where it fits in the rest of the table.

- If you use a numbered outline format, try to have at least two numbered points in each section. If you have just one, reword the point to which it is subordinate.

1. Numbered outlines can be tricky to edit when auto-arrangement is on.
   a. Ensure that the parts remain numbered correctly.
   b. Check for coherence between sections.
      i. Do not have single-item subsections.

For Graphs

- Throughout the entire report, ensure that the *scale* of all similar graphs is the same. For a survey, design your satisfaction scales to have the same number of points, for instance, 5, 3, or 10. When you display the data, make sure that each separate chart visually has the same size and scale. This is because the readers' eyes will *assume* that they are the same, while chart-creating software often simply puts the highest score at about 80% of the height of the chart, no matter if "highest" is 3.0 or 4.9. It is seriously misleading to have graphs with different scales.

- In most instances, answers to scale questions such as "on a scale of 1 to 5" will group on the positive side. The overall average for satisfaction is usually somewhere around 4.0 on a 5-point scale, or halfway between the midpoint and the highest point. If all of your averages are above 3.0, consider having the graph use a scale of 2.0 or 3.0 to 5.0. Always have the maximum at the maximum possible.

- Column graphs or vertical bars are the most versatile. They can display category data either separately, stacked, or as scores. Start with a column graph format and *only* use pie or line charts in specific circumstances.

- Pie charts can *only* display parts such as percentages of a *whole*. If one answer eliminates another, then it is suitable for a pie chart. For example, if you answer "student" to a status question, that means you did not answer "faculty." This is the choose-only-one multiple-choice type of question. Pie charts cannot show
  ○ Scores or scales.
  ○ Multiple-choice choose-any, *except* if you treat each individual choice as yes or no.

- Line charts should only be used when the horizontal axis consists of things that must be in a certain order. If you can rearrange the order, use a column chart, not a line chart. The most obvious applications of line charts are for progression across time, such as database usage by month.

For Tables

The purpose of tables is to give complete details. These are useful for some readers who want the details and are essential when it is time to repeat the evaluation and compare findings.

- When available, include data from previous evaluations. Note what year they took place, as well as how much data were collected, such as number of respondents or numbers of items examined. Put overall demographic information on the sources of data at the beginning so you do not need to repeat it throughout.

- Avoid misleading precision. Under most circumstances, report only one informative decimal point for scores, such as a satisfaction score average of 4.5; leave percentages without decimals (87%, not 87.4%). Mathematics will spit out lengthy decimals, but your actual measures are not that precise. If you have 201 respondents and 100 select one option, it is unnecessary to report that 49.7513% chose that option; 50% is a better match for your data.

- Include overall Ns. That is, if your table shows average satisfaction scores on different items, include how many people answered that question or that group of questions.

- Center or decimal-center all columns of data.

- Keep table formatting consistent. Style manuals such as APA give extensive directions for table formatting, but those are generally intended for publication. Use simple table formats that your particular audience will be able to read and understand.

- Use a small amount of highlighting and bolding to point readers' attention to important data.

- It is traditional to use an asterisk (*) to indicate statistically significant findings. Please see the data analysis section in Chapter 3 for more on this point. For most audiences, use wording, for instance, "the difference is large," or visuals or graphs to show when a difference is worth paying attention to.

In general, avoid using tables in slide presentations; if you use them, make sure the font is large enough to be readable, which will mean a relatively short and simple table.

Appendix A

Study Questions Answer Key

Chapter 1

Surveys

Bridges, Laurie M., and Tiah Edmundson-Morton. "Image-Seeking Preferences among Undergraduate Novice Researchers." *Evidence Based Library and Information Practice* 6.1 (2011): 24–40.

Target audience:

"Undergraduate novice researchers" (p. 26)

"novice" assumed by their being freshmen.

Surveyed:

Random sample (N = 1,000) out of 4,376 freshman (p. 27)

Who responded:

63; response rate of 6%; 52% female, 48% male

Question types:

Open-ended:

Please explain your search process for finding a picture. (p. 34)

Category question:

- Multiple choice choose-only-one: What college are you primarily associated with? (p. 36) (Agricultural Science, Business, Education, etc.)

- Multiple choice-choose-any: [to search for images]

  Flikr/Google/Archives

  Have heard of this site but not used to search for images

  Have used for an assignment to search for images etc.

- No numerical questions.

There were no cross-tabs reported. A possible cross-tab might have been:

Google	Male	Female
Have used this site . . .	55%	43%

Another might have cross-tabbed "school" (major, field of study) with familiarity with Google, other sites, and the library archives.

It is possible that the authors chose not to report cross-tabs because of the low overall number of respondents. They reported primarily on the open-ended question, treating this as a primarily qualitative study.

Bancroft, Donna, and Susan Lowe. "Helping Users Help Themselves: Evaluating the Off-Campus Library Services Web Site." *Journal of Library Administration* 45.1/2 (2006): 17–35.

Target audience:

Potential patrons of the Off Campus Library Services Office (OCLS) (p. 22): students of the university unit responsible for off-campus learning.

Surveyed (p. 22):

- Captive audience: in-person classes at satellite centers and interactive TV classes

- Solicited specific group: Web-based surveys embedded in courses

- Drive-by: Other distribution by staff

Who responded (p. 23):

67 returned out of 335, 20% response rate; 85% female; 78% were already users of the service.

Question types:

Open-ended

15. Please comment on the usability of the URSUS (book catalogue) link from the OCLS homepage. (p.30)

Category:

- Multiple choice choose-only-one: 10. The Article Request Form was easy to fill out. I agree. I disagree. Have not used the form. (Not answered).
  This is not a Likert-type scale because "have not used" is one of three alternatives rather than "agree strongly/disagree strongly."

- Multiple choice choose-any: How did you find out about Off-Campus Library services? Select all that apply.

Numerical:

Likert-type; After using the Article Request Form I was _____ with the length of time it took to receive my article(s)

Very satisfied

Satisfied

Dissatisfied

<Not applicable>

<Not answered>

Results here were reported only as categories and percentages for each answer. However, this could have been treated as a three-point Likert-type scale.

Interviews

Adkins, Denice, and Lisa Hussey. "The Library in the Lives of Latino College Students." *Library Quarterly* 76.4 (2006): 456–80.

General group:

Latino college students; how did they use the library?

Participated:

People belonging to the Latino Student Services mailing list; probably those who had summer activities on the campus (invitation was sent in the summer); incentive of $10. 7 total.

One question:

Do you consider yourself a reader?

Two findings:

1. These students do not necessarily find themselves alienated from the library, though not all were comfortable.

2. The fact that the library building was "large" signaled to the students that it contained more information.

Dulock, Michael. "New Cataloger Preparedness: Interviews with New Professionals in Academic Libraries." *Cataloging and Classification Quarterly* 49.2 (2011): 65–96.

General group:

MLS-educated people in a new entry-level cataloging position

Participated:

Members of either a cataloging or a new-librarian listserv; volunteers; graduated in 2004 or later; in a first position. 17 total (4 via email).

One question:

Upon graduation, how comfortable were you with the theoretical basis behind cataloging?

Two findings:

1. Of those who described themselves as "moderately" comfortable with the theoretical background, many pointed to experiences rather than coursework as being important; a theme was "the course can't cover everything."

2. Many felt that they did not know how to handle the practical aspects of cataloging.

Focus Groups

Howard, Vivian. "What Do Young Teens Think about the Library?" *Library Quarterly* 81.3 (2011): 321–44.

General group:

12–15 year olds; selected from students in the regional school district

Groups, participants:

Nine groups. Students in the regional school district (randomly sampled, stratified geographically); selected/invited from returned surveys (27% of survey respondents volunteered). Each group consisted of both male and female students from one particular school.

Specific question:

Do you prefer to borrow books from the library or buy them from a bookstore?

Findings:

- Participants disliked the three-week loan limit.
- Focus groups expressed dissatisfaction with the local library collections (this contrasted with survey results).

Seeholzer, Jamie, and Joseph A. Salem Jr. "Library on the Go: A Focus Group Study of the Mobile Web and the Academic Library." *College & Research Libraries* 72.1 (2011): 9–20.

General group:

College students (both undergraduate and graduate)

Groups, participants:

Three groups; total of 20 participants, number in each session not noted. Graduate and undergraduate students; traditional- and nontraditional-aged.

Specific question:

What capabilities [for mobile websites] would you like to have?

Findings:

- Using a mobile option to access library links and databases was seen as a source of convenience, particularly when beginning a project.
- Participants wanted the ability to contact the librarian from a mobile device.

Usability

Fear, Kathleen. "User Understanding of Metadata in Digital Image Collections; or What Exactly Do You Mean by 'Coverage'?" *American Archivist* 73.1 (2010): 26–60.

Population:

Undergraduates

Participants:

10 undergraduates. No further details given. Sessions were conducted at the library.

One task:

Select five images for a class project from a specific digital image collection.

Two findings:

1. Participants had trouble with terminology used.

2. The thumbnail (image) was more important than any text.

Imler, Bonnie, and Michelle Eichelberger. "Do They 'Get It'? Student Usage of SFX Citation Linking Software." *College & Research Libraries* 72.5 (2011): 454–63.

Population:

Students

Participants:

Undergraduates in a course-based bibliographic instruction session (on the system being tested). All 40 students were solicited, and 39 completed the study.

One task:

Using a given search string (video games AND boys, limited to scholarly journals), select and print full-text of the five most relevant results.

Two findings:

1. Median length of time to complete the task was 8:15 minutes.

2. 67% of participants used the SFX feature button

Instructional Evaluation

Tests

Sobel, Karen, and Kenneth Wolf. "Updating Your Tool Belt: Redesigning Assessments of Learning in the Library." *Reference & User Services Quarterly* 50.3 (2011): 245–58.

Participants (control group?):

English courses (six levels); no control group

Measurement required:

Participation was voluntary, and the scores were not provided to the course instructor.

Specific question:

Which of these citations is for a book?

Summary finding:

80.3% of students were correct on the "general library information" question; the least number were correct on the "library catalog" question.

Observation

Cmor, Dianne, Alison Chan, and Teresa Kong. "Course-Integrated Learning Outcomes for Library Database Searching: Three Assessment Points on the Path to Evidence." *Evidence Based Library and Information Practice* 5.1 (2010): 64–81.

Participants (control group?):

Students in an introductory information management technology course

Measurement required:

In-class exercises and oral presentations were part of the course grade. Librarians provided in-person feedback and coaching on the worksheets.

Specific question:

(given a specific topic and instruction on Boolean logic): Write out two possible searches for the topic

Summary finding:

71% of students were able to construct a search strategy.

Projects/Portfolio (Rubrics)

Sharma, Shikha. "Perspectives On: From Chaos to Clarity: Using the Research Portfolio to Teach and Assess Information Literacy Skills." *Journal of Academic Librarianship* 33.1 (2007): 127–35.

Participants (control group?):

Students in a stand-alone one-credit information literacy course

Measurement required?:

Yes

Specific question:

Draw a concept map of their topic and its relation to various disciplines. Research log: record every database and search statement used

Summary finding:

Students generally selected appropriate resources in terms of quality but did not cover all areas of their stated research questions.

Citation (Bibliography) Analysis

Leeder, Chris, Karen Markey, and Elizabeth Yakel. "A Faceted Taxonomy for Rating Student Bibliographies in an Online Information Literacy Game." *College & Research Libraries*. 71.2 (2011): 115–33.

Participants (control group?):

Students in a freshman-level information-sociology course; 30 participated in an information literacy game, 70 did not (control group). Weighted sample of 15 yes, 15 no bibliographies.

Measurement required:

Bibliography was part of required project. Scoring not connected to course grade.

Specific question:

n.a.

Summary finding:

Players of the information literacy game were much more likely to use blogs as an information source (this was appropriate to the topic for their papers: Web 2.0 features).

Event Surveys

Figa, Elizabeth, Tonda Bone, and Janet R. MacPherson. "Faculty-Librarian Collaboration for Library Services in the Online Classroom: Student Evaluation Results and Recommended Practices for Implementation." *Journal of Library & Information Services in Distance Learning* 3.2 (2009): 67–102.

Participants (control group?):

Students in an online MLS course

Measurement required?:

No. Students were solicited but for post-instruction, only 12% returned the anonymous survey.

Specific question:

Was the bulletin board a good forum for communication?

Summary finding:

Most respondents had NOT used the discussion board format for questions (75% of respondents; respondents were only 12% of students).

Reflections

Gilstrap, Donald L., and Jason Dupre. "Assessing Learning, Critical Reflection, and Quality Educational Outcomes: The Critical Incident Questionnaire." *College & Research Libraries* 69.6 (2008): 407-26.

Participants (control group?):

All students in an English composition course at one college for one year (N = 752)

Measurement required:

All students filled out the questionnaire at the end of each (of four) sessions, but identities were deleted.

Specific question:

At what moment in the class today did you feel like you most understood the instructional content?

Summary finding:

Students had many questions about search formation.

Mystery Shopping

Cavanagh, Mary. "Re-Conceptualizing the Reference Transaction: The Case for Interaction and Information Relationships at the Public Library Reference Desk." *Canadian Journal of Information and Library Science* 30.1/2 (2006): 1–18.

Service or area:

Information services (reference) at public libraries

Who carried out:

Unknown; possibly the author only

Concrete observations/criteria:

Transactions were "reference" or not: 38% reference at the pilot branch and 27% at a small branch.

Chit-chat occurred in 18% of interactions.

Thematic conclusion:

Staff become knowledgeable about particular patrons, something that is not captured in a recording of a particular interaction but that influences how staff handle that interaction.

Tesdell, Kate. "Evaluating Public Library Service—the Mystery Shopper Approach." *Public Libraries* 39.3 (2000): 145+.

Service or area:

Information visits and physical facilities

Who carried out:

Unknown; "trained researchers," possibly staff (it was a collaboration between nine public libraries)

Concrete observations:

Cleanliness of the floors, signage, sound, and humidity and light levels (results not reported). 6.4 on a scale of 1 to 7 for "friendliness and helpfulness."

Thematic conclusion:

Based on a combination of several items, the "added value" score was only 5.4 ("presence or absence of an understanding of the questions . . . the display of a can-do attitude"). (145)

Observation

Tallies

Applegate, Rachel. "The Library Is for Studying: Student Preferences for Study Space." *Journal of Academic Librarianship* 33.4 (2009): 341–46.

Time period:

Last six weeks of academic semester

Items:

People

Characteristics:

Where they were located; if they were using laptops; if they were in groups; male or female

Finding:

> Outside-classroom area usage was constant through the semester, but usage of the library peaked during the final weeks of the semester.

Arnason, Holly, and Louise Reimer. "Analyzing Public Library Service Interactions to Improve Public Library Customer Service and Technology Systems." *Evidence Based Library and Information Practice* 7.1 (2012): n.p.

Time period:

> Three-day sample period (public library, no other data given)

Items:

> Interactions at the reference desk

Characteristics:

> Date, venue (desk, roving, phone, or email/chat); actual question

Finding:

> Staff fielded more technology-help interactions (31%) than finding books or materials questions (25%).

Unobtrusive Observation (Testing)

Agosto, Denise, and Holly Anderton. "Whatever Happened to 'Always Cite the Source?': A Study of Source Citing and Other Issues Related to Telephone Reference." *Reference & User Services Quarterly* 43.1 (2004): 44–54.

Libraries:

> 25 largest public library systems (United States and Canada)

Questions chosen:

> Ready-reference (short-answer) solicited from MLS students from their personal experiences

Questioner:

> By phone; two authors of the study

Finding:

> Complete citations of sources were provided in only 6% of responses.

Chapter 2

List-Checking

Crawley-Low, Jill V. "Collection Analysis Techniques Used to Evaluate a Graduate-Level Toxicology Collection." *Journal of the Medical Library Association* 90.3 (2002): 310–16.

Library/unit:

Academic medical library, toxicology unit

List/list type:

Stand-alone published bibliography (*Information Resources in Toxicology*)

What constitutes a match?:

Not noted

One finding:

Collection contained 50% of the titles in the bibliography.

Monroe-Gulick, Amalia, and Lea Currie. "Using the WorldCat Collection Analysis Tool: Experiences from the University of Kansas Libraries." *Collection Management* 36.4 (2011): 203–16.

Library/unit:

Research university, all areas (45 sections, by LC number)

List/list type:

WorldCat

peer libraries (ARL, Big 12, Kansas academic)

What constitutes a match?:

WorldCat accession number

One finding:

Some collections are strong but not unique; this matches the goals for the academic programs involved (e.g., KU has no specialty in that area).

Citation Analysis

General

Weissinger, Thomas. "The Core Journal Concept in Black Studies." *Journal of Academic Librarianship* 36.2 (2010): 119–24.

Collection/topic area:

Black Studies/African American Studies

Source of bibliographies:

Articles in two specific years of two core journals in the field

Information (other than journal title):

Journal is a Black Studies journal (specialized) or is a "traditional disciplinary journal."

Finding:

80% of citations in the Black Studies articles were to traditional disciplinary journals.

Local

Dewland, Jason C. "A Local Citation Analysis of a Business School Faculty: A Comparison of the Who, What, Where, and When of Their Citations." *Journal of Business & Finance Librarianship* 16.2 (2011): 145–58.

Collection/topic area:

School of Business, all full time tenure track faculty

Source of bibliographies:

All faculty articles published in last 5 years

Information (other than journal title):

- Age
- Publisher
- LC classification
- Department of author

Finding:

Finance faculty cited journals almost exclusively (93%) compared to 72–80% for those in other departments.

Instructional

Cooke, Rachel, and Danielle Rosenthal. "Students Use More Books after Library Instruction: An Analysis of Undergraduate Paper Citations." *College & Research Libraries* 72.4 (2011): 332–43.

Collection/topic area:

General topics (for general composition class)

Source of bibliographies:

All students in a Composition I course (fall freshmen); papers needed to have at least one scholarly source.

Information (other than journal title):

- Number of citations per paper
- Source/format type (journal articles, books, Websites, other)
- Scholarly/not scholarly

Finding:

Many students used one source exclusively

Collection Mapping

White-Lesniaski

Lowe, M. Sara, and Sean M. Stone. "Testing Lesniaski's Revised Brief Test." *College & Undergraduate Libraries* 17 (2010): 70–78.

Units covered:

University; 12 subject areas in which the goal was level 2 or greater (instructional, research, comprehensive)

Technique; source of list:

Lesniaski approximation; Choice Reviews Online

Finding, use of results:

In most subject areas, the actual collection level fell one level short of what their collection development plan (conspectus) specified.

Collection Mapping/Overlap

Culbertson, Michael, and Michelle L. Wilde. "Collection Analysis to Enhance Funding for Research Materials." *Collection Building* 28.1 (2009): 9–17.

Units covered:

Academic areas supporting doctoral programs

Techniques used:

- Books: Overlap, against identified peer group (WorldCat Collection Analysis); size/quantity
- Journals: Faculty input, size, citation scores (ISI), usage, ILL

Purpose of evaluation:

Determine cost to cover gaps (e.g., amount required to increase book holdings to the peer-appropriate size); demonstrate library alignment with curricular goals.

Usage

Circulation

Jones, D. Yvonne, et al. "Simple Marketing Techniques and Space Planning to Increase Circulation." *Collection Management* 36.2 (2011): 107–18.

Tool:

Circulation data, integrated library system

Data:

Circulated (yes/no) during specified period; particular display theme

Two findings:

1. Browsing book collection had a large increase in circulation, comparing month to previous month.
2. Books featured in thematic displays circulated at a higher rate than the general collection.

Reshelving and Vendor Data

Ugaz, Ana G., and Taryn Resnick. "Assessing Print and Electronic Use of Reference/Core Medical Textbooks/Brief Communications." *Journal of the Medical Library Association* 96.2 (2008): 145–47.

Tool:

- Vendor data, title-specific usage (with local authentication)
- Reshelving: captured in integrated library system via sweep of the reference area and scanning

Data:

- Usage not defined except as "vendor-supplied data."
- Reshelving: apparently, books left out in the reference area
- Title, use

Two findings:

1. Electronic use was much higher than the (recorded) in-house use.
2. Usage varied among titles much more in the electronic versions than in the print versions (print usage was more clustered in key texts).

Website Data

Brown, Christopher C. "Knowing Where They Went: Six Years of Online Access Statistics via the Online Catalog for Federal Government Information." *College & Research Libraries* 72.1 (2011): 43–61.

Tool:

Within the integrated library system, placed a "URL tracking prefix."

Data:

- Time/date of access
- Off- or on-campus user
- URL (here, a government document) requested
- = SuDocs number, date of publication of item

Two findings:

1. Some agencies had consistent popularity (D = Defense), while another had a giant leap (E= Energy, from 129 to 671 in one year).

2. Use of older documents increased substantially over the five years studied: at the beginning only 7% of clicked documents were over 10 years; by the end 27% were.

Database/Electronic Resource

Metz, Paul. "Two Universities in One Place: Reflections on Seasonal Variations in the Use of Library Resources." *College & Research Libraries News* (2010): 311–13.

Tool:

Project COUNTER and other vendor reports

Data recorded:

Downloads (of documents)

searches

sessions (monthly)

Three findings:

1. Peak months were March or April; least popular was July.

2. Some databases are more seasonal than others: there is a greater difference in peak versus off-peak usage. These tend to be full-text databases.

3. Nonseasonal databases were very specialized.

Availability

Nisonger, Thomas E. "A Review and Analysis of Library Availability Studies." *Library Resources and Technical Services* 51.1 (2007): 30–49.

Kinds of libraries:

Almost all, academic libraries

Reasons for nonavailability:

Bibliographic (incorrect citation), acquisitions (ownership), catalog (inability to read catalog record), circulation (checked out)

Senkevitch, Judith J., and James H. Sweetland. "Evaluating Adult Fiction in the Smaller Public Library." *RQ* 34.1 (1994): 78–89.

Methods:

- Most libraries (98%): circulation
- Age (publication date): 78%
- Availability: 8%

Process Evaluation

Murphy, Sarah Anne. "Leveraging Lean Six Sigma to Culture, Nurture, and Sustain Assessment and Change in the Academic Library Environment." *College & Research Libraries* 70.3 (2009): 215–25.

Process:

Ask-a-Librarian, large research library

Who conducted?:

Librarian with assistance of MBA students

Measure—time:

Turn-around time

Measure—quality:

Incorrect or incomplete answers

Measure—quantity:

Number of queries

Piorun, Mary, and Lisa A. Palmer. "Digitizing Dissertations for an Institutional Repository: A Process and Cost Analysis." *Journal of the Medical Library Association* 96.3 (2008): 223–29.

Process:

Digitizing dissertations into an institutional repository

Who conducted?:

A census approach: data captured about all items in the project process

Measure—time:

Time taken to scan the dissertation (including time to "replace the signature page")

Measure—quality:

Image sharpness; orientation of pages in the scan

Measure—quantity:

Number of dissertations

Transaction Log

Chen, Hsin-Liang, et al. "Analyzing Users' Retrieval Behaviours and Image Queries of a Photojournalism Image Database." *Canadian Journal of Information and Library Science* 34.3 (2010): 249–70.

Setting:

The Picture of the Year International website, an image database.

Search system:

Used Google Analytics code to capture search terms used when accessing particular pages

Data:

- Search strings extracted from query strings:
                    /browse?search=walla&submit_search=Search
- Also captured chronological data.
- Individual search terms were placed into conceptual categories (e.g., people, color).

Two findings:

1. Very few queries used advanced features (72 out of nearly 10,000).
2. The most common type of inquiry was about art history.

Mardis, Marcia A. "Classroom Information Needs: Search Analysis from a Digital Library for Educators." *D-Lib Magazine* 15.1/2 (2009).

Setting:

Michigan Teachers Network (continuing education resource)

Search system:

Oracle database with search box and logging function

Data:

- Selected strings from three 2-week periods in one year; one entire year and another entire year (337,598 cases)
- Terms entered
- Time/date stamp

Two findings:

1. Some terms were very common; "classroom management" had 9,000+ inquiries.
2. Overall average time of day was 2:30 pm.

Formatting Data

Quantitative data lives in a spreadsheet format for summary and analysis. In this format, each row is one unit of data, each column is a variable or a type of data, and each cell is the particular value that that unit possesses for that data type.

The underlying structure of data in statistical software programs such as SPSS and SAS also consists of a flat, spreadsheet-style format. Survey templates will form data into spreadsheets. If you intend to use statistical analysis, generally you need to format your data in a spreadsheet where there is a *single* row at the top with variable names, such as AGE or AGEGROUP or STATUS or CIRCS. If you are using a spreadsheet yourself, you can format the top two or three rows to improve readability, such as putting the stem of a question on an upper row and the particular answer choices on the next row.

On the following pages are example spreadsheet grids for 12 different types of evaluation data. The most extensive discussion of spreadsheet format is in the "Surveys" section of Chapter 1. The short-answer grid shows how to use a spreadsheet to code (and sort) simple statements such as from brief, open-ended questions on a survey. You can break down interview notes or transcripts into short statements and use spreadsheets for coding, or use word processing or qualitative analysis software, as described in the "Interviews" section of Chapter 1.

These are not depicted because their data is already formatted by the systems you use to retrieve it:

- Collection mapping: overlap analysis, size, and age

- Transaction log analysis

The last section shows the mathematical formulas behind chi-square grids. You need the grids in order to generated "expected" values for Excel to compare with the actual results of your study (the chi-test formula).

Chapter 1 Surveys

Quantitative Data

Respondent Number	Gender	Township	Please Rate		Have You Attended?
			How Friendly Are Our Staff?	How Good Is Our Collection?	Computer Workshop
1	1	Delaware	4	3	0
2	1	Monroe	5	2	0
3	0	Fall Creek	4	3	1
4	0	Delaware	4	3	1
5	0	Delaware	3	4	0
6	1	Monroe	4	5	0
7	1	Fall Creek	3	3	1
8	0	Fall Creek	5	3	1
9	0	Monroe	5	2	1
10	1	Delaware	3	3	0
Summary:	*50%*	*Female*	*4.00*	*3.10*	*50%*
			Where 1 is poor and 5 is wonderful		
	4	Delaware			
	3	Fall Creek			
	3	Monroe			

Coded Short-Answers

Notice that each line is *one comment*, not *one person* (see the "Respondent Number" column). That is so you can count and sort the different programs.

Respondent Number	Gender	Township	Name One or Two Programs You Would Be Interested in	Code (Added)
1	1	Delaware	How to choose a smartphone	Technology
1	1	Delaware	Reading with movies	Reading
2	1	Monroe	Knitting	Crafts
2	1	Monroe	Selling crafts	Crafts
2	1	Monroe	eBay selling	Crafts

Respondent Number	Gender	Township	Name One or Two Programs You Would Be Interested in	Code (Added)
3	0	Fall Creek	How to write a résumé	Work
4	0	Delaware	What a business plan is	Work
4	0	Delaware	How to get government money	Work
5	1	Monroe	Reading with your family	Reading
5	1	Monroe	Reading fiction	Reading

Summary:

With five respondents, the most popular program suggestions were:

5	Reading
3	Crafts
3	Jobs/work
1	Technology

Chapter 1 Interviews and Focus Groups

Group ID	Prompt	Participant	Gender	Code (*added*)	Opinion about Graphic Novel Collection
Group 1	Where do you get your GNs?	Student 1	Male	Circ	It is an okay collection but the good ones are never in. Suspects that the good ones are checked out by the students who work in the library.
Group 1	What could we do to improve the GN collection?	Student 2	Male	Unknown	Did not know we had a GN collection. Is it back of the SF books?
Group 1	Where do you get your GNs?	Student 3	Female	Recent	Always checks with the student worker to see if something new has been returned.
Group 2	What could we do to improve the GN collection?	Student 4	Male	Manga	Wishes we would buy manga and not "illustrated classics."
Group 2	What could we do to improve the GN collection?	Student 5	Male	Anime	Thinks that anime is the best thing and not many other people like it so he can get what he wants.
Group 2	What could we do to improve the GN collection?	Student 6	Female	Condition	The good ones get worn out quickly—there are dirty pages and someone took out the most exciting pages of the last two she read.

For Interviews, omit the Group ID column. For focus groups, report according to numbers of groups where a comment was made. This example has six different codes for six comments; in real analysis, your number of codes will be less than the number of comments so that you can group them.

Chapter 1 Usability

This is a table of the quantitative information from a usability test. Analyze comments as in interviews.

			Clicks to Get to		Seconds to Find	
Tester	Gender	Major	ILL Policy Page	Specific Database	Hours on Sunday	Advanced Search in MyCAT
1	Male	Business	4	6	6	125
2	Female	Business	4	6	14	40
3	Female	English	5	5	24	49
4	Female	History	9	6	98	15
5	Male	English	3	4	10	44
		average	*5.0*	*5.4*	*30.4*	*54.6*

Chapter 1 Instruction

	TEST			Posttest: Specific Questions		
Student	Course	Pretest Total	Posttest Total	Identify Source	Identify Publisher	Cite Formatted Correctly
1	Comp101	5	6	1	0	1
2	Comp101	6	7	1	1	0
3	Comp101	5	7	1	1	0
4	Comp101	5	5	0	1	0
5	Comp101	4	6	1	0	0
15	SWK201	5	7	1	0	1
16	SWK201	5	7	1	0	1
17	SWK201	6	8	0	1	0
18	SWK201	7	7	1	1	1
	Average	*5.3*	*6.7*	*78%*	*56%*	*44%*

Rubric

Student	Course	Length of Bibliography	High-quality Items	Percent High Quality	Websites	Peer-reviewed Journals
1	Comp101	13	9	69%	1	8
2	Comp101	10	6	60%	2	3
3	Comp101	11	6	55%	2	5
4	Comp101	14	11	79%	2	6
5	Comp101	8	7	88%	1	5
15	SWK201	5	5	100%	1	4
16	SWK201	6	5	83%	0	5
17	SWK201	10	8	80%	1	5
18	SWK201	10	4	40%	1	6
	Average		*For Comp*	73%		
			For SWK	70%		
				76%		

Chapter 1 Observation/Mystery Shop

1 (not) to 3 (entirely)

Visit	Time	Day	Staff					Other patrons		Facilities	
			Greeted	Dress Appropriate	Left Desk	Asked Follow-up		Quiet	Behavior	Clean	Well-lit
1	10:00	Monday	3	3	2	2		3	3	3	3
2	8:00	Monday	3	3	2	2		3	3	1	3
3	16:00	Thursday	3	3	2	1		2	3	3	3
4	19:00	Thursday	3	3	1	1		2	2	3	3
5	14:00	Friday	2	3	3	1		1	3	3	1
		Average	*2.8*	*3.0*	*2.0*	*1.4*		*2.2*	*2.8*	*2.6*	*2.6*

All of these items would be defined in rules for the observation. This assumes that each visit involved a question for the staff.

Chapter 1 Observation

Seat-Sweep Type

Observations of everything at specific times

Observation		Number of People			
Day of Week	Time of Day	In the Café	In the Reading Room	In Carrels	At Study Tables
Monday	11:00	2	5	0	6
Monday	15:00	3	5	5	6
Tuesday	11:00	2	4	1	8
Tuesday	15:00	3	7	4	5
Tuesday	19:00	7	3	6	9
Wednesday	11:00	4	2	2	10
Wednesday	15:00	4	8	5	11
Wednesday	19:00	11	9	9	5
Thursday	11:00	2	3	3	10
Thursday	15:00	1	8	3	3
Thursday	19:00	5	8	4	9
Friday	11:00	4	3	2	4
Friday	15:00	5	2	3	2
Saturday	15:00	10	16	10	8
	Available seats	16	24	30	24
Summary	Midafternoon average:	4.3	7.7	5.0	5.8
	Percentage of Available Seats	27%	32%	17%	24%
	Midmorning	2.8	3.4	1.6	7.6
		18%	14%	5%	32%
	Evening	4.7	4.7	4.3	9.3
		29%	19%	14%	39%

Continuous-Stream Type

Observing people as they enter a library

Gender	Time	With Children (number)	In a Nonfamily group?	First Stop	Second Stop
F	11:05	2	0	Children's area	n.a.
M	11:15	0	0	Reading room	n.a.
M	11:10	0	1	Café	n.a.
M	11:10	0	1	Book return	Café
F	11:15	1	0	Reading room	n.a.
F	11:16	0	0	Book return	Reading room
F	11:18	0	1	Book return	Café
F	11:18	0	1	Café	n.a.

Gender	Time	With Children (number)	In a Nonfamily group?	First Stop	Second Stop
Summary					
Number of visits to the book return:					
	Female	2			
	Male	1			
Those visiting the café:					
		With Children	Not with Children		
	Female	0	1		
	Male	0	2		

Chapter 2 List-Checking

List-checking: *list against collection*	1 = owned	
Book Titles *on the list*	**MyTown Library**	**Big City Library**
My Life in Pictures	1	0
More about Me	1	0
My Future as a Senator	1	0
My Early Years	0	1
What Lies Ahead for Me	1	0
Me, Myself and I	1	0
Should I Be Multiple?	0	1
Reproducing Me	1	1
Many Are My Ideas	1	0
Poems about My Life	1	0
Summary	**8**	**3**
Percent owned	80%	30%

List-checking: *Collection against lists*	1 = owned			
Book Titles *in your collection*	**OurState: Historical**	**U.S. Local History Gems**	**On Any List**	**Number of Lists**
History of OurTown	1	0	1	1
The McAnys vs. the O'Others	0	0	0	0
Feuding in OurTown	0	1	1	1
North School: The Early Years	0	0	0	0

(*continued*)

List-checking: *Collection against lists*	1 = owned			
Book Titles *in your collection*	**OurState: Historical**	**U.S. Local History Gems**	**On Any List**	**Number of Lists**
Schooling in OurState	1	0	1	1
Early Development of OurState	1	1	1	2
O'Garza: The Founders	0	0	0	0
McBrown: Land Baron	1	1	1	2
Many Rivers in OurState	1	0	1	1
Climate Change during OurState founding	1	1	1	2
Summary	**6**	**4**		
Percent on that list	60%	40%		
Percent on any list			70%	
Average number of lists the collection items are on				1.0

This assumes that you are comparing your local history collection to two lengthy lists relevant to it.

Chapter 2 Citation Analysis

					Cited Items				
Source Bibliography	**Author Code**	**Author Department**	**Source Type**	**Source Age**	**Date**	**Age***	**Type**	**Title**	**Library Owns**
1	SW1	SocWork	Thesis	2010	1998	12	Book	*Broken Windows*	1
1	SW1	SocWork	Thesis	2010	2008	2	Journal	*J of Social Work*	1
1	SW1	SocWork	Thesis	2010	2005	5	Journal	*J of Social Work*	1
1	SW1	SocWork	Thesis	2010	2010	0	Website	*NCEChildren*	1
1	SW1	SocWork	Thesis	2010	2006	4	Book	*Evergreen*	0
1	SW1	SocWork	Thesis	2010	2003	7	Journal	*Research in Social Work*	1
2	SW2	SocWork	Thesis	2010	2009	1	Journal	*Gender Research*	0
2	SW2	SocWork	Thesis	2010	2009	1	Journal	*Gender Research*	0
2	SW2	SocWork	Thesis	2010	2004	6	Book	*Questions about Gender*	0
2	SW2	SocWork	Thesis	2010	2008	2	Journal	*J of Social Work*	1
2	SW2	SocWork	Thesis	2010	1956	54	Journal	*J of Social Work*	1
2	SW2	SocWork	Thesis	2010	1999	11	Journal	*Research in Social Work*	1
					Average Age	8.75		Percent owned	67%

This example assumes you are examining theses from several disciplines; the first two you look at are from social work. You code the authors so you can check on any errors with the original material. The "Age" column is calculated from the other data.

Chapter 2 Collection Mapping

Brief Tests, Random Sample from Your Collection

Mytown Library: Books Found Using su=Applegate

Book Titles	OCLC Holdings
Details about My Life	526
The Bright Side of Being Me	1004
Small Towns in My Life	800
Most of My Autobiography	774
The Final Chapter	204
Lost Poems by Me	101
Applegate in Modern Indiana	955
Average (is at "Basic" level)	623.4

LocalCollege Library: Books Found Using Subject Keyword = Applegate	OCLC Holdings
Why Applegate Is a Menace	127
Insanity in the Applegate Family	404
Critical Reflections on Narcissism	542
Secret Files: The Applegate Mystery	95
Applegate, Nixon, and Our Times	144
Autobiographical Fragments	24
Impact of Applegate Studies	221
Allegiances of Applegates and Others	152
Average (is at "Instructional" Level)	213.6

Data from overlap analysis will depend on the vendors involved.

Chapter 2 Usage Analysis

This is a hypothetical example from a check of a particular subject area that was checked manually because it could not be captured with a call-number range. Most usage reports will use the integrated library system with call-number ranges.

Books Owned	Number of Circs Total	Year of Publication	Circs per Year
Applegate: The Sequel	0	1994	0.00
Stalking: Is It Justified?	0	2001	0.00
Applegate Mysteries	4	2001	0.40
My Life	15	1990	0.71
Following Applegate	15	2007	3.75
Applegate Mysteries Demystified	6	2000	0.55

(*continued*)

Books Owned	Number of Circs Total	Year of Publication	Circs per Year
Why Applegate?	0	1992	0.00
My Life	1	1992	0.05
Summary	**Average Circs**	**Average Pub**	**Average Circs**
	5.125	1997.13	0.68
		Number with any circulation	
		5	
		Percent with any circulation	
		63%	

For web hits and journal usage, see current examples at the sites for Google Analytics and Project COUNTER.

Chapter 2 Availability

Availability: Data from Patron Survey Type

Type of Search	Item Searched	Found	Not Owned	Patron Error	Misplaced	In Circ	Lost/Other
Subject	Cruising	1					
Subject	Shipwrecks	1					
Subject	Sea monsters	0	1				
Subject	Boat building	0				1	
Author	Applegate	1					
Author	Smith	0				1	
Author	Chen	0	1				
Author	Carson	1					
Title	*Baking with Brie*	1					
Title	*Crochet Cat Christmas*	1					
Title	*iPhones and Videos*	0			1		
Title	*Keeping Dogs Safe*	0					1

Availability studies that use a random sample from the shelflist will not have "Not Owned" or "Patron Error" columns. Patron error means the book is owned, not in circulation or lost, and is in the correct place.

Chi-square Calculation Grid

Excel Formula

Place your *observed* data in the gray-shaded areas.

Cramer's V is a way to show how much of the variation (change) in one variable is associated with a change in the other variable.

	Observed		row totals	
Topic	Var-a	Var-b		
Variable-1			=SUM(B3:C3)	
Variable-2			=SUM(B4:C4)	
column totals→	=SUM(B3:B4)	=SUM(C3:C4)	=SUM(D3:D4)	total
Expected				Formula: (column total * row total)/total
	=(B5*D3)/D5	=C5*D3/D5		
	=B5*D4/D5	=C5*D4/D5		
			=SUM(B8:C9)	
Chitest	=CHITEST(B3:C4,B8:C9)			Difference IS significant if value is < .05
Chi statistic				Formula: o = observed, e=expected
	=((B3-B8)*(B3-B8))/B8	=((C3-C8)*(C3-C8))/C8		cell = ((o-e)*(o-e))/e
	=((B4-B9)*(B4-B9))/B9	=((C4-C9)*(C4-C9))/C9		
			=SUM(B16:C17)	sum of cells
Cramer's V				Formula: square root of (chi stat/$)
	=SQRT(D18/(D10*1))			where $ = Total / (smaller of row or columns-1)
Square Cramer's V	=B21*B21			x% of the variation in A-B can be explained by the difference between 1-2.

2 x 3 grid

	Observed		row totals
	Var-b1	Var-b2	
Var-a1			=SUM(B3:C3)
Var-a2			=SUM(B4:C4)
Var-a3			=SUM(B5:C5)
column totals→	=SUM(B3:B5)	=SUM(C3:C5)	=SUM(B3:C5)
	Expected		
	=(B6*D3)/D6	=C6*D3/D6	
	=B6*D4/D6	=C6*D4/D6	
	=(B6*D5)/D6	=(C6*D5)/D6	
			=SUM(B9:C11)
	Chitest		
	=CHITEST(B3:C5,B9:C11)		Difference IS significant if value is < .05

Index

Academic department assessment, 176–77
Accreditation, 175–77
Affective domain, 46–47
Anecdotes, compared to interviews, 29
Annual reports, 185–87
Anxiety (affect), 47
Approval, for focus group research, 33
Article downloads, as usage measure, 109
Assessment for accreditation, 175–77
Assessment of student learning. *See* Instructional evaluation
Attitudes, as outcome, 177–78
Audience: for reports, 187; for survey, 13–15
Automated list-checking, 83–85
Availability bias and focus groups, 34
Availability measure: collection sampling type, 113–14; collection sampling type procedure, 113–15; defined, 112; formatting data example, 225; patron survey type, 115–16; procedure, 115–17; study questions, 117; study questions key, 209–10
Average, as summary, 146

Balanced Scorecard, 167–68
Behavior, as outcome, 177–78
Behavioral domain, 46
Behavioral observation. *See* Observation tallies
Bibliography analysis, for instructional evaluation, 53–54
Brief Tests of Collection Strength, 98
Bullet points, in reports, 189–90
Burnout (survey), 5, 14

Calendar for evaluation activities, 170
Captive audience, 14
Charts in reports, 188, 190
Chi-square, 22, 152–55; calculation grids, 226–28

Choose-any: data type, 16, survey question type, 6
Choose-only-one: data type, 16; survey question type, 6; pivot tables, 18
Chronological analysis in transaction log analysis, 127
Circulation as a use measure: procedure, 104–6; study questions, 110–11; study questions key, 207
Circulation ratio, 105
Citation analysis for collection evaluation, 87; compared to use measures, 103; procedure, 89–91; study questions, 93; study questions key, 206; using local data, 90–91
Citation analysis for instruction: formatting data example, 222; procedure, 53–54, 91–93; study questions, 58; study questions key, 200, 206
Citations, defined, 87
Coding: comparing human to automated, 157–58; data analysis, 133; in transaction log analysis, 128–29; in unobtrusive observation or testing, 72
Cognitive domain, 46
Collection mapping, defined, 94–95
Collection sampling type of availability study, 113–14
Collection unit, defined, 81–82
Collection-against-list, type of list-checking, 80, 85
Command preference, in transaction log analysis, 127–28
Comparison library, for list-checking, 86
Conspectus, collection level definitions, 96
Conspectus, procedure, 95–96
Consultants, 159–61
Control groups for programming evaluation, 178
COUNTER (Counting Online Usage of Networked Electronic Resources), 109–10
Critical incident, interview question type, 28

Cross-tabs: automated analysis, 156; in reports, 183; survey subgroups, 20–21

Dashboards and evaluation planning, 168–69
Database use measures: 109–10; study questions, 111; study questions key, 209
Data processing, comparisons, 135
Dead-end questions, in interview, 28–29
Dichotomous: data type, 16; survey question type, 6
Double-barreled question, 8–9
Downloads for usage measures, 109–10
Drive-by, interview format, 26–27

Educational Testing Service iSkills Test, 49
Efficiency, in focus groups, 32
Email, interview format, 27
Error rate, in process evaluation, 119
Evaluation, compared to research, 135; defined, vii
Event surveys (instruction), procedure, 54–56; study questions, 58; study questions key, 200–201
Executive summary in reports, 182–83
Exemplar library for list-checking, 83
Extreme-case sampling, 142

Flipped, version of White Strength test, 100–101
Flowchart, in process evaluation, 119
Focus groups: analyzing results, 36–37; compared to surveys, 33; conducting, 35–36; formatting data example, 216; recruiting participants, 34–35; research approval, 33; study questions, 37; study questions key, 196–97
Food and focus groups, 34
Forced-choice, question type, 7

Gatecounts, for observation tallies, 61
Google Analytics, webpage use measure, 107–8
Google Scholar, for citation data, 88
Graphs, in reports, 188, 190
Grid, for observation tallies, 62–63
Grounded theory and interview data, 29

Helping: in interviews, 29; in usability studies, 39
Human judgment in data analysis, 132

ILL (interlibrary loan), as use data, 106
Incentives: for focus groups, 34; for usability studies, 42
Incident: interview question type, 28
Indirect measures of learning, 47
Informant, defined, 1
Information literacy, 46
Inputs, in program reporting, 177

Institutional repositories, 90
Instruction, as a process, 120
Instructional evaluation: by observation, 50–51; by portfolios, 51–53; by post-program surveys, 55; by reflections, 56–57; by rubrics, 51–53; by tests, 48–50; defined, 46; formatting data example, 217–18; study questions, 57–58; study questions key, 198–201
Instruments, compared to surveys, 2
Integrated library system (ILS) and transaction log analysis, 125; and use measures, 105–6
Intensity sampling, 142
Inter-rater reliability and interview data, 31
Interviews: analyzing results, 29–31; compared to surveys, 2–3; conducting, 26–29; defined, 24; formatting data example, 216; recruiting interviewees, 25–26; showing unmet needs, 110; study questions, 31; study questions key, 195–96
Introduction, in survey design, 9–10
ISBN, and list-checking, 84
iSkills Test, 49

Journal Citation Reports for citation data, 89

Key performance indicators (KPIs) and evaluation planning, 169
Knowledge, as outcome, 177–78

Learning outcomes assessment. See Instructional evaluation
Length of survey, 4–5
Lesniaski, David, variation on White Strength test, 100
LibGuides and use measures, 108
LibQUAL™+, 160
Life condition, as outcome, 177–78
Likert-type scale, question type, 7
List-against-collection, list-checking type, 80, 85
List-checking: analyzing results, 85–86; defined, 79; formatting data example, 221–22; procedure, 81–85; study questions, 87; study questions key, 204
Lists for checking, 82–83
Listserv: and sampling, 137; as survey audience, 15
LOEP (Library operations evaluation plan): 164–73; example, 171–73
Lopez, as list-checking method, 83
Low response rate, 140

Machine coding in data analysis, 133
Maps, for observation tallies, 63–64
Margin of error, 21, 155
Maximum-variety sampling, 141–42
Mean (average, type of summary), 146

Median (type of summary), 146

Member-check in qualitative analysis, 147–48

Mission and evaluation planning, 166

Mode (type of summary), 146

Moderator, for focus groups, 35–36

Multiple coders, in qualitative analysis, 147

Mutually exclusive (question answers), 6

Mystery shopping: analyzing results, 76–77; and personnel evaluation, 76–77; defined, 73–74; formatting data example, 219; procedure, 73–76; study questions, 77; study questions key, 201–2

Natural variation, in data, 21, 148–49

Nonmeasures of learning, 47

Nonrandom sampling, 141–43

Numerical data in reports, 188–91

Observation (instruction): procedure, 50–51; study questions, 58; study questions key, 199

Observation tallies: analyzing results, 65–68; compared to surveys, 2; defined, 58–59; limitations, 68; procedure, 59–65; formatting data examples, 219–21; study questions, 58; study questions key, 202–3

OCLC: and conspectus definition, 95; collection management tool for list-checking, 84; and overlap analysis, 97–98

Online survey (web survey): 11, 15, 156–57

OPAC and transaction log analysis, 125

Open-ended questions: coding, 19–20; data type, 16; in surveys , 8

Outcomes-based planning and evaluation, 177–80

Outputs in program reporting, 177

Overgeneralization in population studies, 137

Overlap analysis for collection evaluation, 97–98

Paper surveys: compared to online surveys, 156; design, 11–12

Patron survey type of availability study, 115–16

Patron surveys for strategic planning, 175

Peer library, for list-checking, 83

Periodic organizational reports, 185–87

Personnel evaluation: compared to service evaluation, 69; and mystery shopping, 76–77

Pivot tables for survey data, 18

Population sampling, 137–38

Portfolios (instruction), 51; study questions, 58; study questions key, 199–200

Postprogram surveys, 55

Power test (Howard White), 97

Pretesting surveys, 11

Privacy and use measures, 104

Process evaluation: analyzing results, 123–4; procedure, 118–23; study questions, 124; study questions key, 210–11

Process, library, defined, 117–18

Programming assessment. See Instructional evaluation

Project SAILS, 48–49

Protocol for usability studies, 40–41

Purposive sampling: defined, 141; in unobtrusive observation, 71

Qualitative data: defined, 143; member-check, 147–48

Qualitative methods: in interviews, 23–24; in usability studies, 43–44

Qualitative software: 157–58; and transaction log analysis, 128

Quality assessment in process evaluation, 123–24

Quantitative data: defined, 143

Query type in transaction log analysis, 126

Question order in surveys, 9–12

Question types in surveys, 6–8

Questionnaire, defined as survey, 1

Random assignment in experimental research, 143

Random dialing: in random sampling, 139; survey audience, 14

Random sampling, 138–40

Ranking questions, 8

Rating scale, 7; data type, 16

Recruiting: for usability studies, 38, 42; interviewees, 25

Reference interview compared to evaluation interview, 24

Reference testing. See Unobtrusive testing

Reflections (instruction): procedure, 56–57; study questions, 58; study questions key, 201

Registrations as surveys, 14

Research compared to evaluation, 135

Reshelving: study questions, 111; study questions key, 208; as use data, 106–7

Response rate, 140

Rubrics (instruction): procedure, 51–53; study questions, 58; study questions key, 199–200

SAILS, Project , 48–49

Sample size, 140

Sampling, 134–43; extreme case, 143; intensity, 142; maximum-variety, 141–42; population size, 134, 137; purposive, 141–43; random, 138–40; snowball, 142

Sampling bias, 135

Sampling with replacement, 140

Saturation: and interviewee recruitment, 26; in sampling, 142–43

Scale, Likert-type, 7
Scheduled interview format, 27
Screen-based survey, 11
Search as usage measure, 109
Search in transaction log analysis, 126
Seat sweeps, 61; formatting data example, 220
Secondhand interview question type, 28
Selection: for interviewees, 24, for process evaluation, 121–22. *See also* Sampling
Sequential random sampling, 139
Server data, for webpage use measurement, 108
Set-group random sampling, 139
Shelf-reading in availability studies, 112
Size for collection evaluation, 97
Skills: assessment, 46; as outcome, 177–78
Skip logic, 11
Snapshot counts: in observation tallies, 60–61; in process evaluation, 122–23
Snowball sampling, 142
Sources of lists for checking, 82–83
Split-half analysis and interview data, 31
Spreadsheet: 146–46, 157; for survey data, 17–20
Standard deviation, summary measure, 146, 151
Statistical software, 156–57
Statistical testing: general idea, 149–50; with survey summaries, 21
Status as outcome, 177–78
Stipend. *See* Incentives
Strategic plan: and overall evaluation planning, 167; with a parent organization, 174–75
Stream in observation tallies, 60–61; formatting data example, 220–21
Student learning assessment. *See* Instructional evaluation
Success, defined as outcome, 180
Summarizing numeric data, 146
Survey fatigue, 163–64; in population sampling, 138
Survey questions: and focus groups, 35; compared to test questions 54-55; in interviews, 27–28
Surveys: administering, 13–15; analyzing results, 15–22; audience, 13–15; burnout, 5; compared to usage, 102–3; defined, 1; designing questions, 4–9; formatting data example, 214–15; length, 4–5; overall design, 9–13; showing unmet needs, 110; study questions, 23; study questions key, 193–95

T-test, 22, 150–51
Tables in reports, 188, 191
Tally sheets, 60–64
Targeted evaluation reporting, 182–85
Tasks for usability studies, 38–40, 41
Technology for surveying, 156–57

Test of proportions, 151–52
Test questions in unobtrusive testing, 70–71
Test questions compared to survey questions, 54–55
Test (tasks) for usability studies, 38–39
Tests (instruction), 48–49; study questions, 58; study questions key, 198–99
Thematic coding and interview data, 29
Themes in qualitative data, 144–45
Tiered list-checking, 85
Time as measure in process evaluation, 118, 119
Time period sampling for observation tallies, 64–65
Tour, interview question type, 28
Tracing, in process evaluation, 122–23
Transaction log analysis: analyzing results, 127–29; defined, 125; procedure, 126–27; study questions, 129; study questions key, 211–12
Transaction surveys: for observation tallies, 64; survey type, 14
Transcripts, from usability studies, 44

Undergeneralization in population studies, 137
Unit, collection, 81–82
Unobtrusive measure, citation analysis as, 88
Unobtrusive observation. *See* Unobtrusive testing
Unobtrusive testing: analyzing results, 72–73; defined, 68–69; procedure, 69–72; study questions, 73; study questions key, 203
Usability study: analyzing results, 44–45; compared to use measures, 109; defined, 36; formatting data example, 217; procedure, 29–44; recruiting interviewees, 42–43; study questions, 45–46; study questions key, 197–98.
Usage in citations, 87–88
Use measures: circulation, 106–7; citations, 87–88; compared to surveys, 102–3; formatting data example, 223–24; reshelving, 106–7; webpage use, 107–8

Walk-by, survey type, 14
Webpage usage, 107–9; study questions, 111; study questions key, 208–9
Web survey, 11, 156–57; benefits, 15
White (Howard D.), Strength test: formatting data example, 223; holdings levels, 99; procedures; 98–101; study questions, 101; study questions key, 206–7
White, Howard D., author of *Brief Tests*, 98
Word-processing, and interview data, 29–31
World of Science, 88
Wrap-up: in focus groups, 36; in interviews, 29

About the Author

RACHEL APPLEGATE, MLS, PhD, is an associate professor of library and information science at Indiana University in Indianapolis. She has taught evaluation techniques, directed the Shaping Outcomes online tutorial in outcomes-based evaluation, and served as an evaluator for projects of ALA, PLA, and local public libraries. She was an academic librarian and is the author of Libraries Unlimited's *Managing the Small College Library* (2010).